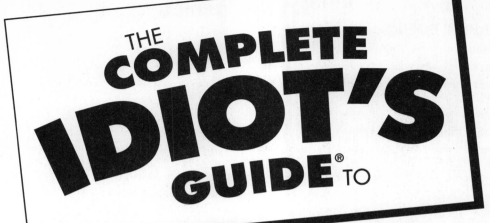

Human Resource Management

by Arthur R. Pell, Ph.D.

ALPHA

A member of Penguin Group (USA) Inc.

Dedicated to my wife, Erica, on the occasion of our fifty-fifth wedding anniversary.

ALPHA BOOKS

Published by the Penguin Group

Penguin Group (USA) Inc., 375 Hudson Street, New York, New York 10014, USA

Penguin Group (Canada), 90 Eglinton Avenue East, Suite 700, Toronto, Ontario M4P 2Y3, Canada (a division of Pearson Penguin Canada Inc.)

Penguin Books Ltd., 80 Strand, London WC2R 0RL, England

Penguin Ireland, 25 St. Stephen's Green, Dublin 2, Ireland (a division of Penguin Books Ltd.)

Penguin Group (Australia), 250 Camberwell Road, Camberwell, Victoria 3124, Australia (a division of Pearson Australia Group Pty. Ltd.)

Penguin Books India Pvt. Ltd., 11 Community Centre, Panchsheel Park, New Delhi—110 017, India

Penguin Group (NZ), 67 Apollo Drive, Rosedale, North Shore, Auckland 1311, New Zealand (a division of Pearson New Zealand Ltd.)

Penguin Books (South Africa) (Pty.) Ltd., 24 Sturdee Avenue, Rosebank, Johannesburg 2196, South Africa

Penguin Books Ltd., Registered Offices: 80 Strand, London WC2R 0RL, England

Copyright © 2001 by Dr. Arthur R. Pell

International Standard Book Number: 978-0-02-864194-2
Library of Congress Catalog Card Number: 2001090184

09   08   07   12   11   10

Interpretation of the printing code: The rightmost number of the first series of numbers is the year of the book's printing; the rightmost number of the second series of numbers is the number of the book's printing. For example, a printing code of 01-1 shows that the first printing occurred in 2001.

Printed in the United States of America

Note: This publication contains the opinions and ideas of its author. It is intended to provide helpful and informative material on the subject matter covered. It is sold with the understanding that the author and publisher are not engaged in rendering professional services in the book. If the reader requires personal assistance or advice, a competent professional should be consulted.

For instance, many of the laws governing human resources that are discussed in this book are federal laws. Many states have similar laws that might be stricter than the related federal statutes. Organizations in those states must comply with the stricter law. In addition the administration and interpretation of these laws come from both administrative rulings and court decisions, which can change from time to time.

This book is not a substitute for the legal advice of a professional. It is always wise to get advice from your legal advisors to assure that you comply with the appropriate laws.

The author and publisher specifically disclaim any responsibility for any liability, loss, or risk, personal or otherwise, which is incurred as a consequence, directly or indirectly, of the use and application of any of the contents of this book.

Most Alpha books are available at special quantity discounts for bulk purchases for sales promotions, premiums, fund-raising, or educational use. Special books, or book excerpts, can also be created to fit specific needs.

For details, write: Special Markets, Alpha Books, 375 Hudson Street, New York, NY 10014.

Publisher
Marie Butler-Knight

Product Manager
Phil Kitchel

Managing Editor
Jennifer Chisholm

Acquisitions Editor
Mike Sanders

Development Editor
Nancy D. Warner

Production Editor
Katherin Bidwell

Copy Editor
Rachel Lopez

Illustrator
Jody Schaeffer

Cover Designers
Mike Freeland
Kevin Spear

Book Designers
Scott Cook and Amy Adams of DesignLab

Indexer
Tonya Heard

Layout/Proofreading
Svetlana Dominguez
John Etchison
Mary Hunt
Gloria Schurick

Contents at a Glance

Contents

Part 3: Building a Collaborative Team

10 Getting Started on the Right Foot

11 Training for Today's Job and Tomorrow's Advancement

Appendixes

Foreword

By Franklin C. Ashby, Ph.D.

President & CEO, The Leadership Capital Group, LLC

As the world of work—and the world in general—becomes faster, more complicated, and more competitive, attracting, retaining, and motivating the human capital becomes more and more critical to organizational success. Although countless "gurus" and other management philosophers have spouted it for years, good people really are the most valuable resource within most every organization. Knowing how to find them, how to handle them, and how to win their loyalty—even in slowing economic times—has finally become a major objective in many organizations.

It has been shown over and over again that the difference between success and mediocrity in management is the quality of the leadership that managers display in obtaining and maintaining the willing and enthusiastic cooperation of the people they lead. Dr. Arthur R. Pell has brought this message to his clients, his classes, the participants in his seminars, and the readers of his books and articles for more than 40 years.

I've followed the career and the writings of Dr. Pell since the mid-1970s when he was a consultant, and as a member of the management team of Dale Carnegie & Associates, Inc. I have seen him in action, and have listened to his concepts both in formal seminars and informal person-to-person discussions. Dr. Pell is without question one of the smartest, most imaginative people I've ever known, and one of the most qualified people in the world on the subject of human resources.

In this book he tackles and does justice to more than 75 key issues of vital importance to managers at all levels with a spicy mixture of sage-like wisdom and Seinfeld-like wit. I know of very few others with his ability to make the difficult both simple and digestible, and the serious both enlightening and entertaining.

This book needs to be in the bookcase of every executive and in the backpack of every serious business student in the country. It is a hands-on manual that contributes significantly to making managers "HR literate." Too many of the old rules have changed, and there's just too much at stake now.

You're going to be pleased and encouraged by much of what you read in Dr. Pell's book. But I also think you're going to be challenged by some of the other things he says, and maybe even a little troubled. That's okay. Regardless, you're about to begin one of the most satisfying journeys you'll ever take into the increasingly complex and important world of human resource management. So sit back, relax, and enjoy the ride. You're going to be stimulated and educated as you wind your way through every page of this terrific book.

—Franklin C. Ashby, Ph.D.

Franklin C. Ashby, Ph.D., is the president and CEO of The Leadership Capital Group, LLC. Headquartered in Princeton, New Jersey, the firm specializes in executive and management development, and executive transition. Dr. Ashby is the former chief learning officer of Dale Carnegie & Associates, Inc., the world's largest for-profit adult training organization, and the former president of Manchester Training. A nationally recognized writer and speaker, recent books by Dr. Ashby include *Revitalize Your Corporate Culture* (Gulf, 1999), *Effective Leadership Programs* (ASTD, 1999), and *Embracing Excellence* (Prentice Hall, 2001). He lives with his wife, Rita, and their son, Danny, on Long Island, New York.

Introduction

How did you get to be a manager? If you are typical of most managers, you were promoted to your position because you are good at what you do. But just because you do your work better than others does not mean that you can qualify as a manager.

Sure, managers should be good performers. But it's not enough. In fact, in many cases being superior in a specialized or technical field may even hinder you from being a good manager. Why? Because being a manager requires people skills.

It's not just getting a job done, but getting it done through other people. No matter how good you might be in doing a job, unless you can get other people—your subordinates or team members—to work together cooperatively and collaboratively, you are doomed to failure. It starts with hiring the right people, training them to perform their jobs and be part of a functioning team, and continuously motivating them to produce over and above the call of duty.

You might think "That's not my job, that's the function of the human resources department." You're wrong. Sure, HR people are experts in that field, but that doesn't exempt you from the responsibility of getting the best from the people you supervise. In this book we'll show you how to apply the tools and techniques of human resource management so you can become a superior manager.

How This Book Is Organized

The book is divided into seven parts—each covering one major aspect of the human resources function that all managers must be prepared to use:

Part 1, "It's the People—Stupid!" outlines the basic concepts of the human resources approach to management and provides an overview of the laws on equal employment, labor relations, and other legal matters that all managers must understand and obey.

Part 2, "Staffing Your Organization," discusses how to staff your department or team. You'll learn the 25 most commonly made hiring mistakes and how to avoid them. You'll be given pointers on where to locate hard-to-find personnel, becoming a better interviewer, and how to evaluate applicants and make better hiring decisions.

Part 3, "Building a Collaborative Team," provides insights into orienting and training employees. You'll learn how to be a better coach and how to use mentors to help you make your staff more effective. You'll also learn how to get your ideas across to your staff orally and in writing and how to elicit their ideas and opinions.

Part 4, "Money, Money, Money," is all about money. You'll delve into the various ways of compensating workers, and compare the various types of benefits and perks that companies offer.

Part 5, "Day to Day on the Job," covers your day-by-day relations with the people you supervise. Among the areas explored are keeping employees motivated, understanding the OSHA rules concerning health and safety on the job, dealing with employee problems and problem employees, and working with a diverse workforce. Special attention is given to how to deal with sexual harassment and racial, ethnic, or religious prejudices.

Part 6, "Keeping Your Staff on the Cutting Edge," is devoted to performance evaluation and handling disciplinary problems. One chapter concentrates on dealings with labor unions.

Part 7, "The End of the Line," discusses separation and termination. In this section you'll learn what "employment at will" really means, and how to fire somebody legally and tactfully. You'll learn how to conduct a meaningful separation interview when somebody quits and all about layoffs and downsizing.

As companies differ in their structure, the titles and terminology used in this book might be somewhat different from those used in your firm. For example, some companies call a work group a "team" and the leader "team leader"; in others a work-group is a "department" or "section" and the leader is a "supervisor" or "manager." Rank-and-file workers might be referred to as "employees," "subordinates," "associates," "staff members," or "team members." In this book these terms are used interchangeably.

How to Make This Book Work for You

Reading a book like this one can be interesting, enlightening, and amusing. I hope that this book will be all these things to you. More important, it should provide you with ideas you can use on the job. You'll find lots of these ideas in the following pages.

However, it will all be a waste of your money, time, and energy if you don't take what you read and put it into effect when performing your day-to-day managerial functions.

Following these five steps should ensure that this book isn't just a reading exercise, but also a plan of action:

1. After you read each chapter, create an action plan to implement what you've learned. Indicate what action you will take, with whom you will take the action, and when you will begin.

2. Share your plan of action with your associates. Get them involved.

3. Set a follow-up date to check whether you did what you planned to do.

4. If not, reread the chapter, rethink what you did or didn't do, and make a new plan of action.

5. Review what you have done periodically. Renew your commitment.

Some Things to Help Out Along the Way

To add to the material in the main text of the book, a series of shaded boxes throughout the book highlight specific items that can help you understand and implement the material in each chapter:

Meanings and Gleanings

You might have a good idea of what most of these expressions mean, but you don't have to guess about their meanings and implications. These definitions will put you in the know so that you won't have to bluff your way through when your boss throws these terms at you.

Tactical Tips

Tips and techniques to help you implement some of the ideas you pick up in this book. Some come from the writings of management gurus; others come from the experience of managers like you who are happy to share them.

Personnel Perils

Common mistakes made by supervisors that could cost you time, money, energy, and embarrassment.

Management Miscellany

Tidbits that might add to your knowledge or just amuse you.

Special Thanks to the Technical Reviewer

The Complete Idiot's Guide to Human Resource Management was reviewed by an expert who double-checked the accuracy of what you'll learn here, to help us ensure that this book gives you everything you need to know about human resource management. Special thanks are extended to Richard Beck.

Richard Beck has been a manager in the computer software industry for over 15 years. He is a frequent author and speaker on technical subjects, and is currently a programming manager for a large software development organization in New York City.

Trademarks

All terms mentioned in this book that are known to be or are suspected of being trademarks or service marks have been appropriately capitalized. Alpha Books and Penguin Group (USA) Inc. cannot attest to the accuracy of this information. Use of a term in this book should not be regarded as affecting the validity of any trademark or service mark.

Part 1

"It's the People—Stupid!"

Have you ever worked in a company in which the boss was a "boss"? You know what I mean. The boss told everybody what to do and how to do it, and anybody who didn't do exactly what the boss ordered was disciplined—even fired. Did it really result in productive workers?

Over the years studies have shown that when people get satisfaction from their work, when they are treated as human beings, when their work is appreciated and their suggestions are welcome, they become more productive workers.

This means you can't treat workers like robots. Dealing with employees is governed by a variety of federal and state laws. You can't ignore these laws, and ignorance of the law is no excuse for noncompliance.

In this part you will learn about changes in the attitudes of employers toward their workers, the policies and procedures related to human resources, and find an overview of the laws you must know as a manager.

Chapter 1

Human Resources— The Key Management Tool

In This Chapter

➤ The not-so-good old days

➤ Attempting "scientific management"

➤ Discovering the human side

➤ What behavioral scientists have learned

➤ The human resources function

➤ Personnel policies and procedures

Do you know what they used to call workers in the old days? "Hands." You still hear that word occasionally in such terms as "farm hands" or "factory hands." You know why? Because that was what the employers were hiring—a pair of hands to do manual labor. They were not interested in brains or personalities—just physical ability.

Today's jobs call for much more than physical labor. Employers must recognize that the people working for them have many talents that can be applied to their jobs. Most large companies have created human resources management departments to devise the best approaches to utilizing the talents of their employees. Human resources is that area of management that coordinates all aspects of employment; this includes hiring, training, compensating, motivating, disciplining, and all day-to-day interactions. Formerly this function was called *personnel administration, employee relations,* or *industrial relations.*

In this chapter we'll look at how the cultures of companies have evolved over the years, from considering workers as a commodity like machinery or materials to utilizing the full capacity of its human resources.

"Leave Your Brains at the Door"

To understand where we are today in dealing with people on the job, let's look at how we got there. There was no such thing as "industry" as we know it today until the 18th century. Before that virtually all workers were engaged in agriculture or considered commodities themselves. Carpenters, blacksmiths, weavers, and other skilled artisans plied their trades from their homes or small shops.

Until the early years of the twentieth century, the concept of human resources—or "personnel administration," as it was called—didn't really exist. True, a few progressive companies had primitive personnel policies, but there was no formal or even semiformal set of principles for dealing with people on the job. With the invention of the steam engine and the introduction of standardized and interchangeable parts, it became more economical to manufacture products by bringing workers together in a factory—the beginnings of mass production. This was the start of the Industrial Revolution. During this time, Adam Smith, the first theoretician of modern capitalism, wrote in his classic work *The Wealth of Nations* that to maximize profits, companies should reduce work to its simplest possible form. In doing so, each worker's task would be minimal and workers could be trained, transferred, or replaced with minimum effort.

Management Miscellany

Eli Whitney, best known for his invention of the cotton gin, introduced the concept of standard and interchangeable parts in the manufacture of firearms, the first essential ingredient in modern mass production.

This concept dominated management thinking for centuries. The workers were "hands," and were treated as such by bosses, who in turn were domineering, often tyrannical. Workers who didn't please their bosses were fired—often for trivial reasons. Hours were long, wages were low, and conditions often were deplorable. By the mid-nineteenth century, the factory system was deeply entrenched. Cities grew around factories and a high percentage of the population was employed in these mills. People started working in factories as young children and worked in these menial jobs until they could no longer cope with the work.

Although working conditions in many industries improved over the years, the basic treatment of workers as "hands" continued well into the twentieth century. It was expected that managers make the decisions and workers carry them out. As one boss told his workers, "I run this department. I don't want your ideas. When you come into my department, bring in your hands and a strong back, and leave your brains at the door." Although rapidly disappearing, there are still some bosses like that.

Scientific Management

The grandfather of what became known as *scientific management* was an engineer by the name of Frederic W. Taylor. Taylor's goal was to find a way to reduce costs of manufacturing in the Midvale Steel plant in Philadelphia. This required developing accurate performance standards based on objective data acquired through time studies for every operation. Once standards were established, workers could be trained to work more efficiently by eliminating wasted time and, as an incentive, rewarded if they met or exceeded the standards.

Enter the Industrial Engineers

Scientific management led to a new class of management experts: the *industrial engineers*. Some of the older readers of this book might recall the days when these "time and motion" specialists would stand behind a worker with a clipboard, stopwatch, and checklist, timing every movement made and marking it down. The engineers then studied the results and devised ways to eliminate unnecessary steps, speeding up the overall process.

Probably the most famous industrial engineers were Frank and Lillian Gilbreth, a husband and wife team who designed a program called "The One Best Way." Its objective was to find the one best way to perform a job, resulting in true efficiency. Some skeptics reported that in their firms, once that "best way" was found, the next step was to keep working for an even better way. There was no end to the process.

What About the Human Side?

What the industrial engineers ignored was the human element. How would you feel if every move you made was timed and you were required to work like a robot? Despite the advantages of doing a job "by the numbers," this approach stifles creativity and often leads to boredom and decreased productivity. Industrial engineering has its place in industry, but there's much more to getting out the production than relying on "scientific approaches." You have to consider the human element.

The Hawthorne Studies

The first systematic approach to the human element came about by accident. In the 1920s the Western Electric Company, an AT&T subsidiary that manufactured telephone equipment, began a study at its Hawthorne, IL plant to determine the effects of hours of work, rest periods, and lighting on worker productivity. The research team chose a small group of workers to work in a separate room. Over time they altered various elements of the work environment and measured productivity. For example, the lighting was lowered gradually from bright to dim and then back to bright. They found that productivity rose when the lighting was increased, but to their surprise, continued to rise when it was made dimmer. The same held true with the other factors. Why?

The researchers concluded that the reason for the increase in productivity was the social environment. The workers developed a team relationship, which resulted in their working together more effectively. To prove the point, the research team replaced some of the workers. After factoring in the time needed for training the new people, they noted that productivity fell for a while; but once the social relationship developed, it rose again. These findings encouraged many companies to explore further the human side of managing people. The Hawthorne studies thus provided the foundation for what became the human resources movement.

Enter the Behavioral Scientists

As the human resources movement developed, more and more aspects of its effect on productivity were studied. Experts in psychology, sociology, anthropology, economics, and education were called upon to contribute their expertise to the *behavioral sciences*. Following are some of the major contributions of notable behavioral scientists.

Meanings and Gleanings

Behavioral science is the study of how and why people behave the way they do. It includes psychology, sociology, anthropology, and some phases of linguistics, economics, and education.

The Hierarchy of Needs

Abraham Maslow, a mid-twentieth-century psychologist, conducted a series of studies on what motivated people and came up with his "Hierarchy of Needs," which became the basis of the motivational programs of most companies. Briefly, Maslow stated that all humans have five basic types of needs. Starting with the lowest level, they are as follows:

➤ **Physical**   People have basic needs for food, clothing, and shelter. In the working environment these needs usually are met if workers are paid enough so that they are not concerned about life's essentials. Most people with steady, full-time jobs satisfy their basic physical needs.

➤ **Security**   People need to feel that they have some stability in their lives, that their jobs will be there for them over a reasonable period of time, and that working conditions are safe. This is why companies with a high turnover history have difficulty motivating their people—the feeling of security just isn't there.

➤ **Social**   People need to identify with a group, to be associated with others, to belong. Added to this is the desire for approval by others in the group, and to feel liked and respected.

➤ **Ego**   People want to be recognized for what they do. We all need praise and the feeling that our bosses and companies appreciate our work.

➤ **Self-actualization**   The highest need also is the most difficult to fulfill. Self-actualization is getting a peak experience from what we are doing in the workplace. It can be manifested in knowing that our job is helping us achieve our goals and the work is not only satisfactory, but also satisfying.

Tactical Tips

One of the major contributions of behavioral science to management is the belief that all people are individuals and differ from one another. To work effectively with people, get to know them and tailor your way of dealing with them to their individual personalities.

According to Maslow, these needs are hierarchical. Once a lower need is satisfied, it no longer is a motivator; to motivate that person you must go to the next level. For example, you offer a good meal to a hungry person if he will work. He does the job and eats the meal. Now you say, "I'll give you another meal for more work." It won't help because the hunger has been satisfied. It's no longer a motivator. Now reverse this: You pat a hungry person on the back and tell her, "You're a great person." It won't do any good unless you feed her first. You'll learn how this can be applied to the job in Chapter 17, "Motivating Your Staff for Peak Performance."

Theory X and Theory Y

Another behavioral scientist who has impacted greatly on human resource management is Douglas McGregor. According to McGregor, the essential task of management is to create a climate in which people can best actualize their own goals by directing their efforts toward organizational objectives. He presented two theories on the manner in which management deals with employees:

➤ **Theory X**   McGregor asserts that most management thinking is mistakenly based on the concept that people do not want to work and that leaders can get work from them only by promise of reward or threat of punishment. McGregor further asserts that if companies understood the true nature of people, they would change their approach, resulting in higher productivity.

➤ **Theory Y**   This is based on what behavioral scientists believe is the true nature of human beings: All people have within themselves motivation, potential for development, capacity to assume responsibility, and the ability and willingness to direct their behavior toward organizational goals. Management does not create these traits, but can encourage people to recognize and develop the traits themselves.McGregor's theory was that people do not need sticks or carrots to be motivated; they'll work because they want to work and will work better if they have a say in how they are to meet their objectives. Satisfaction from doing work they enjoy is enough motivation. When McGregor proposed this theory in 1950, it was considered radical. Now, a half-century later, a large percentage of companies apply Theory Y in supervising and motivating their employees to overall company management (more on this in Chapter 17).

The HR Function

Over the years the function of what now is called the human resources (HR) department has evolved from that of an auxiliary unit—sort of a support group to the operations activity—to a major department. Often it is headed by a senior vice president.

In large companies, the human resources department will actively engage in all HR functions. In smaller organizations, supervisors and team leaders might have to handle these functions with little or no guidance. In any case, all managers should be familiar with every aspect of HR functions.

Human Resources Department Functions

The human resources department is responsible for many important aspects of management. Let's look at some of the activities essential to HR management:

➤ **Hiring**   This was the main responsibility of the early personnel departments, as supervisors were too busy to handle the time-consuming function of filling job openings. This area includes setting employment policies, recruiting and screening candidates for open positions, and orienting new employees.

➤ **Training and development**   This includes designing training programs, conducting training, training department supervisors to conduct training, creating management development programs, and contracting with outside training organizations when necessary.

➤ **Compensation**   This includes setting compensation policies, keeping tabs on industry- and community-wide wage and salary rates, making job analyses, and approving recommendations for salary adjustments.

➤ **Benefits**   Today, benefits make up a significant part of the compensation package. Most companies have specialists to administer these programs. These include insurance, pensions, health, and a variety of other benefits such as 401(k), stock options, and health club memberships.

➤ **Medical**   Most larger companies have a medical section, which usually is part of the HR department. Some areas they cover are physicians and nurses at company facilities, health maintenance programs, and coordination with the benefits section for health insurance issues.

➤ **Safety**   Responsible for OSHA compliance, conducting safety campaigns and inspections, investigating accidents, and dealing with workers' compensation claims.

➤ **Labor relations**   If a union is involved with the company, this section deals with grievances, contract negotiations, and day-to-day contact with the union.

➤ **Equal employment**   Responsible for compliance with all federal and state civil rights laws. Establishes programs to keep managers and employees alert to these laws; deals with complaints of discrimination, harassment, and other violations; and administers affirmative action programs.

➤ **Personnel administration**   This section keeps all personnel records including employment papers, disciplinary documentation, official commendations, performance reviews, termination papers, and any other pertinent material about the employee. Increasingly, companies are adding comprehensive computerized personnel systems that facilitate some of these administrative areas.

Relationships Between HR and Line Managers

The HR staff is there to help *line managers*. By learning as much as possible about human relations from these specialists, department supervisors and team leaders can build their strengths in working effectively with employees. If you are a line manager, take advantage of the HR department's know-how in this critical area. Here is a list of some of the things you can learn and apply to your job:

➤ **How to become a better interviewer.** Although a member of the HR Department usually conducts the preliminary interviews with applicants, the supervisor with whom the person will work conducts subsequent interviews. It takes training to become a successful interviewer; HR staffers are equipped to help you. You'll learn some of the fundamentals of good interviewing in Chapter 8, "Becoming a Better Interviewer."

➤ **How to train.**   You probably are well qualified to show the new worker what has to be done on the job. However, the HR Department can give you new ideas for communicating ideas and implementing new training techniques on the job. We'll give you some hints on training in Chapter 11, "Training for Today's Job and Tomorrow's Advancement."

Meanings and Gleanings

A **line manager** is a supervisor who directly supervises the activities of workers. As differentiated from **staff manager,** who provides services and specialized expertise, but does not direct the work of others.

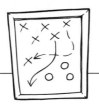

Tactical Tips

If your company does not have a human resources department, consult the person in the company who is responsible for personnel policies.

➤ **The laws.** Here is another area in which HR expertise is important. You are responsible for complying with all of the equal employment and other labor laws. You'll get an overview in Chapters 2 and 3 ("You Gotta Know the Laws" and "Still More Laws," respectively) but you should consult the HR experts for the specifics of how they apply to your company.

➤ **Company policies and procedures.** This includes motivation, discipline, and day-to-day dealings with your people. As this varies from company to company, it's important to become thoroughly familiar with them.

➤ **Union management contracts.** If there is a contract with a labor union, read the contract carefully and discuss it with someone from the HR or legal department to ensure that you don't violate any of its provisions.

➤ **Performance appraisals.** Learn the company's procedures on performance reviews. Be sure to know just what is expected of you when conducting and reporting the assessments. If there is no formal policy, consult a senior executive on this.

➤ **Termination of employees.** This is a critical area. If not properly handled, termination can lead to serious problems—even litigation. Be sure to know the company's practices. Consult with the HR manager before terminating anybody.

Personnel Policies and Procedures

Most companies have a set of policies and procedures governing their human resources. This might take the form of a detailed manual specifying exactly what must be done in every phase of the personnel activity or might be a loose set of guidelines.

Human resources policies usually are established by top management and administered by the HR department. However, the responsibility for implementing the policies rests with the department managers, supervisors, and team leaders.

HR Policies and Procedures (P&Ps)

HR *policies and procedures* (P&Ps) should start by stating the company's objectives. It's important that these objectives be realistic and meaningful to all staff members. Although primarily concerned with the relations between the company and its employees, policies and procedures also might include relations with customers, the community, and shareholders. P&Ps serve as a guide to all employees so that they understand what must be done to meet the company's overall objectives.

Well-thought-out policies are essential to human resource management because employees are sensitive to variations in the treatment they receive when compared to others. When policies are clearly stated, it is less likely that problems will arise regarding salaries, raises, vacations, work schedules, promotions, disciplinary actions, and other work-related actions. It enables managers to be consistent in their decisions.

P&Ps should be in writing. They should be communicated to all employees—not just in a manual that gathers dust on some upper shelf—but by periodic discussions with staff members and feedback to ensure that the policies are understood and accepted. Many companies give each employee an employee handbook that contains the policies and procedures. Make this handbook user-friendly. It should not be a closely printed legalistic hodge-podge of rules and regulations, but easily readable and easily understood. Gear it toward the reading level of your average worker.

Meanings and Gleanings

Polices indicate the viewpoint of the organization concerning various aspects of its activities. For example, human resources policies indicate the firm's philosophy of management and overall concepts in its dealings with employees. **Procedures** are the techniques specified for carrying out various aspects of the policies. For example, the policy provides "X" days vacation each year. The procedures show methods of setting vacation schedules and related matters.

What's the Downside of P&Ps?

There's no question that P&Ps serve a useful purpose. If a supervisor faces a human resources problem, all he or she has to do is look in the manual for the solution. This works well for most routine matters, but not every problem is routine. The supervisor looks in the manual and finds no mention of the problem—or worse, the "solution" indicated might not fit the actual situation. What to do?

One of the major problems in using a rigid manual is that often there are facets to situations that make it inadvisable to follow the recommended procedure. For example, the manual states that if an employee is late three times, he or she will be suspended for one day. Susie, one of your best producers, is late for the third time, but in your judgment she has a legitimate excuse. The manual

Personnel Perils

In recent years employee handbooks have been deemed by the courts to have the force of a contract between the employer and employee. To avoid legal complications, include a disclaimer in large print in a prominent place, stating that the contents of the manual do not constitute a contract.

doesn't give you discretion in this matter. Over-rigidity can lead to decisions that work against the best interests of both the worker and the manager. There should be some flexibility built into the P&Ps.

Another problem with P&Ps is that they stifle creativity. Managers depend too much on the manual rather than stretching their brains to come up with even better solutions to problems. Does this mean that P&Ps should be abandoned? Not at all. In general, they serve a valuable purpose, but managers should be trained to use the P&P as a guideline and be given some discretion in following it.

Over the past 100 years, the attitude of management toward the people it hires has changed significantly. True, there are still employers who are dogmatic and tyrannical, but more and more companies have recognized that the men and women on their staffs are major contributors to the success of the organization and have made human resources management a key factor in their corporate culture.

The Least You Need to Know

➤ Scientific management is developing accurate performance standards based on objective data acquired through time studies for every operation.

➤ The "Hawthorne Studies" provided the foundation for what became the human resources movement.

➤ According to Maslow's "Hierarchy of Needs," once a lower need is satisfied, it no longer is a motivator; to further motivate that person, you must go to the next level.

➤ The major functions of the human resources department include employment, training and development, compensation, benefits, medical, safety, labor relations, equal employment, and administering the personnel records.

➤ Line managers should learn as much as possible about human relations from the human resources specialists in their organization.

➤ Policies and procedures (P&Ps) manuals serve a valuable purpose, but managers should have some discretion in following them.

Chapter 2

You Gotta Know the Laws

In This Chapter

➤ Laws on race, religion, and national origin

➤ Laws on gender, pregnancy, and family issues

➤ Laws on age discrimination

➤ Understanding affirmative action

➤ The Americans with Disabilities Act

As a manager, the laws governing employment affect most of the decisions you make about the way you hire, supervise, compensate, evaluate, and discipline personnel. It begins even before your first contact with an applicant and governs all your relations with employees: how you screen candidates, what you pay employees, how you treat employees on the job—all the way to employees' separation from the company, and sometimes even after that. This chapter looks at these laws and discusses some of the problems you might have in applying them in your job. It explores some of the problems that have plagued other employers and what you can do to avoid similar troubles.

The Civil Rights Act of 1964

The primary law in this area is the Civil Rights Act of 1964, as amended, which prohibits discrimination in employment on the basis of race, color, sex, religion, or national origin. The section of the law that covers employment (Title VII) is usually referred to as the Equal Employment Opportunity (EEO) law and is administered by

Personnel Perils

In addition to federal employment laws, most states also have employment laws. In this book we'll cover only federal laws. Make it a point to check with your attorneys or local authorities on special state laws that might affect you.

Tactical Tips

The interpretation of EEO laws comes from both administrative rulings and court decisions. As in many legal matters, what seems simple often is complex. It's strongly recommended that you consult an attorney to clarify any actions you take to which these laws apply.

the Equal Employment Opportunity Commission (EEOC). All companies or organizations with 15 or more employees are subject to this law. The EEOC also administers the Age Discrimination in Employment Act (ADEA) and the Americans with Disabilities Act (ADA).

Discrimination—Race, Color, National Origin

Among the areas covered by Title VII of the federal Civil Rights Act of 1964 is the prohibition of discrimination on the basis of race, color, or national origin.

Although many states had already passed fair employment laws—some as far back as the 1940s—this was the first all-inclusive federal law to address this issue. Most companies recognize the importance of these laws and have made strong efforts to train and support staff to comply with them. Many large organizations have added equal employment officers to their human resources departments to be responsible for compliance with the laws. Smaller firms have assigned this responsibility to members of their management teams.

The Civil Rights Act made companies rethink and disregard many of the myths that kept them from hiring minorities. Such myths included the following:

➤ "White people will never work for a black supervisor."

➤ "To have a harmonious department, employees should all come from the same ethnic group."

➤ "You invite trouble if you put Poles and Germans, or Irish and Italians, or X's and Y's in the same unit."

➤ "Blacks can do only menial work."

However, the law changed more than just stereotypes. Practices and procedures such as the following had to be reconsidered:

➤ Questions on application forms and in interviews that directly or indirectly queried national origin had to be deleted (more on this in Chapters 7 and 8, "Screening Candidates" and "Becoming a Better Interviewer," respectively).

➤ Employment tests that discriminated against minorities had to be eliminated or rewritten (see Chapter 9, "Making the Hiring Decision").

➤ All employees who interviewed or processed applicants had to be trained to comply with the new laws and guidelines.

Religion

Prior to the passage of the Civil Rights Act, it was not uncommon for companies to refuse to hire people whose *religious practices* and beliefs differed from theirs. Help wanted ads often specified such requirements as "Protestants only," and application forms included questions on religion. Such requirements were prohibited by the Civil Rights Act.

In addition to prohibiting religious discrimination in hiring, the law requires companies to make *reasonable accommodation* for a person's religious practices unless doing so results in *undue hardship* on the company. This will be discussed further in Chapter 21, "Working with a Diverse Workforce."

Gender, Pregnancy, and Family Issues

In addition to the prohibition of discrimination on the basis of race, religion, and national origin, the Civil Rights Act also prohibits discrimination on the basis of gender. Interestingly, when the Civil Rights Act of 1964 was introduced in Congress, it covered only race, color, religion, and national origin. An opponent of the act added sex discrimination to it because he believed that such a radical provision would make the law unpassable. As they say, the rest is history.

Until the Equal Employment Opportunities laws, traditionally many jobs were associated with a particular gender. For the most part, skilled jobs such

Meanings and Gleanings

According to the Equal Employment Opportunity Commission Guidelines, **religious practices** include not only traditional religious beliefs, but moral and ethical beliefs, and beliefs individuals hold "with the strength of traditional religious views."

Meanings and Gleanings

Reasonable accommodation is the requirement for employers to adjust working conditions or schedules of employees to meet their religious needs or disability status. However, such accommodation is not required if it will cause the company **undue hardship,** usually defined as incurring excessive expense to make the accommodation.

15

as carpentry, machining, and plumbing were considered suitable only for men (as were engineering, accounting, outside sales, and virtually all management positions). Women's jobs usually were lower-paid positions such as nurses, typists, retail sales clerks, and low-skilled factory jobs.

Although there have always been exceptions, until this law was passed, few men were hired as secretaries and receptionists, and few women were hired or promoted to supervisory or management jobs. This law radically changed the gender structure of most companies. You now will find women in most type jobs and more men performing jobs that formerly were considered "women's work."

Bona Fide Occupational Qualifications

The gender provision of the EEO law, however, includes an additional element not found in the other categories. There are some positions for which a company is permitted to specify only a man or only a woman for the job. However, clear-cut reasons must exist for why a person of only that gender can perform the job. Within the law, these reasons are referred to as *bona fide occupational qualifications,* or *BFOQs.*

For example, if a job calls for heavy lifting, is it a BFOQ for men only? Not necessarily. There are women who have the capacity to do the job; there also are men who might not have the required strength. This can be determined by requiring that all applicants—both men and women—pass a weight-lifting test.

Additionally, let's suppose a job calls for driving a forklift truck and that the operator is occasionally required to do heavy lifting. A woman applicant might be able to drive the truck but not be able to do the lifting. If the lifting is only a small part of the job, you cannot reject her. She is capable of performing the major aspect of the work, and other people can be assigned to handle the lifting.

Meanings and Gleanings

A **bona fide occupational qualification** (**BFOQ**) exists when the gender of the employee is essential to performing the job. Some cynics have commented that the only undisputed bona fide occupational qualifications are a wet nurse (for a woman) and a sperm donor (for a man).

Here's another scenario: Suppose you have always had an attractive woman as your receptionist and the job is now open. Is being an attractive woman a BFOQ? Of course not. There's no reason that a man—with the personality and skills for the position—cannot be just as effective.

Don't Base Decisions on Stereotypes

Employers often have claimed that their policies on hiring women were not based on prejudice, but had sound business reasons. Women often have children at home and can't travel, can't work overtime, and typically stay home when a child is sick. The EEO laws do not recognize these as legitimate reasons to reject the application of a woman.

The sex discrimination provisions of the EEO laws also cover maternity and pregnancy. Although this was implied in the Civil Rights Act of 1964, it was clarified and strengthened by the Pregnancy Discrimination Act of 1978. The basic principal of this law is that women who are pregnant must be treated the same as other applicants and employees. In screening a pregnant applicant, she must be judged on her ability to perform the job for which she applies without regard to her current condition. The law also applies to current employees who might be terminated, denied benefits, or otherwise be penalized on the basis of their pregnancy or maternity.

Personnel Perils

Today, despite the laws, many employers still ask female applicants about their family responsibilities. In Chapter 8, you will learn what questions you may or may not ask and how to get the information you need lawfully.

You might be concerned that if you hire her, she will have to take time off for delivery and care of the infant, and perhaps will not even return to work. Under this law, you must assume that she will be away from the job for only a relatively short period of time. The law says that pregnancy should be considered the same as a "temporary disability." There's no question that it's temporary and in most cases it will be only a minor inconvenience to the company.

Workplace Risks

There are some jobs in which working conditions such as exposure to certain chemicals might be dangerous to unborn children. Until just a few years ago, many companies had fetal protection policies that excluded pregnant women and sometimes all women of childbearing age from these jobs. The U.S. Supreme Court ruled that such policies were illegal and that women could not be barred from these jobs.

Lawyers specializing in employment law strongly recommend that when a woman is hired or later assigned to work in such a position, she be carefully informed about the workplace risks and be asked to sign a release. Because recent studies show that certain workplace substances can affect the male reproductive system, men hired or assigned to such jobs also should be informed of the risk and required to sign releases.

Age Discrimination

The Age Discrimination in Employment Act of 1967 prohibits discrimination against individuals 40 years of age or older. Additionally, some state laws cover all persons over the age of 18. Unlike the Civil Rights Act of 1964, which covers all employers with 15 or more employees, the ADEA applies to organizations with 20 or more employees.

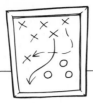

Tactical Tips

When you interview older applicants, avoid the stereotypes that might keep you from hiring highly qualified people. Maybe you "can't teach an old dog new tricks," but people are not dogs and usually can be trained to do the job for which they apply. And they may know a few tricks themselves.

The original law protected only people between the ages of 40 and 65; companies could legally refuse to hire people over 65. This was changed by later amendments; now there is no maximum age. You may not refuse to hire an applicant so long as he or she is otherwise qualified even if that person is 100 years old. The law also prohibits mandatory retirement at any age with a few exceptions (for example, companies might require senior executives to retire at a specified age).

Note that the federal law does not apply to people under 40. Theoretically, you can turn down a 35-year-old applicant for being too old for your "trainee" job—but don't try it. First, many states cover everybody over the age of 18. However, even if your state has not reduced the age, you can still get into trouble.

For instance, a few years ago a company rejected a 30-something applicant and told her they wanted a younger person for that position. She was advised that as she was under 40, she couldn't file a complaint of age discrimination under federal law or in that state.

Here's what happened: The State Job Service sent a 43-year-old applicant for an interview and when she was rejected, filed an age discrimination charge against the firm.

Even though most company application forms don't ask a person's age or date of birth and most people omit that information from their resumés, it's still easy to guess an applicant's age range within a few years. A team leader who prefers that young people join his or her team might overlook potential members who could be of great value to the team.

Affirmative Action

There's no law that requires any company to give preference to members of a minority group. In fact, Title VII of the Civil Rights Act of 1964 (the Equal Employment Opportunity law) specifies that "nothing contained in this subchapter shall be interpreted to require any employer, employment agency, labor organization … to give preferential treatment to any individual or to any group because of the race, color, religion, sex, or national origin of such individual or group."

So, why are so many companies practicing affirmative action? Some civil rights leaders assert that many discriminatory practices of the past remain so deeply embedded in basic institutions of society that they result in extreme exclusion of certain groups. This happens even when the employer has no conscious intent to discriminate. To help members of these groups catch up with the majority groups, these advocates suggested that affirmative action programs should be established. To meet this objective,

President Lyndon B. Johnson issued an *executive order* (#11246), which required not only special preference for certain minority groups, but an active program of affirmative action to recruit members of these "protected classes" into companies that held contracts with the government.

Who Is Covered? The "Protected Classes"

Executive Order #11246 requires affirmative action programs by all federal contractors and subcontractors that have contracts of more than $50,000 and have 50 or more employees. In addition to the organizations covered by the executive orders, any company that violates EEO laws might be required by the EEOC to establish an affirmative action program.

Although discrimination against all minority groups is illegal, only five groups have been designated as "protected classes." They are as follows:

Meanings and Gleanings

An **executive order** is not a law. It is an edict promulgated by the president without being passed by Congress. Executive orders do not apply to the entire population—only to government agencies or organizations that do business with the government. Violation of an executive order can lead to cancellation of the government contract and debarment from future business with the government.

➤ **Blacks**   This covers all individuals who are of African American background (however, in reporting, blacks of Hispanic background are listed under Hispanics).

➤ **Hispanics**   This group includes all people who derive from countries in Latin America. (People from Spain are not considered "Hispanics," they are considered "white" like other Europeans.)

➤ **Asians or Pacific Islanders**

➤ **Native Americans or Alaskan natives**

➤ **Women**

Determining the Numbers

Companies that are required to engage in affirmative action programs must hire members of each of the protected classes, in proportion to the population of people in each class within their communities. These numbers are based on figures issued by the Department of Labor and can be obtained from the Office of Contract Compliance, U.S. Dept. of Labor, Washington, DC, 20010.

Contractors then must survey their current work force to determine the number of employees in each category for each job classification. This is to set goals to bring

into each job classification a representative group of people from all of the classes within the community. For example, a company might have a staff consisting of 40 percent black employees in a community where the African American population is 12 percent. The company is not in compliance because all of the black employees are in the lowest job classification. To comply, the company must take steps to bring more African Americans into higher-level jobs.

The requirement for affirmative action applies only to the five protected classes noted in the preceding section. For example, even though 40 percent of your community are Italians, it is not necessary that 40 percent of your workforce be Italian. On the other hand, if Hispanics, Asians, blacks, or Native Americans make up 40 percent of the community you must strive to have 40 percent of that group in each level of your workforce. More difficult is determining standards for women. The Department of Labor bases this on the number of "women in the workforce" rather than women in general.

The Americans with Disabilities Act

The newest and probably least understood civil rights law is the Americans with Disabilities Act (ADA). Your company must adhere to this law if it has 15 or more employees. The ADA makes it illegal to discriminate in hiring, job assignments, and the treatment of employees because of a disability. Employers also must make reasonable accommodation so that disabled employees can perform the essential duties of their jobs. This accommodation can vary from building access ramps for wheelchair users to providing special equipment for people who are seeing- or hearing-challenged.

Reasonable accommodation for the disabled is required unless the accommodation will be an undue hardship for the company. Undue hardship usually is defined in monetary terms. If an applicant who uses a wheelchair applies for a job with a small company, the cost of building an elevator or a ramp to create access to the job location might be a financial hardship. If it is not possible to provide a less expensive accommodation, the company could reject the applicant. However, if the same applicant applies for a job in a more affluent company, it might not be considered undue hardship to do the necessary construction.

Accommodation doesn't always require expensive construction. Here are some other ways to meet this requirement:

➤ The small company you work for wants to hire Gregory, an accountant who uses a wheelchair, but the accounting department is on the second floor of your building. The building has no elevator or ramp, and providing one would be an undue financial hardship for your company. However, there might be other ways to accommodate Gregory. Use your imagination. You could let him work on the ground floor or his work could be brought to him. It might be an inconvenience, but it would qualify as reasonable accommodation, and it would enable you to hire a particularly competent accountant.

➤ Dorothy, a highly skilled word processor operator, is legally blind and walks with the aid of a white cane. She can transcribe from dictated material faster and more accurately than many sighted people. You want to hire her, but you're concerned that in case of a fire or other emergency she would be a danger to herself and others. The accommodation you can make is to assign someone to escort Dorothy in case of an emergency.

➤ Pete, an applicant for an assembler in a factory was badly injured in an automobile accident. The job requires him to stand at a workbench all day. Pete is unable to stand for long periods of time. Is this a legitimate reason to reject him? Accommodations can be made. Perhaps a high stool could be provided so that Pete could reach the workbench without having to stand. If that option isn't feasible, the job structure could be changed so that he could work part time on that job and do other work that doesn't require standing for long portions of the day.

Alcohol and Drug Users

Alcohol and drug users are considered disabled under the ADA. If a person can perform a job satisfactorily, a previous record of alcoholism or drug addiction is not reason enough to refuse hiring. However, if an applicant is still addicted and it resulted in poor attendance or poor performance in his or her previous job, you can reject the person—not because of the addiction, but because of poor work habits.

Most companies prohibit drinking on company premises or coming to work under the influence. If an employee violates this rule, he or she can be disciplined according to company rules. This may vary from just being sent home to a suspension or termination.

As using drugs is illegal in all states, companies have stricter rules on drugs. In most companies taking drugs on the job is a serious offense, and suspected drug users, even if they are not caught taking the drugs, may be required to be tested.

If you suspect that an employee cannot perform a job because of alcohol or drug abuse, have the person sent to the medical department. Drug testing is a medical procedure. Employees should be made aware that this policy will be enforced, and it should be clearly stated in the company's policy manual.

Utilizing the Talents of Physically and Mentally Challenged People

Even in this day of computers and technological sophistication, many types of work are still routine and repetitive, resulting in high turnover among workers who are assigned to that work. Many companies have found that people who are mentally challenged can do this work and are not bored by it. These people often are capable of learning much more than you might expect.

Training the mentally challenged requires more patience and some tasks might have to be simplified; however, trainees who master these tasks retain the skills and often improve on them. Coaches who are specially trained to work with mentally challenged people are available in many communities. Your local mental health association can tell you whether this type of help is available in your area.

When you interview a candidate for a new job or consider someone for a promotion, don't focus on disabilities. Concentrate on that person's abilities. In this way you will not only give that person a chance to do his or her best on the job, but will give your department or company the opportunity to utilize the very best talents of all its people.

The Least You Need to Know

➤ The Civil Rights Act of 1964 prohibits discrimination in employment based on race, color, national origin, or sex.

➤ Women who are pregnant must be treated the same as other applicants and employees.

➤ The Age Discrimination in Employment Act of 1967 (ADEA) prohibits discrimination against individuals 40 years of age or older. Some state laws cover all persons over the age of 18.

➤ Companies that have government contracts of more than $50,000 and 50 or more employees must establish and implement an affirmative action program.

➤ The Americans with Disabilities Act makes it illegal to discriminate in hiring, in job assignments, and in the treatment of employees because of a disability.

Chapter 3

Still More Laws

In This Chapter

➤ Laws related to wages and salaries

➤ Laws on hiring noncitizens

➤ Laws on labor relations

➤ The Family and Medical Leave Act

In the previous chapter, we covered laws relating to various aspects of fair employment. These are the laws that many of us are most concerned about, but there are other laws that are just as important. These include laws governing wages and hours, immigration laws, laws on labor relations, and more recently a law that requires employers to give employees time off to deal with family and medical problems. Let's see how these affect your human resources responsibilities.

Wage and Hour Laws

Until the administration of Franklin D. Roosevelt, there were no federal laws governing wages and hours. Although some states had such laws, unless there was a union, employers could pay as much or as little as the market would bear, and workers could be required to work long hours without extra compensation. The first comprehensive federal law regulating wages and hours was the Fair Labor Standards Act of 1938. Over the years it has been amended many times and is still the basic law governing these issues.

The Least You Can Pay

The minimum wage is established periodically by Congress and has become something of a political football. Every few years it is raised to be at least congruent with the cost of living, but the exact amount of the increase is always a battle between the "pro-labor" groups, which want it to be high, and the "pro-employer" groups, which fight to keep it down. In addition, the relationship between the available supply and demand for workers in various fields influences Congress in making these decisions. For example, when demand for workers is high, wages go up no matter what the law requires. During the past few years when most wages have been high, Congress has not changed the minimum wage, even though there are still many workers being paid low rates. The pressure to raise the rate has been mitigated by the higher wages paid to most workers.

Meanings and Gleanings

An **exempt employee** is one who is engaged in management, administration, professional work, and others who use "independent judgment" in their work. In addition, outside salespersons are considered exempt. Persons falling into this category can be required to work overtime with no extra compensation. All others are considered **nonexempt** and are subject to the overtime requirements of the law.

The one standard that has been consistent since the passage of the original act has been the 40-hour work week. *Nonexempt employees* must be paid at the rate of one and one half their hourly pay for each hour in excess of 40 hours worked in any week. *Exempt employees* need not be paid for overtime.

If you have any question about whether a job is considered exempt, contact the local office of the U.S. Department of Labor (listed in the phone book under U.S. Government) for specific rulings. Most states have similar laws. Inasmuch as some state laws vary from the federal law, be sure to check the laws that govern business in the state or states in which your company has facilities.

Special Laws Related to Government Contractors

Even before the Fair Labor Standards Act was passed in 1938, there were two laws on the books governing companies that had contracts to construct public works for the federal government. Although they were chiefly designed for the construction industry, the courts have ruled that they apply to any company engaged in work for any federal agency. These laws are the Davis-Bacon Act and the Walsh-Healy Act.

➤ **The Davis-Bacon Act (1931)** The minimum rate paid to companies engaged in public works projects must be at least equal to the *prevailing rate* in the community in which the work is being done. The prevailing rate is defined as that paid to 30 percent of the workers in that area. As this law primarily applies to the construction industry, and usually at least 30 percent of these workers are in labor unions, the rate paid often is actually higher than the average rate in the area. Attempts to repeal the act—or at least the 30 percent rule—have consistently been defeated in Congress.

➤ **The Walsh-Healy Act (1936)**   This act also only covers companies engaged in public works projects. It reiterates the prevailing wage rule of the Davis-Bacon Act and adds the provision that time and a half (overtime) be paid for all hours worked over eight hours in any one day or 40 hours in one week, depending on which is higher.

If your company is engaged in a federally contracted public works project, non-exempt employees must be paid at the rate of time and a half for all hours worked over eight in any given day, even if they don't work a full 40-hour week. Some union contracts also have such a provision.

Equal Pay Act

The Equal Pay Act of 1963 requires that an employee's gender not be considered in determining salary (equal pay for equal work). As this act is an amendment to the Fair Labor Standards Act, all employers engaged in interstate commerce are covered no matter how many employees they have. The law was passed to eliminate the common practice of paying women less than men who were doing similar work.

For example, a male "porter" on the cleaning crew was paid more than a female "maid." Often this was justified by claiming the porter had heavier work such as climbing ladders and lifting heavy loads. However, this often represented a minuscule part of his work. Most work was the same as that of his female counterpart.

In the "olden days," it was assumed that men should be paid more because they supported a family and women worked only if they were single and had to support only themselves. If a married woman worked, it was to earn "pin money," to supplement her husband's income. Now, of course, we don't accept these myths; but the practice of paying less to women persists. According to the latest figures from the U.S. Department of Labor, women in the workplace paid on an hourly basis earn only 73.2 percent of what men earn; women paid on a weekly basis, 76.3 percent; and women paid on an annual basis, 81.8 percent.

The Immigration Reform and Control Act of 1986

You're worried. You continually read about companies that get into trouble for hiring undocumented aliens (no, not Martians—people from foreign countries). You're almost afraid to hire anyone who has a foreign accent. Uh, oh! Not hiring someone because of this fear is illegal.

Personnel Perils

Failure to obtain the proper documentation when hiring noncitizens, such as their "green card" or other authorization to work, can lead at minimum to loss of production due to deportation of the undocumented workers; at most to fines or imprisonment.

You cannot discriminate against a person because he or she isn't an American. However, you must ensure that an applicant is legally allowed to work in this country; noncitizens who work in the United States must have proper documentation. There are two types of scenarios most often involved in the hiring of non–United States citizens. I'll examine both in the following sections.

It's Up to You to Find Out

Many immigrants come into this country—some legally; many more illegally—looking for work. Most of these people seek lower-level positions as farm hands, factory workers, hospital and nursing home attendants, taxi drivers, and similar positions. Your main concern is to ensure that the applicant has the proper documentation.

To ensure that you comply with government regulations …

➤ Make sure all new employees (not just those that you suspect are foreign) fill out an I-9 form. You can obtain copies from the Immigration and Naturalization Service. This form should not be completed until after a person is hired. When a starting date is agreed upon, the employee should be advised that he or she must submit proper documentation before being put on the payroll.

➤ Make sure new employees provide documents to prove their identity. You have to be sure that a new employee isn't using someone else's papers. Acceptable documents include a driver's license with photo, a school ID with photo, and similar papers. A telephone or utility bill can prove that the employee has provided a correct address.

➤ Require new employees to provide documents to prove citizenship. These documents include a current U.S. passport, certificate of naturalization, birth certificate, or voter registration card.

➤ Require that noncitizens provide documents that authorize employment. The most commonly used authorization is Form I-551, usually called the "green card" (originally it was green; now it's white). The employee's photograph is laminated to the card. (Other forms are acceptable for students who might work while in school and some other exceptional cases.)

Most applicants will be able to provide the necessary papers, but some applicants may have misplaced or lost them. Assuming they are legitimate, these documents can be obtained.

26

If the person you hire cannot show you the required documents, advise him or her to do everything possible to locate them. If they cannot be located, they should be applied for at once. When the application is made, the employee must show proof that an application for the document has been made. This can be in the form of a receipt from the appropriate agency or of certified mail sent to the agency.

These receipts should be photocopied and kept until the documents are received and shown to you. The law requires that the employee present the documents to the employer within 21 days of starting the job, or that person's employment must be terminated. When the documents are received and examined, notations should be made on the Form I-9 indicating the type of document and identification number (if any). Make photocopies of the documents; the originals should be returned to the employee.

Employers who hire undocumented aliens are subject to fines and, in cases of repeated offenses, imprisonment. If you have any doubts about a document or any questions concerning the law, contact the local office of the Immigration and Naturalization Service.

Personnel Perils

The immigration laws do not prohibit you from hiring non-citizens. Refusal to hire a person who is legally permitted to work in this country because of his or her nationality is unlawful under the Civil Rights laws.

Hiring Foreign Students and Specialists

There are situations in which an employer actively recruits men and women from foreign countries for hard-to-fill jobs. Most of these people are professionals or highly skilled workers. Hospitals need physicians and nurses, which are in short supply in their communities. Technical organizations need engineers and technicians to staff their teams. In this section, you'll learn what is required to bring these specialists into the United States and onto your payroll.

Here are some situations in which you may put foreign nationals on your payroll:

➤ Foreign students may come to the United States to study in a field in which practical training is desirable. The student's university can apply for a practical training visa (F1 visa). This will allow the student to work for one year in his or her field of study. If the person you want to hire has this visa, you can hire that person immediately and you need not take any further action. However, remember that the visa expires one year after it is issued and that person is no longer allowed to work in the United States unless some other visa is obtained. If you are interested in hiring such students, a good source of referrals is the universities that train them.

➤ Exchange students (students from foreign universities) may come here to continue their studies and pick up practical experience in their fields of expertise. To hire such students, contact an exchange student organization, which arranges for the necessary documentation (J-1 visa).

➤ Those who have a nonpermanent work authorization (H-1 visa) may work temporarily in the United States. (There are several different types of visas depending on the kind of work the individual engages in. For example, registered nurses require form H-1A; technical workers, form H-1B.) If you can prove to the INS that the skills needed to fill a job cannot be found among American citizens or permanent residents, you may obtain permission to recruit the needed employee from a foreign country. Employees who come to the United States under this program may stay here for six years. However, during this time, if they wish, they may apply for permanent residence (the green card), and if granted, have the same rights as any other permanent resident, including application for U.S. citizenship.

Once you locate a suitable candidate, you must apply for the H-1 visa. Even if you find a qualified candidate who is already in the United States and has an H-1 visa to work in another company, you will need to apply to the Immigration and Naturalization Service to transfer it. This takes four to eight weeks. The processes and rules governing this visa are very complicated; an attorney or consultant specializing in immigration should be retained.

The National Labor Relations Act

In 1935—long before the Civil Rights Acts were passed—Congress enacted the Wagner Act, which prohibited employers from discriminating against workers on the basis of union membership or activity. This law is still in effect.

Discriminating Against Union Members

The Wagner and Taft-Hartley Acts cover a variety of matters related to employer-union relations. One section of the law applies to the hiring process. It is illegal to discriminate against a person because he or she is a member of a union. An employer may not even inquire whether an applicant is a union member.

The basic provisions of the National Labor Relations Act (NLRA), usually called the Wagner Act, are as follows:

➤ Employers may not interfere, restrain, or coerce employees into organizing or participating in unions.

➤ Employers may not contribute to the financial support of a union (this is to restrict formation of phony, company-dominated unions).

➤ Employers may not discriminate in the hiring or tenure of applicants or employees because of their union membership or activities.

➤ Employers may not refuse to bargain collectively with unions that have been certified to represent their employees.

The Taft-Hartley Act (1947) added these restrictions on unions:

➤ Unions may not restrain employees from or coerce employees against the exertion of their rights.

➤ Unions may not restrain or coerce employees in their selection of a bargaining unit.

➤ Unions may not require employers to discriminate against employees who choose not to join the union.

➤ Unions may not refuse to bargain with an employer.

➤ Unions may not charge excessive initiation fees or dues.

In addition, the National Labor Relations Board, which enforces these laws, has added a variety of interpretations and administrative rulings.

Before the passage of the Taft-Hartley Act many management-union contracts called or a *closed shop.* The company was required to hire people who were members of the union—often through the union's hiring halls. This was outlawed by the Taft-Hartley Act. However, contracts may call for a *union shop* in which nonunion members can be hired, but must join the union within a specified period of time after employment.

> **Meanings and Gleanings**
>
> A **closed shop** is a company that is required to hire only members of the union with which it has a contract. In a **union shop** a company may hire nonunion members, but employees must join the union within a specified time after being hired.

What About "Right to Work" Laws?

When the Taft-Hartley Act was proposed, one of the major areas of contention in Congressional debates was the right of workers to decide whether they want to join a union. Many union contracts included clauses that required all employees working for the company join the union, whether they wanted to or not. This was referred to as a union shop.

Conservative congressmen wanted to completely outlaw such a requirement. A compromise was reached on this point: Instead of the federal government making it illegal for a union to require that all employees of the company be compelled to join the union shop, the decision was left to the states. Several states have passed these laws, called "right to work" laws. In these states, it is illegal to require any employee to join a union as a condition of employment. A company is not allowed to ask applicants if they are members of a union, even if the contract calls for a closed shop. Bring up the subject of union membership only after you've made a job offer. If your company has a union or is facing union organization, it's best to obtain the services of an attorney who specializes in labor relations.

The Family and Medical Leave Act

Conflict between work and family obligations has become an inevitable aspect of modern work life, often resulting in absenteeism, work interference, job turnover, and other detrimental impacts. Although conflict between work and family responsibilities cannot be eliminated, family leave and other work/family policies can make it easier for America's workers to fulfill their responsibilities as parents, family members, and workers.

In 1993 Congress passed the FMLA (Family and Medical Leave Act), which requires companies with 50 or more employees to provide eligible employees with as much as 12 weeks of unpaid leave in any 12-month period. Family and Medical Leave may be taken for any of the following reasons:

➤ The birth or adoption of a child or the placement of a child for adoption or foster care.

➤ To care for a spouse, child, or parent with a serious health condition.

➤ The employee's own serious health condition.

To be eligible, the employee must have been employed by the company for at least 12 months and, in the case of a child, must request this leave at least 30 days before the expected birth, adoption, or foster care placement. When this notification isn't possible, such as in the case of a serious illness of a family member, employees are required to provide as much notice as possible. Both men and women are eligible for leave under this law; however, if both husband and wife work for the same employer, the total amount of leave is limited to 12 weeks for the couple.

The key provisions of the law require the following:

➤ When the employee returns from leave, the company must provide him or her with the same position or a position with equivalent pay, benefits, and other conditions of employment.

➤ Health insurance must be continued during the leave period and paid for in full even though the employee is no longer being paid wages or salary at that time.

As with most laws, variations apply in special circumstances. For example, Dick's mother receives outpatient chemotherapy every Tuesday. He brings her to the hospital on Tuesday and stays with her on Wednesday while she regains her strength. Although the law primarily calls for continuing periods of leave, special arrangements can be made so that Dick can take off the time he needs. However, if the type of work Dick does makes this arrangement infeasible, the company has the right to transfer him temporarily to another job—with the same pay and benefits—that enables him to take the days off.

Secretary of Labor Alexis Herman reported in August 1998 that an estimated 20 million people have benefited from the Family and Medical Leave Act. To obtain the details about how this law might affect you or a team member, check with your human resources department, legal department, or local office of the Wage and Hour Division of the U.S. Department of Labor (listed in the U.S. Government pages of most local telephone directories).

Laws on Safety and Health

In 1970, Congress passed the Occupational Safety and Health Act (OSHA). The act was designed to "assure so far as possible every working man and woman in the nation safe and healthy working conditions and to preserve our human resources." Enforcement of this law is in the jurisdiction of the Occupational Safety and Health Administration (also referred to as OSHA) of the U.S. Department of Labor. Many states also have enacted similar legislation.

Regulations on health and safety are publicized by OSHA and must be adhered to by all companies engaged in interstate commerce. These are published in the Federal Register. It is the obligation of all companies to study and implement these rules. A more detailed discussion of this and other health and safety issues will be found in Chapter 19, "Keep 'Em Safe and Healthy."

Personnel Perils

Companies must ensure that all managers, supervisors, and team leaders are thoroughly familiar with the OSHA regulations and, where pertinent, state safety and health rules related to the works and facilities they supervise. Failure to comply can be very costly.

Managers at all levels must be aware of all of the laws that affect management-worker relations. If you have any doubts, questions, or concerns about how the laws affect your actions, get in touch with your company's legal counsel to ensure that you don't violate these laws.

The Least You Need to Know

➤ The Fair Labor Standards Act requires that all nonexempt employees be paid time and a half overtime for all hours worked over 40 hours in any week.

➤ The Equal Pay Act of 1963 requires that an employee's gender not be considered in determining salary (equal pay for equal work).

➤ You cannot discriminate against a person because he or she isn't an American. However, you must ensure that an applicant is legally allowed to work in this country.

➤ You cannot refuse to hire or discriminate against a person on the job because he or she is a member of a labor union.

➤ All managers and supervisors must be prepared to implement the OSHA regulations concerning their company and workplace.

Part 2
Staffing Your Organization

Hiring people is time consuming, expensive, and to many managers a side issue that takes them away from their real duties—getting out production.

Even if you have a human resources department that does much of the work in seeking new employees, the manager must be actively involved in the process. You have to be involved in determining just what qualifications the new employee must have to succeed in the job. You have to participate in the interviewing and almost always, it's you who makes the final decision to hire or reject.

Even the best supervisors can use help in this function. In the following chapters I'll show you how to avoid the major hiring mistakes and then steer you through the steps that will enable you to make better hiring decisions.

Chapter 4

Twenty-Five Mistakes Companies Make in Hiring

In This Chapter

➤ Starting off on the wrong foot

➤ Not using all available resources

➤ Failure to properly prescreen applicants

➤ Making unwise decisions

➤ Losing applicants you want to hire

What do you do when a vacancy develops in your department? Most managers hate expending the time, energy, and emotional drain that the hiring process involves. It takes them away from their regular duties; adds extra hours to their day; and worst of all, often they fear they will make the wrong choice and have to go through the whole process over again in a few months.

In most large companies (and in many smaller firms), the human resources department handles recruiting and selection of new employees. Even so, line supervisors and team leaders have to participate in the process; almost always, they also will interview prospects. After all, they are the people to whom the person hired will report and ultimately they are responsible for the new employee's success or failure.

In some companies there might not be an HR department or, if there is one, it is situated at the home office; so managers at branch facilities are required to do the hiring themselves. Unfortunately, although these managers usually are skilled in performing work in their own specialty, they don't have the training and experience required for successful hiring.

I have had the opportunity to observe the hiring processes in hundreds of companies. I've witnessed countless errors that have resulted in wasted time and effort at minimum, and in hiring people who were doomed to fail at worst. This chapter will identify the 25 most frequently made hiring mistakes and will provide suggestions on how to overcome them.

Getting Started All Wrong

The hiring process, like all effective processes, must be carefully planned. You cannot wait until a vacancy occurs. It takes careful thinking about the job, a thoughtfully developed job analysis, and a continuous updating of all of the jobs in your organization.

Management Miscellany

According to the Society for Human Resources Management (SHRM), the cost of hiring an employee is 1.5 times the annual salary. This includes recruiting costs, training time, and lost productivity as co-workers and supervisors pitch in during the time the job is left unfilled.

#1—Not Updating the Specs

It might seem logical to start by pulling out the current job description and specifications, and searching for somebody who qualifies. But is it really logical? The job description might have been written several years ago—and jobs change over time. What is being done today might be somewhat different from what was done then. It's a good idea to review carefully and critically every job description before starting the search to refill it.

For example, one common reason for a job to become available is the voluntary resignation of an employee. An example of this is Lisa, a customer service representative, who notifies you that she's decided to go back to school and will leave the job in two weeks. When Lisa was hired, customer service reps wrote out customer complaints on a form, checked them out, and then telephoned or wrote to the customer with the results and suggested solutions. During her tenure all this became computerized so that many of the problems could be checked and adjusted during the first telephone call.

Although Lisa was very good in her dealings with customers, her computer skills were poor and she was much slower than other reps. Thus, the *job description* and *job specifications* should be rewritten with more emphasis placed on computer skills. Details on *job analysis* and how to write job descriptions and specifications will be given in Chapter 5, "Starting the Search."

#2—Inflexible Specs

Job specs can be so rigid that you're unable to find anyone who meets all your requirements. Sometimes you have to make compromises. Re-examine the job specs and set priorities. Which of the specs are nonnegotiable? These requirements are the ones a new employee absolutely must bring to a job; otherwise, there is no way the job can be done. For example, a candidate must have a jet pilot's license to fly the company plane; another candidate must be able to do machine work to precise measurements in order for the work to pass inspection.

Meanings and Gleanings

Job analysis includes a description of the duties and responsibilities of the job (**job description**) and the background required to perform the job (**job specification**).

Other specs are not essential but preferable. For example, the job calls for using spreadsheets. It is preferable that the applicant is experienced with Microsoft Excel, but having worked with other spreadsheets or similar programs should be acceptable as software specifics can easily be learned on the job.

Suppose that your specs call for sales experience. One of the applicants has no job experience in selling, but as a volunteer was a top fundraiser for the local community theater. That person might be able to do the job. In seeking to fill a job, the manager or supervisor should make every effort to abide by the job specs. However, the manager also should have the authority to use his or her judgment to determine when deviation from the job specs is acceptable.

#3—Establishing Unrealistic Specifications

You may dream up specs that you would ideally like to have, but are rarely found in candidates for the open job. Don't make the mistake of establishing unrealistic specifications that really are not needed to perform the job. By mandating them, the best candidates might be eliminated for the wrong reasons.

For example, when the Property Development Corporation expanded its Minneapolis division, one of the jobs it created was that of a divisional controller. The job included managing the accounting department, dealing with banks and other financial institutions, and coordinating financial matters with the home office. In determining the specifications for the job, the company required comprehensive experience in similar work, a degree in accounting, an MBA, and certification as a CPA (certified public accountant).

Are these educational requirements truly needed for success in the job? Because the job calls for extensive knowledge of accounting, the degree in accounting most likely is an essential factor—but why an MBA? Graduate degrees in business can provide a good deal of knowledge and analytical skills. However, the specific skills needed to be a successful controller also can be acquired, not in graduate school, but by extensive, hands-on work experience.

If an MBA is a requirement, men and women who have the necessary skills but not the degree will be eliminated. To avoid this, the MBA instead should be considered as only one method of acquiring the skills needed to do the job. Lack of the degree should not eliminate an otherwise viable candidate.

Let's look at the requirement for certification (CPA). Certification is required for accountants working as public accountants, whose work involves dealing with clients' accounts and certifying their accuracy. The CPA license is needed for a career in public accounting, but is not necessary for accounting positions in companies or organizations. A background in auditing and other public accounting activities might be a valuable asset for controllers—and it certainly is not a negative factor. However, to make it a job requirement also might eliminate the best-qualified applicants.

#4—Waiting for Vacancies

Sometimes you know when a person plans to leave. She might be reaching retirement age; he might decide to be a stay-at-home dad once his child is born. This gives you weeks or months to find a replacement. But often, it's a complete surprise. Sarah finds a better job and gives you two weeks notice; Tom is badly injured in a car accident and will be out for months.

Some jobs are more difficult to fill than others. Unless there's a plan for hiring new people, the job might go unfilled for a long time. Implementing an ongoing recruiting policy can minimize such problems. Even if there is no vacancy in your department, accept applications from good prospects and keep an active resource file; this way, when an opening does occur you have a head start in the recruiting process.

#5—Settling for a "Warm Body"

The job is open and the right candidate just hasn't come along; so you hire a marginally qualified person to just "do the work." Big mistake. This is how companies often wind up with a glut of marginal workers. You figure you can train them to become at least "satisfactory"; but the time, energy, and money spent rarely pays off. It's better to get the work done by utilizing other team members to meet work schedules, employing temps, or outsourcing the work. Take your time and aim for well-qualified people.

#6—Cloning the Incumbents

In seeking to replace an effective employee who has moved on, companies often seek that person's mirror image. For example, you loved Diane. You wish you had 10 like her. When she left because her husband was transferred to another city, you were devastated. Your goal: Hire another Diane. So you use her background as the specs for her replacement. Diane graduated from an Ivy League college; therefore, her replacement must come from an Ivy League school. Diane always dressed in bright colors—really made the place more cheerful—therefore, applicants with bright clothes will be preferred. Before she worked in your company, Diane worked in a bank; bank experience is important, and so on.

Conversely, if he or she was not effective, an employer might search for the exact opposite. For example, you fired Alfred. Alfred was from New York; thus, his successor should come from a smaller community. Alfred was an avid sports fan—he always talked about sports. People like that don't really concentrate on their work; no sports fans. Alfred had a background in Macintosh computers. Although he did learn our PCs, he always complained that Macs were better. Therefore, no Mac users, and on and on.

Such trivial factors often enter into the unofficial job specs. It is unwise to use the incumbent or a predecessor's personal characteristics as significant factors in determining the qualifications for a job. Not only can it keep you from hiring the best-qualified person; it might overly influence you to hire an unqualified person.

Recruiting Resources

To get the best possible candidates for a job, it's a good idea to use as many sources as possible. Just because the last administrative assistant you hired came from an ad in the local paper doesn't mean you can depend exclusively on running an ad. Open your mind, open your Rolodex, and use your imagination to broaden the market.

#7—Up from the Ranks

Promoting or transferring a current employee to a new position is commendable and should be encouraged. Internal candidates are known factors. The company has seen them in action and knows their strengths and weaknesses, personality quirks, work habits, attendance and punctuality patterns, and all the little things that months or years of observation uncover. Additionally, promoting and transferring from within are good for employee morale and motivation.

However, a problem arises when a company tries to limit the candidates for a position to only current employees. In this highly competitive world, a company should attempt to find the very best candidate for an open position. That person might not currently be on your payroll.

Management Miscellany

When companies fill advanced positions primarily with current employees, they tend to perpetuate the racial, ethnic, and gender makeup of the staff. To achieve a diverse workforce, expand the resources from which you choose candidates for all positions.

There was a time when companies boasted that when the chairman retired, they hired a junior clerk; everybody moved up a notch. In today's large organizations it is more likely that there are many highly competent people available to fill the new openings—and of course they should be seriously considered. However, a search for outside candidates might bring to the company skills and expertise currently lacking, and new ideas that often elude people already established in the organization.

#8—Relying on a Friend of a Friend

Personal contacts are excellent sources for referrals. People you know from your business and social worlds often might be ideal candidates themselves or might recommend highly qualified people from their networks. Indeed, networking can be a prime source of potential applicants.

However, using personal contacts has its downside. First, the people you contact might not know anybody at this time who is qualified. Worse yet, they might palm off a friend or relative who needs a job but has limited abilities applicable to your opening. Turning down a friend of a friend might jeopardize your personal or business relationship with the person who made the referral.

Another problem might occur when you are overly impressed with the personality or sociability of a person you know, but fail to consider his or her true capability for the open position. A good example of this is Harry, the sales manager of Amalgamated Products. Harry was always looking for good salespeople. He had known Jim for years; they belonged to the same golf club and occasionally played together or socialized in the restaurant or bar. When Harry learned that Jim was looking for a job, he offered him a position on his sales force.

It didn't take long for Harry to realize that Jim needed considerable training and supervision if he was to succeed. It was only after months of wasted effort and frustration that Harry finally let him go. Had Harry used even minimum screening, he would have learned that Jim had a pattern of failure in his previous jobs.

Many companies encourage their current employees to recommend friends and acquaintances for open jobs. This can be a valuable resource and should be used. However, it should be made clear that a referral by a current employee is not a guarantee of a job and that the applicant will be treated as any other applicant.

#9—Ads That Don't Pull

Help wanted advertising is expensive. You might be running a classified ad in the local paper to fill a clerical or blue-collar position, or a display ad in a national publication for a technical expert or an executive. Either way, the results can range from just a few replies to a deluge of resumés.

No matter how many responses you receive, the key is whether the respondents actually fit the job. Too many companies place ads that either do not pull at all or bring in a plethora of responses from unqualified people. Too many managers write help wanted ads without giving them adequate thought. They scribble the ad on a scratch pad while waiting for a phone call to go through or on a paper napkin while eating lunch. It's worth the time to learn how to write and place effective ads. You can get help in writing ads from your own advertising department or an ad agency.

Management Miscellany

Studies show that when screening responses received from an ad, employment specialists spend an average of 30 seconds reading each resumé before deciding whether the applicant should be given further consideration.

#10—Failure to Take Proactive Steps in Seeking Candidates

Are your recruiters surfing the Internet on a 24/7 basis? Are they visiting the Web sites of competitors to identify their top producers and attempting to entice them away? Are they reviewing the constant flow of listings on the Internet referral services such as Monster.com, Careerpath.com, and others to look for the talents needed by your firm?

Management Miscellany

According to a poll of 400 employers taken by Recruiters Network of Milwaukee, Wisconsin in August 2000, 59 percent of respondents reported that Internet recruiting significantly reduced the cost per hire.

Screening Fiascos

Whether you have located the candidate through an ad, a referral, or online, it takes time—lots of time—to filter out the unqualified and select those you think are worthy of an interview. Once an applicant is invited for an interview, depending on the type of position, an initial interview can take anywhere from 10 minutes to more than an hour.

How much time do you have to devote to interviewing? Even if you are a full-time interviewer in the human resources department, there are only so many hours each day you can schedule. If you are a team leader, department head, or senior executive

41

your day probably is already full and interviewing means putting in extra hours. You must be able to prescreen candidates so that those you interview are viable prospects for the position.

#11—Resumé Fantasies

The prescreening tactic most often used is the resumé. Most employers ask prospective employees to provide a resumé either before the first meeting or at the interview. As resumés are written to impress prospective employers, you must learn how to separate the facts from the fluff.

Beware of the functional-style resumé. In this format, the writer describes the functions performed in previous jobs. This is very helpful in learning about the applicant's background but often is used to play up functions in which the applicant has only superficial knowledge. If the applicant wishes to hide it, the resumé might not indicate the duration of the experience or the name or type of company in which it was obtained.

For example, Gertrude has used a functional format. She lists four functions: administration, data processing, human resources, and secretarial. Although 80 percent of her job was secretarial, her resumé gives the impression that she was equally involved in all four functions. This doesn't mean you should not consider Gertrude for the job. It does mean that you must be prepared to ask very specific questions about the details of her experience in each of the functions listed.

When seeking an information technology (IT) position, Ted used the more traditional chronological resumé. However, instead of listing the dates of his employment, he noted only the number of years spent in each position followed by a description of the duties performed. For example:

> Systems Specialist, ABC Co. (5 years)
>
> Programmer, XYZ Co. (3 years)
>
> Sales Representative, Apex Insurance Co. (8 years)

This gives the impression that the past eight years were in computer work; in reality, the most recent job was the last one listed—selling insurance. He has been away from computer work for some time—and the field has changed significantly during those years.

#12—Prescreening Foibles

Sometimes when companies are in a rush to fill a job, they might ask applicants to call for appointments or come right to the office, making it difficult to prescreen candidates. Despite all the problems of reading and evaluating resumés, they do help to eliminate unqualified people, which saves interviewing time. When no resumé is used, it is more difficult to weed out time-wasting candidates. One way to overcome this is by a carefully structured telephone interview. Asking good questions will help determine whether or not to invite the candidate in for an interview. This will be discussed in more detail in Chapter 7, "Screening Candidates."

Personnel Perils

Remember, a resumé is written to promote the applicant. Don't take it at face value. In studying it, read between the lines and try to determine what the applicant really has accomplished.

#13—The Casual Interview

An interview should be more than a polite conversation. Yet, many interviewers sit down with the applicant and expect that by asking a few questions about his or her background and discussing the job requirements, they will get enough information to make a hiring decision.

To ensure that you obtain significant information about a candidate, you must ask very specific questions. The answers should indicate whether that person can perform the job and what he or she can offer in comparison with competing applicants. (This may or may not develop into a pleasant conversation.)

You also must design a definite interview structure that will elicit key points of the position, allow the candidate to discuss credentials and accomplishments, and enable the interviewer to size up the applicant's personal characteristics. Some methods of doing this will be discussed in Chapter 8, "Becoming a Better Interviewer."

#14—Overly Structuring the Interview

In their efforts to cover all the bases, some interviewers overly structure their interview plan. They make a list of questions and read them to each candidate. This way, they will get responses that enable them to determine basic qualifications. Because the questions are the same for each applicant, answers can easily be compared and the differences among the candidates clearly defined.

Sounds good? Maybe. The problem is that quite often an answer requires a follow-up question. If you stick to the structure—with no flexibility—you might miss an important point. For example:

> **Interviewer:** What was your greatest accomplishment on that job?
>
> **Applicant:** I saved the company a lot of money.
>
> **Interviewer:** What was your greatest disappointment on that job?

Note that the interviewer asked the next question on the list instead of following through and finding out what the applicant did that saved the company money. The

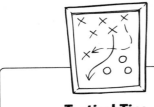

Tactical Tips

Make every question count. If the answer is vague or unclear, ask an appropriate follow-up question.

answer to that might have opened the door to even more questions that would give considerable insight into the prospect's qualifications. As noted, there will be many more suggestions for improving your interviewing skills in Chapter 8.

#15—"You Can't Ask That!"

It's been over 30 years since the federal Equal Employment Opportunity law was established. You'd think companies would no longer be asking applicants questions that are considered unlawful. Yet, every day some interviewer in some company—maybe yours—will ask a question that shouldn't be asked.

Why? Sometimes it's ignorance of the laws. Most employment professionals know the laws and abide by them. However, as noted before, team leaders, managers, and often team members participate in the interviewing process. Many of these people have only vague concepts of the laws. And, as in many matters with legal implications, it's not always clear just what the law allows and prohibits.

To determine whether the candidate will be available for overtime work, you might think you should ask if she has any young children. Uh oh! Illegal! Perhaps the applicant has an unusual name. You're curious, so you ask, "What kind of a name is that?" When the applicant is rejected for whatever reason, he files a complaint against you claiming discrimination because of national origin. This might not have had anything to do with his rejection; but because you asked, the burden is on you to prove otherwise.

Make it your business to learn what the laws require. You can get much of the information you need to make a hiring decision without violating any laws. A list of lawful and unlawful questions is provided in Chapter 8.

#16—Telling Too Much Too Soon

One of the major errors interviewers make is to tell the applicant all about the job early in the interview. Often they might give the applicant a copy of the job description before the interview begins. Why is this bad? This enables the smart applicant to tailor his or her background to fit the job description. For example, the open job calls for somebody who has extensive experience in administering employee benefits. In her last job, Shirley had some exposure to benefits. Knowing that this is an important aspect of the open position, Shirley might play up—perhaps exaggerate—her background in this field.

Of course, the applicant should have some concept of the job for which he or she is being interviewed. The best way to do this is to first ask questions about the applicant's background in the pertinent area. After the response, describe how that experience relates to the job. Some ways to structure the interview to get an unbiased response will also be discussed in Chapter 8.

#17—Verify, Verify, Verify!

The applicant has presented you with a slick resumé and comes across well in the interview. Before you make the decision, you should verify that what the applicant claims is true. The purpose of the reference check is to verify the applicant's statements and perhaps catch the "artful liar."

Unfortunately, this essential part of the employment process often is disregarded or treated much too casually. Often the background check is assigned to a junior employee who might send reference letters to previous employers or telephone them—with little training or know-how in asking probing questions and interpreting the responses.

Additionally, in recent years many companies have been advised by their attorneys to avoid giving any reference information for fear of defamation suits. Companies often limit responses to reference inquiries to the dates of employment and some general information about job duties. Because of this, some organizations don't bother to check out potential employees and take them at face value. This can be a costly mistake. It's important that you make every effort to get as much information as possible about an applicant before you make the hiring decision.

Personnel Perils

Automatically rejecting an applicant because of a poor reference can be a mistake. You might lose a good applicant for the wrong reason. Arrange for another interview. Don't mention the poor reference, but ask questions that might uncover the reason for it. Hold your judgment until you know the entire story.

Decision Making Goofs

The bottom line in the hiring procedure is selecting the best candidate for the open position. There are times when there are very few qualified people and you might be tempted to lower your standards; this can be a costly mistake. It's far better to keep looking. On the other hand, you might be blessed with a choice of several good candidates; you want to pick the best. Watch out for some of the following mistakes when making that important decision.

#18—"The Applicant's So Charming"

There's an old saying that the decision to hire or not to hire often is made in the first 30 seconds of the interview. There is some truth to this. One of the major factors in hiring is the interviewer's first impression of the applicant—and that is primarily physical appearance. This has been categorized as lookism—overemphasis on appearance.

Common sense tells us that just because a person is attractive is no indication of competence. However, it's a well-known fact that good-looking people are far more likely to be hired than equally qualified but less attractive people. Both men and women usually will decide in favor of the better-looking applicant.

For instance, in an informal exercise I administered at a series of seminars a few years ago, I distributed to the participants a job description and several resumés of equally qualified prospective candidates. Half the class received resumés with photos of the applicants attached; the other half had no photos. In virtually every instance, the participants who received photos selected the more attractive candidate. The selections of the nonphoto group were about equally divided among all the candidates.

Some first impressions create a *halo effect:* Because you are so impressed by some superficial facet, it is assumed that all other aspects of a candidate are outstanding. He's so charming; he must be a good salesman. She speaks so well; she'll make a great supervisor. However, halo effects are not limited only to appearance.

Meanings and Gleanings

The opposite of a **halo effect** is called a **pitchfork effect.** In this case, one poor characteristic causes you to assume that the person is unsatisfactory in all aspects.

Sometimes because an applicant is highly competent in one aspect of a job, it is assumed that he or she is equally competent in others. For instance, Charles could type on the word processor at 90 words per minute. With that speed, the supervisor figured he had hired a winner. It wasn't until after Charles started work that they realized speed was his only asset. He was temperamental, a poor organizer, had a poor attendance record, and had other unsatisfactory work habits.

Poor first impressions might cause you to reject an otherwise well-qualified candidate. An applicant might be downgraded in your mind because he or she does not speak well—important if the job calls for oral communication. However, this should not be a factor in jobs in which extensive oral communication is not required.

For instance, one of my clients wouldn't even consider an applicant who had a straggly beard and long, unkempt hair. He hired him only after the person who referred the applicant persuaded him that the man was a computer whiz. The employee has since solved countless technical problems for the company and has saved it tens of thousands of dollars.

#19—Watch Your Biases

We all have biases. Biases are not limited to prejudice against people because of race, religion, or sex. They can be based on long-held beliefs, stereotypes, personal tastes, or idiosyncrasies.

At one seminar I asked participants to share with the group some of their hiring mistakes. Most people told about people they hired who didn't make the grade. However, one participant told about a salesman he had rejected. At a luncheon meeting for a trade association, the sales manager of a competitor was bragging about his top sales rep, who in his first year broke all records for acquiring new accounts. When the competitor mentioned the rep's name, it rang a bell. After recalling having interviewed him some time ago, he checked his files. Sure enough, he had interviewed and rejected him. Why? His notes on the application just said "not suitable." Then he remembered that he had turned him down because he was wearing a bow tie. His stupid bias against bow ties kept him from hiring a potential winner.

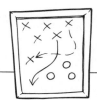

Tactical Tips

To get the best people, recognize your own biases and do your best to keep them from influencing your decision. (For example: "He fits this job and I won't eliminate him just because he's short.")

#20—Is It a Good Match?

The whole purpose of developing a list of realistic job specifications is to ensure that the person hired can fulfill all (or most of) the responsibilities of the job. Often it is difficult—if not impossible—to find somebody with all of the requirements. In such cases, choose the specs that are absolutely essential and identify those areas in which a new employee can be trained.

There are certain aspects of most jobs in which experience or technical know-how is essential and cannot be taught on the job. The big mistake organizations make is to hire a candidate who might be qualified for several of the specs but is weak in the essential areas. For example, the job calls for background in A, B, and C; the most important is C. Even though Betty has experience in all three, her weakest area is C. Keep looking.

#21—Don't Overlook the Intangibles

When making a hiring decision, it's extremely important to evaluate the intangibles. Too often, the employer limits the selection procedure to determining whether the applicant is technically qualified. Many interviewers overlook such factors as ability to work in a team, communicate ideas, work under pressure, be flexible, and countless other personality factors that make up the human being.

These intangibles are just as important as education, skills, and experience and really determine the degree of success on a job. In making your job analysis, be as diligent in determining the intangible factors as you are in the tangible factors. More on this in Chapter 9, "Making the Hiring Decision."

Losing Good Applicants

You have screened hundreds of resumés, interviewed dozens of applicants, tested or sent many of them for evaluation, and checked references. You finally make up your mind and make an offer—only to have it rejected by the applicant. This is the most frustrating experience one can have in the hiring process. Why does this happen?

#22—Making Unrealistic Job Offers

The terms of employment should be well thought out long before an offer is made. However, too many companies have a preconceived idea of the offer before they even interview applicants. This makes for sound business, but unless the offer is shaped to fit the needs of the applicant, there's a good chance it will not be accepted.

The major part of the job offer is the salary. We'll talk about this in the following section. Other key aspects of the job should be clarified to the candidate before you make an offer. This includes the amount of travel required, hours of work including the likelihood of extensive overtime, whether the job will call for relocation now or in the future, and any other special aspects of the position. Don't surprise the applicant at the time of the offer with, "By the way, you will have to go to our plant in California for three months of training."

#23—The Compensation Package Is Too Low

With lower-level employees, salary is nonnegotiable. It's "take it or leave it." However, when the position at any level is hard to fill, you must be more flexible or you'll lose the best applicants. Companies may have to rethink their compensation policies in periods when applicants are in short supply.

It's not necessary or even advisable to commit to a salary too early in the interviewing process. There are many factors that should be considered when determining the final financial package. However, it makes sense to clearly establish the salary range early on. If your idea of salary differs radically from that of the applicant's there is no point in considering him or her seriously for a position.

Perhaps your benefits package is significantly poorer than other firms in the community or industry. For example, one of the most sought-after benefits is health insurance. The plan you have is not as good as other firms competing for the same type personnel. You'd better improve your medical plan to bring it in line with those of other firms or many applicants will turn you down.

Most benefits plans are standardized. However, increasingly organizations are constructing individual benefit programs for each employee. The amount paid into the package might vary with the position and pay scale. The specifics of what is covered within the package can be tailored to fit the desires of the employee. Salary and benefits will be discussed further in Part 4 of this book, "Money, Money, Money."

#24—The Spouse Is Unwilling to Relocate

Everything seemed to go okay. You've brought the applicant to your facility on three separate occasions. You agree on the terms of the job. He appears to be enthusiastic about the job. And then, surprise! He phones and tells you that his wife doesn't want to move to your city. How could this have been avoided? When a job calls for relocation, it's imperative that you spend considerable time with both husband and wife to ensure that both are amenable to the relocation.

Let's look at Tom and Geri. Tom is being considered for a senior position in your IT (information technology) department. You recognize early in the interviewing process that Tom is a viable candidate. This is when you should point out that the job calls for relocating and invite his wife to the facility so she can observe the new community for herself.

When Tom and Geri come to town, have one of your staff give Geri a tour of the town and try to uncover any special concerns she might have. Be prepared to discuss schools (if there are school-age children), cultural and entertainment activities, religious facilities, and housing. If Geri is interested in finding a job in her own field, give her information about that field and help her locate a suitable job.

If Geri has any reservations, try to bring them out into the open and discuss them with both her and Tom; preferably over lunch or dinner. If she is still not happy about the move—and you cannot persuade her to change her mind—it is better to find out in the early stages of the interviewing process. This way, Tom can withdraw from consideration before the decision is made to hire him.

#25—A Counteroffer Is Made

Talk about frustration—here is one of the worst examples: After all the time, energy, thought, and emotional turmoil you have experienced in the hiring process, you offer the job to Tom, and he accepts it. You think your troubles are over and you can get back to work. A week later, Tom calls and tells you he gave notice to his boss and was made a counteroffer, so he has decided to stay. You have to start all over again.

You must expect that counteroffers will be made to good workers. You probably have done the same when one of your best people gave notice. To beat this, you have to be proactive. You must prepare the person to whom you make a job offer to expect and reject a counteroffer. Some methods of doing this will be discussed in Chapter 9.

Hiring staff is one of the most important roles a manager has. Picking the wrong people can cost you money, time, and emotional upset. By keeping these 25 hiring errors in mind every time a job has to be filled or refilled, you'll be a more effective manager and do a more credible job for your company.

The Least You Need to Know

➤ Plan the hiring process before you even look for applicants and stick to the plan. Develop job specs that are realistic and have direct bearing on job success.

➤ To get the best possible candidates for your job openings, it's smart to use as many resources as possible. Prescreen candidates so those you do interview are viable prospects for the position.

➤ Interviews must have a definite structure designed to elicit the key points, allow the candidate to discuss credentials and accomplishments, and enable the interviewer to size up the applicant's personal characteristics.

➤ In addition to salary and benefits, factors that should be made clear before making a formal job offer are travel requirements, hours of work including the likelihood of extensive overtime, whether the job calls for relocation, and any other special aspects of the position.

➤ You must expect that counteroffers will be made to good workers. Be proactive. Prepare the person to whom you make a job offer to expect and reject a counteroffer.

Chapter 5

Starting the Search

In This Chapter

➤ Making the job analysis

➤ Writing the job description

➤ What an applicant needs to fill the job

➤ Your current staff—a primary source

➤ Creating a job bank

➤ Encouraging referrals

In this chapter you will learn several ways to analyze jobs and write job descriptions that truly depict what that job really entails from day to day, week to week, year to year. You also will learn how to determine the education, experience, and personal traits candidates should bring to the job to perform the duties effectively. We'll also examine how to use your present employees as a source for filling open positions.

A Job Is Open

Jobs can develop for a variety of reasons. What is needed to fill that job depends to a great extent on why the vacancy exists. The process differs significantly depending on whether you are replacing a worker who has left, or expanding the team or department.

Tactical Tips

Be just as thorough in making a job analysis whether the opening is a replacement for somebody who left or it's an entirely new job.

When Refilling a Position

One of your employees notifies you she is leaving. If you work for a medium- or large-sized organization, you probably will notify human resources and request a replacement. In some companies you will notify your boss and start the process to find a new employee.

When It's a Brand-New Position

Your team is overworked. You need a larger staff. You succeed in persuading your manager to add one or more positions to your team. What kind of jobs will you add?

In some teams all members do the same kind of work. For instance, in a data entry team, all members usually enter the same kind of data; in a quality control team, all members might perform the same analysis functions. In these cases you can just review the job descriptions to ensure that they are current.

What Does This Job Entail?

The way you obtain information about what a job entails is called *job analysis.* In some companies specialists perform these analyses. These specialists might be industrial engineers, systems analysts, or members of your human resources staff. If your company employs these people, use them as a resource. However, the best people to make an analysis are those closest to a job—you and other members of your staff. The following sections will discuss several ways to develop information for a job description. It is very helpful to design a worksheet to use in making the job analysis. A well-structured form will assure that all the bases are covered and result in a thorough analysis. A sample worksheet is shown later in this chapter.

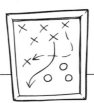

Tactical Tips

A good job description is not a rigid depiction of functions. It should allow for reasonable deviations, additions, and variations.

Observing the Action

For jobs that are primarily physical in nature, watching a person perform the job will give you most of the material you need to write the description. If several people are engaged in the same type of work, observe more than one performer. Conversely, in jobs that are not primarily manual there is little you can learn from observation alone. For example, just watching someone sitting at a computer terminal isn't enough to learn what's being done.

Also, even a good observer might not understand what he or she is observing. Sometimes the job involves much more than meets the eye. Additional steps must be taken to get the full picture. Supplement your observations with discussions of what is being done with both the workers performing the jobs and their supervisors. Suggestions on how to do this will be given later in this chapter.

Interviewing the Worker

Ask the people who perform a job to describe the activities they perform. This technique makes clearer what you're observing. Of course, you must know enough about the work to understand what's being said and be able to ask appropriate questions.

It's a good idea to prepare a series of open-ended questions in advance. Ask only questions that are specific to the job being analyzed. Avoid questions that can be answered in a single word, such as "yes." Such questions yield very little information. Questions such as the following will elicit good information:

Personnel Perils

When several people perform the same type of job, don't select the most or least experienced or skilled workers to observe. Highly experienced workers often tailor the job to their own style and newcomers haven't mastered the work. Studying a few mid-level performers will give you a more realistic concept of what that job actually entails.

➤ Tell me about how you spend a typical day.

➤ Tell me about some of the other work you occasionally do—how often and when do you do this work?

➤ What positions do you supervise (if any) and how much of your time is spent in supervising others?

➤ What responsibilities do you have for financial matters such as budgeting, purchasing, authorizing expenditures, and similar decisions?

➤ What equipment do you operate?

➤ What performance standards are you expected to meet on this job?

➤ What education and experience did you have prior to taking this job that prepared you for it?

➤ What training did you get on this job to help you do it effectively?

The answers to these questions should give you considerable insight into the job. But, to assure that you have the entire picture, it's a good idea to also interview the person who supervises or leads the team.

Interviewing the Supervisor or Team Leader

If you're analyzing a job other than those you supervise, speak to the team leader or supervisor of that group to obtain that person's perspective of the position. The questions you ask the supervisor or team leader should be similar to those you asked the worker. Note variations in their answers. Probe to determine which is the more accurate description.

If you are evaluating a job that you personally supervise, try to take an objective view of the position and review it as if you were a stranger. Review in your mind how you view the position, what you believe the performer should be doing, and the standards that are acceptable. It's not easy to do, but you'll be amazed at the results. You'll see things you never noticed before and interpret aspects of duties and processes in a different light. Companies have found that when the performance standards are developed collaboratively by managers and the people who perform the work, they are more realistic and more likely to be accepted and achieved.

Meanings and Gleanings

The major aspects of a job that must be accomplished by the employee are referred to as **key results areas.**

Indicate Performance Expectations

Some companies prefer to call the job description a "position results description" or a "job results description." In this approach the true objective of this document is to determine what is expected of the people performing the job. Each description should include the major goal (why the job exists), the *key results areas* or KRAs (the main objectives of the job), and the standards for which performance will be measured.

By indicating performance standards and expected results, managers and employees can measure performance and use the results as motivation toward desired goals. Tailor the form you use to the type of job you're analyzing. The following job description worksheet is a helpful tool:

Job title: _____

Reports to: _____

Duties performed: _____

Equipment used: _____

Skills used: _____

Leadership responsibility: _____

Responsibility for equipment: _____

Responsibility for money: _____

Other aspects of job: _____

Special working conditions: _____

Performance standards: _____

Analysis made by: _____

Date: _____

What You Seek in a Candidate

After you know just what a job entails, you can determine the job qualifications and personal qualities you seek in the successful candidate. In some situations the job specifications must be rigidly followed. For example, in civil service jobs or in cases in which job specs are part of a union contract, even a slight variation from job specs can have legal implications.

In some technical jobs, a specific degree or certification might be mandated by company standards or to meet professional requirements. For example, an accountant making formal audits must be a certified public account (CPA); an engineer who approves structural plans must be licensed as a professional engineer (PE).

Other job specs might allow for some flexibility. If there's no compelling reason for the candidate to have a specific qualification, you might deviate from the specs and accept an equivalent background. For example, one job spec may be completing a course in computer technology. If the candidate never took the course, but has excellent experience in that technology, you should have the flexibility to hire that person, if so desired.

Components of a Job Spec

The objective of the job specification is to provide a list of the aspects of a candidate's qualifications that will enable him or her to perform the job satisfactorily. The usual components of the job specs are ...

➤ **Education**   Does a job call for college? Advanced education? Schooling in a special skill?

➤ **Skills**   Must the candidate be skilled in computers? Machinery? Drafting? Statistics? Technical work? Any other skills necessary to perform a job?

➤ **Work experience**   What should be the type and duration of previous experience in related job functions?

➤ **Physical strength or stamina**   Does the job require heavy lifting or hard physical labor? If so, is it a significant part of the job or does it occur only occasionally?

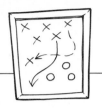

Tactical Tips

To ensure that the person you hire can do a job, the job specs should emphasize what you expect the applicant to have accomplished in previous jobs—not just the length of his or her experience.

➤ **Intelligence**   Some jobs call for a high level of intelligence. Decisions must be made that require deep thinking, complex problem solving, or ability to think on one's feet.

➤ **Communication skills**   The job specs should indicate exactly which communication skills you need; for example, one-to-one communication, the ability to speak to large groups, innovative telephone sales methods, or creative writing skills.

➤ **Accuracy of work**   If a job calls for "attention to detail," specify what type of detail work. In some jobs there is no margin for error. Work must be done right the first time or serious problems might result; for example, working on a nuclear reactor or piloting a jet plane.

➤ **Dealing with stress**   If a job calls for "ability to work under pressure," indicate what type of pressure; for example, daily deadlines, occasional deadlines, round-the-clock sessions, difficult working conditions, or a demanding boss.

➤ **Special factors**   Many other requirements might factor into the job specification such as fluency in a foreign language, willingness to travel, willingness to work weekends, willingness to work overtime on short notice, and anything else with which an employee must comply to perform the job satisfactorily.

Eliminating Good Prospects for the Wrong Reason

One of the most common problems in determining the specifications for a job is requiring a higher qualification level than really is necessary. This can knock out potentially good candidates for the wrong reason. The following identifies some of the areas in which this can occur:

➤ **Education**   Suppose certain job specs call for a college degree. Is that degree necessary? Often it is, but just as often the degree has no bearing on a person's ability to succeed in a job. Requiring a higher level of education sometimes has more disadvantages than advantages. You might attract smart and creative people; but the job might not challenge them, resulting in low productivity and high turnover. More important, you might turn away the best possible candidates for a position by putting the emphasis on a less important aspect of the job.

➤ **Duration of experience** Your job specs might call for 10 years of experience in accounting. Why specify 10 years? No direct correlation exists between the number of years a person has worked in a field and that person's competence. Lots of people have 10 years on a job but only one year of experience (after they've mastered the basics of the job, they plod along, never growing or learning from their experience). Other people acquire a great deal of skill in a much shorter period. Rather than requiring a number of years, set up a list of skills a new employee should bring to a job, specifying how qualified the person should be in each skill. By asking an applicant specific questions about each of these factors, you can determine what he or she knows and has accomplished in each area.

Personnel Perils

Don't clone your current team. It's best to get people with diversified backgrounds who can augment the work of others on the team. When you set up specs for a job, ask yourself, "What must the applicant be able to do that other team members cannot do. Your team will be stronger if it includes people with different but complementary skills.

➤ **Type of experience** Job specs often mandate that an applicant should have experience in "our industry." Sure, there are some jobs in which the necessary skills and job knowledge can be acquired only in companies that do similar work. However, in many jobs a background in other industries is just as valuable. A different background might even be better because the new associate isn't tradition-bound and will bring innovative concepts to the job.

Internal Transfers and Promotions

When a change of job involves a promotion, most people are delighted and welcome the opportunity. However, not every transfer is a promotion. Often it's a transfer—an opportunity for someone to learn, gain experience, and take a step toward preparing for career advancement. Most companies use a judicious mixture, combining internal promotion and transfers with outside recruitment to get and keep the best candidates for their openings.

Seeking to fill a vacancy from within a company has many advantages:

➤ People who already work in your company know the "lay of the land." They're familiar with your company's rules and regulations, customs and culture, and practices and idiosyncrasies. Hiring these people rather than someone from outside your company saves time in orientation and minimizes the risks of dissatisfaction with your company.

➤ You know more about these people than you can possibly learn about outsiders. You might have worked directly with a certain person or observed him or her in action. You can get detailed and honest information about a candidate from previous supervisors and company records.

➤ Offering opportunities to current employees boosts morale within the company and serves as an incentive for all employees to perform at their highest levels.

➤ An important side effect is that it creates a positive image of your company in the industry and in your community. This image encourages good people to apply when jobs for outsiders do become available.

Although the advantages of internal promotion usually outweigh the downsides, there are disadvantages to consider:

➤ The job might require skills not found in your company.

➤ If you promote only from within, you limit the resources from which to draw candidates and might be restricted to promoting a person significantly less qualified than someone from outside your company.

➤ People who have worked in other companies bring with them new and different ideas and know-how that can benefit your team.

➤ Outsiders look at your activities with a fresh view untainted by overfamiliarity.

One of the major problems in interdepartmental transfers is the reluctance of department heads to release efficient and productive workers to other departments. It's not easy to overcome this. A company implementing internal recruitment should notify all management that it will overrule any attempts to keep people who could be more valuable if transferred.

It also should be mentioned that people who are passed over for better positions in other departments are unlikely to remain with the company. These employees probably will seek jobs elsewhere. Unfortunately, both the department and the company could lose valuable employees.

Finding the Right Candidate from Within the Company

Many organizations have developed training programs that provide them with a steady stream of trained people for their expanding job needs. In some companies there's a plethora of talent to choose from. However, there are times when there are no obvious candidates for a vacant job. You might have people in the company who are qualified to do the job—but you don't know it. What can you do?

Search the Personnel Files

If properly maintained, personnel records can be a major resource. Examination of these records can uncover people working in jobs below their education or skill levels. It also might reveal people who have had additional training since they were employed.

Any training given by the company, whether internal or outside seminars or programs should be noted. If the company has a tuition reimbursement policy, any courses falling into this category should be noted. Employees should be encouraged to inform the human resources department of other courses, programs, or outside training they might have completed.

Tactical Tips

Send periodic questionnaires to all employees to bring their personnel records up to date. At their annual reviews, ask about new skills or knowledge acquired. All this should be incorporated in their personnel records.

Personnel records can be an important method of locating people urgently needed by a company. A major aerospace firm recently spent several thousand dollars advertising for specialized engineers needed for a new project in one division of the company. The recruiters were shocked to receive letters in reply to the ad from engineers in another division of the same company. The engineers claimed that their specialized knowledge was not being used in their current jobs and were seeking a position where it would be. Had the HR department known of them, it would have saved the company money and time.

Ask the Supervisors

Supervisors and team leaders know a good deal about their associates. Take advantage of this. Let them know what jobs are open in other departments—they might have associates who are qualified.

However, there are dangers here. One danger, as stated in the preceding section, is that often supervisors or team leaders are reluctant to lose a good worker. The other is that the supervisor might refer somebody he or she wants to get rid of. Carefully screen applicants referred by their team leaders just as you would any other candidate.

Job Banks

To systemize internal searches, many firms have established databases listing all the skills, talents, experience, education, and other background information of its employees. As new skills are acquired, internal training programs completed, and outside training reported, they are added to the database. These databases usually are referred to as *job banks,* sometimes called *skill banks,* and are used to match job openings against current workforce.

For instance, under "Microsoft Excel" are listed the names of all persons who have worked with this program at any time in their careers, whether or not they are currently using this skill. Here's an example of how this is useful: Let's say a need for a team member with this background occurs in Unit A. The job bank indicates there is a person in Unit B who has that experience but is employed in another capacity. He or she might be approached about transferring to Unit A.

Job Posting

Many companies make a practice of posting job openings on bulletin boards or listing them in company newsletters so that any employee who believes he or she is qualified can apply.

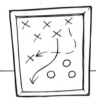

Tactical Tips

Consider posting jobs on the company *intranet*—the internal variation of the Internet that is accessed only by company employees.

Posting a job opening encourages current employees who might qualify for the job, but are not known to the manager or team leader seeking to fill the job. For example, Sandra works in the order processing department, but her career goal is in sales. Everybody tells her she has a "sales personality," and she has had some part-time selling experience. When an opening for a sales trainee is posted, she applies. The sales manager interviews her and recognizes her talent. She is transferred into the sales training program and in time becomes one of the company's star sales reps. Had the job not been posted, Sandra would not have known there was an opening, the sales manager would not have known about Sandra, and the company would have missed a high-potential employee.

There are still companies in which minority and female employees are not usually considered for certain jobs. Job posting enables members of these groups to apply and be given serious consideration. For this reason, many compliance agreements with the EEOC include a requirement that all jobs be posted. In addition many union contracts require that all jobs be posted so that union members who might have been overlooked by management know of openings for which they believe they are qualified and can apply for them.

However, there's a downside to posting jobs. When a current employee applies for a posted job and is rejected, you have a disgruntled employee. Some might quit, causing the loss of a possibly good employee. Some of those who stay might lose confidence and make little effort to build up their competence. Some go back to work and badmouth the company to their co-workers, leading to low morale.

When rejecting an employee for an internal transfer or promotion, take the time to explain in detail why he or she did not qualify. Point out what might be done so that next time this type of job is posted, he or she will be better equipped to compete for it. Suggest additional training and if pertinent, state what the company will do to help the person attain that training.

When several employees apply for a posted job—and there is only one opening—assure the unsuccessful candidates that they were seriously considered and, if true, that they will be considered for future opportunities. Guide them to improve their chances in the future.

Using Current Employees as a Recruiting Source

The men and women who work for you are an excellent source for bringing in talented people like themselves. Many of them have friends from school or previous jobs who have similar backgrounds and who might be prospects for your open positions. Many companies have instituted programs to encourage referrals by employees.

This has not always been the case. In fact, many companies had policies to refuse employment to friends and relatives of current employees. Before the EEO laws banned such questions, application forms often inquired whether the applicant had relatives or friends within the company. One reason for this policy was the fear that if friends or relatives worked together they might form cliques, which would disrupt the smooth flow of operations. This fear has diminished over the years due to better understanding of group dynamics and the decentralization of business functions. It has made it possible for friends and relatives to work in departments in which they have little contact with each other.

Another reason companies have lifted these restrictions is that because of the shortage of skilled personnel, they cannot afford to overlook any qualified person.

Management Miscellany

Fortune Magazine (Jan. 22, 2001) reported in its list of the 100 Best Companies to Work For that at least 20 percent of new hires in those companies came from recommendations from employees; 83 of those companies paid bonuses for successful new hires. *The Wall Street Journal* recently reported that one company paid a bonus of $12,000 to an employee for referring a highly specialized engineer. It justified this by pointing out that if it had hired this engineer through an executive recruiter, the fee would have been even higher.

Encouraging Employee Referrals

The most important factor in developing a program of employee referrals is company morale. The morale and attitudes of the people in a company can make or break a referral campaign. If employees are discontented, it's unlikely they will refer friends.

Managers often kid themselves into thinking their organization is "one big, happy family," when under the surface it is seething with dysfunction. Periodic employee attitude surveys or evaluations by outside consultants can educe the true status of morale. If it is not satisfactory, the referral program will not work until steps are taken to correct the problems causing the poor morale.

Some programs might entail only occasional suggestions by the management that friends are welcome to apply for jobs. Others might involve formal campaigns with prizes, rewards, and publicity—usually contingent on the new employee remaining with the firm for a specified period of time. How much the reward should be varies from company to company and usually depends on the difficulty of locating qualified candidates. Most companies pay a set fee—from $100 for referring a semi-skilled factory worker or office clerk to several thousand dollars for technicians, engineers, and professional staff members.

To assure that the company's personnel needs are met, human resources specialists and all managers must be constantly on the alert for qualified people. They must use every resource available to them starting with the people currently in the company. Make the most of their qualifications. Place them in jobs where they can use their talents. Call on them for referrals of potential new employees.

The Least You Need to Know

➤ Base your job requirements on job factors, not on the background of people currently doing the job.

➤ When you analyze a job, observe the people performing the job and discuss what they do with them and their managers.

➤ Clarify with employees results expected and performance standards by which they are measured.

➤ Base job specifications on an accurate job description.

➤ Develop job banks listing the skills and experience of each employee.

➤ Posting a job opening encourages current employees who might qualify for the job, but are not known to the manager or team leader seeking to fill the job.

➤ Rewards and bonuses for referring successful applicants should be commensurate with the difficulty in filling the job.

Chapter 6

Where the Applicants Are

> ## In This Chapter
>
> ➤ Writing effective employment ads
>
> ➤ Using employment agencies and headhunters
>
> ➤ Building resource networks
>
> ➤ Is the job fair right for you?
>
> ➤ The Internet—a new source of applicants

Once you have determined just what a person needs to qualify for your job opening, you are ready to look for candidates. As pointed out in the previous chapter, one source is your current employees. However, it also pays to look outside the company to ensure that you select from the very best people available. In this chapter, we'll look at various approaches to locating these candidates.

Using Help Wanted Ads

Probably the most frequently used method of attracting applicants is the classified ad section of a newspaper or trade magazine. Choosing the most effective medium depends on the type of position that is advertised. If the job is one that is most likely to be filled by a local resident, the logical source is a local newspaper; if you are willing to relocate a candidate, your best bet is a publication that the type of person you are seeking will most likely read. When the candidates for your job are not likely to be in

Tactical Tips

A great source of advertising for local people is "drive time" radio because you have a captive audience. While they are riding in their cars, you hit them with your ad. If your ad sounds exciting enough, they'll contact you when they get home—or even immediately from their cell phones.

Tactical Tips

If you list a telephone number in your help wanted ad, use a dedicated phone—one not used for any other purpose. This will prevent the switchboard or direct lines used for regular business from being tied up with job inquiries. The same is true of an e-mail address—set one up for this purpose only.

your vicinity, advertise in newspapers in cities where they work. In addition, most industries have trade journals that cover their specific fields and many professional organizations have magazines devoted to their special needs.

Classified Ads

Most help wanted ads are placed in the classified columns of the newspaper—the best location for routine jobs. Classified ads usually are listed alphabetically by job title. When writing your ad, it's important to choose the appropriate job title, even if it differs from the title used by your company. For example, your title for the open job is "Engineering Associate" but the job does not call for an engineering education; it's a clerical position keeping engineering records. If you use the company title, it will appear under "engineers" and you will not attract the desired type of candidate. Study the help wanted columns to see what kind of title best describes the job.

Display Ads

If a job is hard to fill, such as engineers, information technology specialists, professional staff, managers, and executives, it might be more effective to run a display ad. Display ads are much larger than classified ads and can be placed in any section of the paper, although most of these ads appear on the business pages. As these ads also cost considerably more than classified ads, a company does not use them unless it feels that the prospects for such a job will not usually read the classified section of the newspaper.

Unlike classified ads, which are restricted by limited typefaces, in a display ad you can use a variety of typefaces or specially designed layouts. As most managers are not familiar with the nuances of display advertising, assistance in writing these ads should be obtained from your company's advertising department or ad agency. To ensure accuracy of content and style of your ads, ask the paper to send you print proofs of all display ads and, if possible, classified ads. Check all ads carefully.

You can place help wanted ads by phoning them in to the classified advertising department of the newspaper if you place only a few each year. They will provide you with the newspaper's guidelines and rules. However, if you place a large number of classified ads or even just one display ad, you are better off using an ad agency. An ad agency won't charge you anything for placing your ads. They get their fees from the magazine or newspaper running the ad. However, if the agency does special work for you such as designing a display ad, it might charge for that service.

Employment Agencies

Your objective is to fill the open job as rapidly as possible with the best-qualified applicant at the lowest cost. Unless you are exclusively engaged in hiring, you have many other duties that might be neglected while you search for personnel. Employment agencies can cut down on the time needed to fill the job; however, they can be a waste of your time if you don't know how to use them effectively.

What They Can Do

Employment agencies will not necessarily solve all your hiring problems, but they can often make the process less time-consuming, costly, and frustrating. Some of the advantages of using employment agencies are listed here:

➤ They can save you money. Ads, time spent interviewing, travel for interviewers and applicants, and hiring all cost money. The fee you pay the agency usually is considerably lower than the amount saved by the work they do.

➤ They can save time. Often agencies have files of qualified applicants who can be referred to you immediately.

➤ If your job opening is in a specialized field, agencies that deal heavily with people in that field have extensive resources. They are able to reach top-level candidates who might be interested.

➤ They prescreen candidates and refer only those whose skills come close to or meet your specs. This saves you the time and energy of reading countless resumés and interviewing unqualified applicants.

➤ If you want to hide from competitors or even your own staff the fact that you are seeking to fill a certain job, the agency can keep your company name confidential until you are ready to interview the applicants.

➤ If you develop an ongoing relationship with an agency, it will inform you about highly qualified people who are available even when you don't have an immediate opening. Often, it might be worthwhile to create an opening for a high-potential individual.

The cost of hiring is more than just the direct costs such as advertising, agency fees, and travel. Often more expensive are the indirect costs: salaries for time spent by your own management people engaged in the hiring process (reading resumés, interviewing applicants, checking references, and related work). By having the employment agency perform many of these activities, the costs are significantly reduced.

What They Cannot Do

Some companies have made the mistake of turning over the entire hiring process to an agency. This doesn't work. Agencies are not substitutes for a company's employment department. They don't know the inner workings of your company or the subtleties of your corporate culture. Plus, agencies often make their money by placing candidates. Their long-term interests may not coincide with yours.

It's up to you to develop job specs and convey them to the agency. The agency's job is to locate possible candidates, do preliminary screening, and refer to you those closest to your requirements. Don't rely on any outsiders to make final decisions about whom you will or will not hire.

Agencies also cannot be used to shield you from charges of discrimination. In order to evade the responsibility of screening out minorities or women for certain jobs, some companies "hint" to agencies about the "type of person" they want to have referred to them with the "understanding" that only applicants of the "right type" will be referred. They wrongfully assume that this will protect them from being charged with discrimination by claiming that they didn't discriminate, "the agency didn't send me any women or blacks," or whatever. This excuse won't fly. The company as well as the agency can be cited for discrimination.

Personnel Perils

Always obtain a fee schedule from an agency. Agency fees differ. You should know in advance what your obligation will be and the refund policy of the agency in case the applicant doesn't work out.

What It Costs You

Employment agencies don't charge you a fee unless you hire a person referred by them and that person starts working for your company. Most agencies charge fees based on the salary paid to the employee—usually 10 to 20 percent of the annual salary.

However, sometimes it costs you nothing. Although employers pay most private agencies for their services, there are some agencies that charge the fee to the applicant. Whether the agency charges the company or the applicant often depends on the job market. When jobs are hard to find, applicants are more likely to be charged; when jobs are plentiful and applicants are hard to find, the burden of payment shifts to employers.

Government Job Services

Every state has its own job service, aided and coordinated by the United States Employment Service (USES), a division of the U.S. Department of Labor. When created in the depression years of the 1930s, the primary function of the state services was to help find jobs for the unemployed; the same agencies usually were responsible for administering unemployment insurance plans.

An unemployed person is still required to register with the state job service to qualify for unemployment benefits. As a result, the public usually refers to these offices as "unemployment offices." State job services have a limited value to most employers. They're a good source for filling some positions, but not too helpful in filling others.

The Upside of Using State Job Services

State job services have always been a major source for hiring blue-collar help. They usually know the needs of the companies in their areas and can serve them rapidly and effectively. In case of shortages of certain types of labor in one part of the state, they can recruit from other parts of the state and occasionally from other states through the USES.

They also test applicants for certain skills and aptitudes. They will work with employers to assist them in planning for job searches, and when large numbers of workers are needed, they have the facilities to recruit statewide or even from other states. Of course, because they are government funded, there is no fee for their services.

The Downside of Using State Job Services

Many employers have found fault with the quality of referrals from the state job services. People who are not really interested in working accept referrals to maintain their unemployment benefits—a waste of time for the companies interviewing them.

Generally, state job services have not been a good source for higher-level positions. Despite government efforts to upgrade the image, employers are reluctant to entrust their more complex job specs to the state services. Additionally, currently employed applicants seeking better professional, technical, administrative, and managerial jobs usually will not register with state services.

Professional and Technical Associations

Most professional associations offer informal placement services to their members. Members seeking jobs send their resumés to the placement committee. When companies list jobs with the association, appropriate resumés are referred to them.

Management Miscellany

A good source to locate professional or technical associations in any field is Gale's Encyclopedia of Associations, which can be found in most libraries. Internet sources include Internet Public Library Associations on the Net at www.ipl.org/ref/AON and Gateway to Associations Online at www.asaenet.org/OnlineAssocSlist.html.

The problem with this is that volunteers often run the services or committees. Because the members are not trained in employment screening, they might refer unqualified candidates, wasting the employers' time. In some organizations, the committee meets once a month or less frequently, resulting in delay in sending out the resumés. However, some organizations do have full-time professionals doing the placement. When contacting a professional association for referrals, learn how they are organized and operated.

Schools and Colleges

Most colleges, community colleges, and trade schools are anxious to place their graduates and usually offer placement services for this purpose. It pays to contact the schools in your area and list your company's job openings. Most large companies make regular visits to college campuses throughout the country to recruit graduating students. If you seek trainees with specialized education, it pays to keep in regular touch with schools and colleges that teach those specialties.

Using Temps

You don't have to hire people to have them work for you. At some time during each year almost all companies use "temps" (temporary personnel) who work on their premises, but are on the payroll of a temporary staffing or employee leasing service. According to a survey by the American Staffing Association, 90 percent of companies in America use temporary help services.

Temporary services differ from employment agencies in that they don't place people in jobs, but hire the employees themselves and "lease" them to employers who require either full-time or part-time workers for short periods of time. These jobs range from simple clerical or low-skill laborers all the way to professional and executive positions.

The temp services charge a fee to the company based on the skill level and the number of hours worked by the people they supply. As the workers are not on your payroll, you pay no benefits or payroll taxes. You are free from the burden of withholding income taxes. Temps accrue no sick leave or vacation time. If the temp is absent, the temp service will send another person to do the work. If you are not satisfied with one temp, the agency will send a replacement. You don't have the hassle of hiring, disciplining, and perhaps firing people.

Rent-a-Worker

Some business executives have a dream—to run a company without the problems of hiring, administering, and dealing with employees. Believe it or not, it can be done. Instead of hiring people, you can lease them just as you would a car or a piece of equipment. This is much different from using temps to fill in for absent workers or to handle a work overload. Companies using rent-a-workers maintain only a core group of key personnel and have most of their work done by leased employees. Many of the leading temp services have expanded into this field. In most cases, leased employees work on company premises. They might even be employees who were downsized by the company, and then hired by the staffing service and leased to their former employer.

The advantages of leasing employees are that the company is relieved of having to recruit staff and deal with all of the administrative headaches. However, there are many drawbacks to leasing people. When you lease a car, you're still responsible for maintaining it. When you lease personnel, you still have to train them and direct their work. They might not be your employees, but they are your associates. It's up to you to keep them motivated. This is not easy when you have no control over their compensation. It's tough to instill a sense of loyalty and ownership when the team member doesn't identify with the company.

Because leased employees don't receive the same benefits as regular employees, a climate of resentment might develop that impairs morale and productivity. To overcome this, many leasing companies are providing equivalent benefits to their people—of course, this is reflected in higher charges to the employer.

Executive Recruiters— Headhunters

Executive recruiters (also known as headhunters) have been a major resource for locating senior managers and hard-to-locate technical and professional people since the rapid expansion of business that followed World War II. They have helped to fill many top-level positions for some of the major corporations in this country and abroad.

Differences Between Agencies and Headhunters

Many people think of executive recruiting or "headhunting" firms as just another type of employment agency. There are some similarities;

Tactical Tips

Often, the qualified person for your particular job opening is not actively looking for different employment. In these cases, an executive search firm might be your best resource.

indeed, some employment agencies will do proactive searches for clients. However, executive recruiters generally operate in a different fashion from employment agencies.

Employment agencies obtain applicants primarily through advertising, their own reputations, and referrals. Most people who register with an employment agency are active job seekers. They are either not currently employed or, for whatever reasons, have chosen to seek a job while still employed.

The agency usually will interview the applicant and check his or her background against its list of job openings. If there is a match, it refers the applicant to the client. Often when an agency receives a job order it will send several resumés to the employer, which then will choose those people who should be invited for interviews. If there are no open jobs to fit the applicant, the agency will retain the applicant's information in its files and when new job orders develop, will search these files to locate qualified candidates. Such files are one advantage of using an agency.

Executive recruiters work quite differently. The focus of the recruiter's activity is the employer—not the applicant. An executive recruiter will spend time studying the job the client is seeking to fill, research to determine in what companies the type of person they want probably is working, identify possible candidates, and then contact them to sell them on considering the job.

Management Miscellany

If you are seeking a job, don't expect executive recruiters to help you; their function is to fill their clients' openings. However, it can't hurt to send them your resumé on the possibility that it might fit a job they are seeking to fill.

Once a candidate expresses interest, the recruiter will meet with him or her for an informal interview. Usually the name of the employer is kept confidential until an interview with the employer is arranged. If there is mutual interest, the candidate will be invited back to the recruiter for a more detailed interview. At this point, references will be checked; then the recruiter will discuss the candidate's background and qualifications with the client.

Unlike an agency, the executive recruiter does not send a batch of resumés from which the employer selects candidates. The recruiter, who then presents the select few candidates to the employer for consideration, does all of the screening.

The Cost of Using Executive Recruiters

It's not cheap. Fee structures vary somewhat in the field. Be sure to get a full understanding of what it will cost before engaging an executive recruiter. Most search firms base their fees on the salary paid to the person hired. The most common percentage is 25 to 35 percent of the annual salary. If the compensation package also includes bonuses or stock options, some search firms factor the estimated value of these into the fee.

Unlike employment agencies, executive recruiters usually receive a nonrefundable retainer before they start the assignment. This retainer usually is one third of the estimated fee. When the job is filled, the fee is recalculated on the basis of the actual salary minus what has already been paid. If the job is not filled, there is no additional fee. In addition to the fee, the employer agrees to pay expenses incurred in the search. This includes travel costs for the recruiter, travel costs of candidates, telephone costs, and other expenses directly involved in the search.

Some firms charge hourly fees. Just as lawyers charge clients on the basis of billable hours, some search firms will use a similar formula. They set an hourly rate with a maximum fee, such as one third of the annual salary paid the successful candidate. The fee will be calculated on both bases and the client pays whichever is lower; thus, if the job is filled rapidly, you might save money.

Some search firms, particularly those associated with management consulting divisions of the major accounting firms, charge a flat fee, which is paid whether or not the job is filled. These fees usually are lower than the contingency fees. However, you risk the possibility that they won't find a suitable candidate.

Some recruiters dealing with high-tech companies have worked out deals to accept part of the fee in company stock. In this way, the company benefits by conserving its current cash position, and the recruiter benefits by what he or she hopes will be the growing value of the stock.

Most executive recruiters do not refund fees if the selected candidate doesn't work out. However, they usually will seek a replacement at no additional fee other than reimbursement of expenses.

Recruiting Networks

An easy way to fill jobs is through personal contacts; yet we can't depend on knowing somebody who knows somebody when we have to fill a job immediately. One way to improve your odds of getting recommendations is to *network,* meaning to make connections with people who are likely to know people with the skills and experience your company usually hires.

A logical source is people who work for firms that hire the same types of people you do. It's unlikely that your competitors will refer good people to you; however, there are lots of noncompeting firms that might be good sources. Cultivate them.

A competitor or a company in a similar business may lay off staff. Staff who have been laid off through no direct fault of their own are an excellent source of candidates. Sometimes the company that is letting staff go will run your ad in their own internal newspapers or even contact the laid-off workers on your behalf.

Job Fairs

One of the most cost-effective ways to recruit "techies" is the job fair. Job fairs started as an informal part of technical society conventions. For example, when engineers attended the convention, they often would spend more time looking for a new job than attending the workshops and technical programs. Companies would set up elaborate hospitality suites at a nearby hotel and invite prospective employees to visit and learn about the opportunities at that firm.

Management Miscellany

A variation of the job fair is the company open house. The company advertises that it will host an open house and invites people with the special skills they are seeking. Representatives from the various departments in which the jobs exist provide information about the openings to visitors and arrange for interviews when mutual interest is generated.

Today's job fairs are not necessarily tied in with conventions. Recruiters or trade show operators run them. Companies rent a booth at the fair and staff it with representatives of the human resources and technical departments. Applicants are given a guidebook listing the participating companies and the types of positions they are seeking to fill.

The sponsors of the job fair advertise in local and trade papers, and quite often participating companies will advertise their jobs in the papers and invite interested applicants to visit their booths. Users of job fairs have found them to be a relatively inexpensive way to hire people, and many companies participate in job fairs several times a year.

The Internet as a Source for Personnel

Everything now can be found on the Internet. You can purchase all kinds of goods and services by clicking your mouse. So why not seek to fill your jobs through the computer? The applicants you want might be sitting at their terminals right now, surfing the Net for career opportunities.

Often, Internet advertising for open positions is placed on the company's own Web site. Today most companies have Web pages on which they describe the company's activities. These pages are designed primarily so that customers or potential investors can learn about the organization. Many firms include in their Web pages announcements of job openings.

The trouble with many Web pages is that it's not easy to access employment information. To attract applicants, design a special recruiting page and put a connecting link on the home page so applicants can easily access it. Make your recruiting page exciting and enticing. Give prospects an intimate look at the company through video clips, vignettes about successful employees, and meaningful job descriptions. Make it easy to contact the company and provide an e-mail address for submission of resumés.

Using Internet Referral Services

You might be thinking: "Web pages are okay for big companies—but my company isn't that well known. Job seekers are not likely to even know about it, let alone hit our Web page." The solution: Use one of the many Internet job referral services. These are the cyber-equivalent of the help wanted pages in newspapers or technical publications.

A survey of 1000 corporate recruiters found that 71 percent report spending up to 20 percent of their recruitment budget on the Internet—and this is growing exponentially. Of companies that responded, 75 percent plan to increase their Internet recruiting advertising in the coming year. It is estimated that the Internet recruiting business will go from $250 million in 1999 to $5.1 billion by 2003.

There are several Internet referral services currently online and many more are opening every month. With so many, sometimes it can be hard to choose the appropriate server for your needs. Log on to several sites, study their approaches, compare their rates and their records of success before choosing those you wish to use.

According to Media Matrix, an Internet consulting firm, the top 10 job sites are as follows:

➤ Monster.com   ➤ HotJobs.com

➤ Careerpath.com   ➤ Dice.com

➤ CareerMosaic.com   ➤ CareerBuilder.com

➤ HeadHunter.net   ➤ NationJob.com

➤ JobSearch.org   ➤ Jobs.com

Searching the Applicants' Listings

Another source that should not be overlooked is the postings of individuals seeking jobs on the job service Web pages. There are literally thousands of applicants posting their qualifications on one or more of the listing services. If you are able to narrow the field down to a reasonable number of prospects, it will bring to your attention people who might fit your needs.

However, unless there are very few available people in the job you seek to fill, you'll have to spend more time scanning the postings than it might be worth. Keep in mind that a great portion of the postings are from men and women who are currently employed and not registered with agencies, not regular readers of want ads, or not desperate for a job.

When jobs are hard to fill, every possible source should be used so that you can attract the best-qualified applicants. You may have to screen many people in order to make the best selection. Advertise, use employment agencies, executive recruiters, job fairs, and the Internet. Let people know that your company is a company that people want to work for.

The Least You Need to Know

➤ In seeking candidates for routine jobs, run ads in the help wanted section of a local newspaper. For specialized jobs, trade or professional journals are your best bet.

➤ Employment agencies can provide rapid service in filling jobs and you pay a fee only if you hire the person referred by them.

➤ Headhunters (executive recruiters) are best used when a job is hard to fill and proactive steps are needed to find them.

➤ Temporary services hire the employees themselves and "lease" them to companies that require people for short periods of time.

➤ Develop a network of people who are good sources for referring potential employees.

➤ Don't overlook the Internet as a viable source of candidates.

Chapter 7

Screening Candidates

In This Chapter

➤ How to evaluate resumés

➤ Separating the wheat from the chaff

➤ Getting significant information from application forms

➤ Making the application a legal protector

➤ Using the telephone as a prescreener

As a result of your recruiting efforts, you've received a number of resumés. Your next job is to determine which applicants are worth bringing in for interviews. Your time is valuable and good interviewing is time consuming. It's important to study the resumés carefully and pick only those whose backgrounds appear to be closest to the open job. This chapter will offer guidelines on how to select from the many resumés you receive and help you determine which applicants are most likely worth interviewing.

Screening the Resumés

Always remember that the resumé is a promotional piece written by the applicant to persuade you to hire him or her. It is not an objective recap of qualifications. Your job is to find—amid those glowing words—what the applicant really has done in past employment and education.

You might receive hundreds of resumés in response to an ad. It can take hours and hours of your time to read them and make your preliminary judgments. You can save time and uncover hidden problems in the resumés by following these guidelines:

➤ Establish some "knockout factors." These are job requirements that are absolutely essential to performing the job. They might include necessary educational qualifications or licenses; for example, a degree in electronics, certification as a plumber, or a pilot's license. Show some flexibility in using "knockout factors."

➤ Select key results areas (KRAs) of the job and screen for them (see Chapter 5, "Starting the Search"). When you have many applicants for a position, you can narrow the field by looking for experience in those key aspects.

➤ Look for gaps in dates. Some people who have had jobs for only short durations omit them from their resumés. For example, an applicant might indicate only the years (for one job 1998–2001 and 1994–1998 for the previous job), rather than month and year. It might mean only a short period of unemployment between jobs, but it also might mean that a job held for several months between the listed jobs is omitted.

➤ Watch for resumés that devote more space on the page to past positions than to the current or recent one. The applicant might have just updated an old resumé instead of creating a new one. This could be a sign of laziness, or it might just mean that the more recent jobs are of less importance than previous ones.

➤ Look out for overemphasis on education for experienced applicants. If a person is out of school five or more years, the resumé should primarily cover work experience; information about education should be limited to degrees and specialized programs completed. What was done in high school or college is secondary to what has been accomplished on the job.

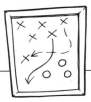

Tactical Tips

Chronological resumés present an applicant's background by listing jobs by the dates of employment. Functional resumés present an applicant's background by listing duties, responsibilities, or accomplishments without regard to the job or company in which they were performed.

None of these tips to screening resumés are necessarily knockout factors; they simply suggest further exploration in the interview. Keep in mind that even if they have a resumé, all applicants should complete a company application form before the interview. Use the resumé as a supplement to the application form; not a substitute for it.

Determining Whom to Interview

The resumé usually is the first source of screening applicants. As interviewing takes a good deal of time, it's necessary to eliminate candidates who are unlikely to be qualified early in the screening process. Here are some suggestions that will help you separate the wheat from the chaff:

➤ Study the job specifications for the open position. Prepare a list of key factors that the applicant must have to qualify.

➤ As you read the resumés, check to see if the specified education and experience significantly include these factors.

➤ If these factors are mentioned, determine whether this experience or training has been acquired in a setting comparable to that of your organization. (For example, cost accounting experience in a chemical company might not be of much value to an automobile parts company as the cost systems are entirely different.)

➤ If these factors are not mentioned, it doesn't necessarily mean that the applicant lacks them. In writing a resumé, an applicant might overlook some important factors in the effort to keep it brief. To avoid eliminating such an applicant, phone him or her to obtain more information.

➤ Determine whether the applicant's experience is comprehensive enough to meet your requirements.

➤ Does the resumé show the accomplishments and results attained by the candidate? If the description of the work is presented in concrete terms, and shows achievements rather than a textbook description of the job duties, it's more likely that the candidate is a clear thinker and is a results-oriented person.

➤ Are the accomplishments significant? If the applicant brags about a routine or superficial achievement, it might indicate a low standard of what he or she considers to be important.

Resumés are only pieces of paper; they cannot possibly describe the whole person. If you choose not to see an applicant based on the resumé, you will lose this prospect—perhaps the best candidate—forever. If you have any doubts before placing it in the reject file, telephone the candidate to obtain more information.

The Application Form

The company application form serves several purposes. It's a rapid way to provide the interviewer with basic information about the applicant. It makes it easy to compare candidates. It alleviates the need for the interviewer to take time asking for routine information. It also provides legal protection. As you will learn in the following, the application is very important and should be a requirement.

All Applicants Must Fill Out the Form

Some candidates might be reluctant to complete an application. They tell you that all of the information is in the resumé; sometimes it is. But, as was pointed out earlier in this chapter, a resumé is designed to play up the strengths of the applicant—and sometimes to cover up negative factors. "I don't have to fill out the application. I have a resumé" is not a good argument. If an applicant doesn't want to take the time to complete your application form, he or she might be hiding something—or it might be an indicator of laziness or unwillingness to follow instructions.

Management Miscellany

Target and Home Depot have substituted computer-based tools for paper job applications. Kiosks have been placed in the stores so shoppers can apply for jobs by answering the questions online. A formatted copy is sent electronically to the manager on duty, who then can set up an immediate interview.

Tactical Tips

Before reprinting your application form when more copies are needed, have your legal counsel review it to ensure that it's in compliance with the latest laws and regulations.

It Protects You Legally

In this litigious age, there have been a rash of suits against companies by applicants who have claimed discrimination when they didn't get the job. Others have claimed that companies jeopardized their current job by calling their employers for references, or that their privacy was invaded when their backgrounds were investigated.

Properly designed application forms can protect companies. For example, if no questions on your application request age or related information, applicants will have a tough time proving you discriminated against them because of age. As noted in Chapter 2, "You Gotta Know the Laws," and Chapter 3, "Still More Laws," make sure that your form complies with the civil rights laws and does not ask questions that are prohibited.

It Provides Information You Need

It's convenient to have essential information in one easy-to-find place. The application form provides name, address, phone number, Social Security number, and educational background. Most useful is the work history with dates of employment, positions, companies, and a brief description of duties and responsibilities. Usually it includes salary, reason for leaving, and the name of a person in the company who can provide information about the applicant.

In short, the application gives you enough basic information to determine whether or not the prospect is worthy of further consideration. Although most forms don't have enough space to give details about a person's activities, responsibilities, and accomplishments, it provides—along with the applicant's resumé—adequate data to make preliminary judgments.

It Makes It Easy to Compare Candidates

Whereas resumés are written in a variety of styles, all applications for jobs within a company are formatted in the same way. This makes it easy to compare applicants. Placing application forms side by side, you can immediately measure the education and experience of each candidate against the others. You can compare duration and types of experience and note salary variations.

Impressive resumés might make a candidate stand out, but when the resumé and application together are considered, you might find that the applicant with a less impressive resumé actually has a better background.

Clauses to Protect You

In addition to being a selection tool, the application form is a contract. Of course, it's a one-sided contract in that it is written to protect the employer. Many attorneys strongly recommend that certain clauses be included in this document; some of the most important are covered in the following.

Permission to Investigate

This covers two different types of investigation: checking references and using an investigative service to look into the applicant's background. Because of concerns about litigation, many companies refuse to give information about former or current employees. By getting a release from the applicant authorizing the employer to provide information, you avert this concern. Many companies include a clause to cover this on their application forms; some provide it on a separate document. The following is an example of such a clause:

> *I understand that the (NAME OF EMPLOYER) follows an "employment at will" policy, in that the employer may terminate my employment at any time or for any reason consistent with applicable federal and state laws. This employment-at-will policy cannot be changed verbally or in writing unless authorized specifically by the president or executive vice president of this company. I understand that this application is not a contract of employment. I understand that the federal government prohibits the employment of unauthorized aliens; all persons hired must provide satisfactory proof of employment authorization and identity. Failure to submit such proof will result in denial of employment.*

I understand that the employer may investigate my work and personal history and verify all information given on this application, on related papers, and in interviews. I hereby authorize all individuals, schools, and firms named therein except for my current employer (unless indicated herein) to provide any information requested about me and hereby release them from all liability for damage in providing this information.

[You may/may not contact my current employer] _____

Personnel Perils

Some lawyers suggest that even if a release clause is incorporated in the application form, a separate form should be signed for each school and employer that will be contacted.

Under the federal Fair Credit Reporting Act, if you use the services of an outside credit or investigative reporting agency, you must provide the applicant with a written notification that such a report might be ordered. The applicant must be advised that he or she has the right to request a copy of such a report from the agency that conducts the investigation. The name of this agency also must be provided to the applicant upon request.

If used, this clause should be printed on the application form in print that is no smaller than the rest of the application and should have space for the signature of the applicant and a witness. If you use investigative reports for only a few positions, develop a separate form to use when appropriate rather than printing it on the application.

Employment at Will

Unless an employee is protected by an individual contract with the employer or a negotiated contract between the employer and a labor union, or is a civil service employee, the employee falls under *employment at will* status. This means that the employer has the right to terminate the services of that employee at any time, for any reason or for no reason at all so long as it complies with applicable laws such as the civil rights laws. You will find more on this in Chapter 25, "How to Fire an Employee Legally and Tactfully."

Most employees in American companies fall into this category. However, to ensure that new employees are aware of this, it should be indicated on the application form (see the example in the suggested application form). By having the applicant sign the application form, he or she indicates understanding and acceptance of "employment at will."

Certification of Truth

After you hire a person, you might find out that he or she lied in his or her application or resumé, or misrepresented an important factor. If this happens you should be able to take immediate action to terminate that person. The prototype application form in the previous section includes sample protective clauses. Have your company's legal advisors word the clauses in a way specific to your company.

Evaluating the Application

There are many things you can learn from the application form (and its accompanying resumé) that can help you narrow your selection of candidates. The following are some of the areas that should be carefully examined.

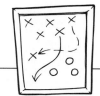

Tactical Tips

When designing your own application form, add questions that are pertinent to the jobs you seek to fill. Check all questions against the "lawful and unlawful" question chart in Chapter 8, "Becoming a Better Interviewer."

Can the Person Do the Job?

In reviewing the application form, determine whether the applicant has the basic requirements to do the job. Application forms usually don't provide much space for details of experience. However, make sure that at least the basic educational requirements are met and the job history reflects the necessary experience. If so, prepare to explore this experience at the interview.

Progress

The applicant's progress and growth in jobs and career should be evaluated as well as specific experience. If your job offers opportunity but demands ambition and drive, the applicant should have demonstrated these traits by the progress made in previous jobs.

Progress can be measured by positions held and salaries earned. A person who has worked for the same firm for many years and has received only automatic annual salary increases actually has made no real progress even though earnings have gone up. Position and salary should be compared with those of other people in that field who have similar education and experience.

The earnings record should not be the only measure of progress. It is more important to determine whether the applicant shows a pattern of increasing responsibility in his or her career. Have promotions been in line with the person's experience? Has he or she moved more rapidly than might be expected? If so, was this due to personal capability and accomplishments? Was it due to growth of the industry or the company rather than individual efforts? Was it based on *nepotism?*

Meanings and Gleanings

Nepotism is favoritism shown by higher-ranking officials or managers to their relatives or close friends.

Management Miscellany

In today's hot market for technical and other hard-to-find personnel, qualified people are likely to move from company to company far more frequently than workers in other areas. Over the past few years the typical job tenure of these specialists has fallen from five to three years.

Stability

Another factor the application form indicates is job stability. Many employers will automatically reject an applicant who has changed jobs too often. Some companies have implemented this rule: If a person has had more than two jobs in five years or some similar combination of years and jobs, he or she is knocked out. There is much to be said in favor of this policy. Frequent job changes might indicate restlessness or boredom with a job; however, it's unlikely that the candidate's next job will be any different.

Some people are "two-yearers"—the time it takes to master the intricacies of the job and then tire of it. Others might be marginal workers—employees who are not bad enough to discharge but are the first to be laid off when business slows down. In other cases there might be personality problems. The employee might never have been able to get along with co-workers or managers.

On the other hand, it might be just bad luck. The person might be on the job only a short time when the company suffers a business reversal, massive downsizing, or a reorganization that eliminates the job. Sometimes a person might start a job and rapidly realize it was a mistake. It's better to quit immediately than stay around just to keep the work record from looking bad.

Before arbitrarily rejecting an applicant as a job hopper, it's important to determine the reason for the apparent instability. There are often good reasons one changes jobs. Don't lose a potentially good employee because of some arbitrary policy on "instability."

Other Factors to Look For

The application form might offer some insight into the applicant's personality. It indicates whether the applicant can follow the simple directions required to complete it. In some employment offices, the length of time taken by an applicant to fill out the form is used as a measure of speed in performing clerical tasks. If the job calls for good handwriting, it also can be observed on the application form.

In some companies receptionists are trained to observe the manner in which applicants act when given the form. Do they get to work on it in a businesslike manner? Do they refer to notes? Do they ask questions about the form? If another person accompanies them, do they confer with that person before answering a question on the form?

The Telephone Screening Interview

Probably the most frequently used prescreening tool is the telephone. In a relatively brief telephone interview, you can acquire a lot more information about a candidate than can be obtained from the application or resumé. Telephoning not only enables you to get more information than shown on the resumé, but you can probe for details on specific areas that are important to the job you seek to fill.

It's not a good idea to call the applicant at work to discuss your job opening. This is not only unethical; it puts the applicant in an awkward position as other people might be nearby who can hear the conversation. The call should be made to the person's home in the evening. This might mean you have to make these calls from your home or work late at the office—that's just one of the sacrifices that recruiters and managers have to make to get the people they want.

Plan the phone call as carefully as an in-person interview. Read the application and resumé and note the areas that require elaboration. Don't be afraid to ask hard questions such as reasons for leaving a job, accounting for periods of unemployment, relations with superiors, and specific details about work or educational background. (Suggestions on how to conduct an interview will be covered in the next chapter; you can adapt these techniques to the telephone interview.)

Be certain you have set up an appointment in advance, so that the candidate expects the call. Otherwise you may be calling when the candidate is rushed and is too polite to say so, or even be mistaken for a telemarketer and hung up on.

Management Miscellany

If there are any possibly negative factors about the position or your company, give the prospect a chance to discuss it before extending an invitation for an interview. For example, you might say, "This job requires that you travel 75 percent of the time. Will this affect your consideration of this job?"

The Least You Need to Know

➤ Set up a series of knockout factors before evaluating resumés. Unless the applicant meets these specs, there's no point arranging for an interview.

➤ Don't take a resumé at face value. Read between the lines and look for hidden negative factors.

➤ Require all applicants to complete a company application. The resumé should be used as a supplement; not a substitute for the application.

➤ Make sure your application form meets all legal requirements.

➤ Telephone interviews can provide enough information to determine whether it's worthwhile to invite the applicant for a face-to-face meeting.

Chapter 8

Becoming a Better Interviewer

In This Chapter

➤ Preparing the groundwork for the interview

➤ Questions you can and cannot ask an applicant

➤ Putting the applicant at ease

➤ Getting meaningful information from the interview

➤ Remembering the applicant

You've done the preparatory work. You've studied application forms and resumés. Now you're ready to see the applicant. Interviewing is both an art and a science. It's an art because the interviewer must be able to tailor the questions and interpret the responses. It's a science because it can be structured to bring out the desired information.

Interviews are more than just pleasant conversations between you and the applicant. The way the interviewing process is planned and followed can make the difference between hiring the best candidate and just selecting one by instinct. This process will be explored in this chapter.

Preparing for the Interview

Before an applicant enters the interviewing room, the interviewer should thoroughly study the application and resumé. Any areas that require more information or are indicators of strengths or weaknesses should be noted so that questions can be asked about them. Keep in mind the objectives of the interview. First you must determine whether the candidate has the technical qualifications needed for the position. Second, you must find out whether the applicant has the necessary personality traits to be successful in the job.

Well-designed questions based on the job specs can help determine skill qualifications; however, personality qualifications are much more difficult to measure. Some of these intangibles might be listed in the job specs. For example, "must be able to work under pressure," or "should be able to present public speeches." It's not easy to reduce many personality factors to a simple statement in a job specification. The interviewer must be able to tailor the questions based on the nature of the job, the people with whom the applicant will have to work, and the company culture.

Management Miscellany

Although many well-known organizations have developed sophisticated selection tools including structured interviews, psychological evaluations, and written assessments by several managers, most companies rely on informal nonstructured interviews by supervisors and managers as their primary selection method.

Plan Your Questions

Some interviewers sit down with the applicant with only a general idea of the questions they plan to ask. They might start with a general question such as, "Tell me about yourself." From the response, they pick aspects of the background to explore. This might be okay for an experienced interviewer who just uses that question as an opening device and has prepared additional questions. However, the applicant might tell you only what he or she wants you to hear—and you might never get around to asking about some important areas.

Make a List of Key Questions

An effective interview is well planned. It's a good idea to prepare a list of key questions that must be asked during the interview. However, don't limit yourself to asking just those questions. Be alert to responses and ask additional questions based on those responses.

Some interviewers write down the questions they plan to ask and refer to them during the interview. Others make notes on the applicant's application form to remind them about areas they wish to explore. Still other interviewers depend on their knowledge of the field to develop questions as they move along in the process. Later in this chapter you'll find a structured interview form listing questions that are effective in obtaining good information.

Can I Ask About ...?

As noted in Chapters 2, "You Gotta Know the Laws," and 3, "Still More Laws," respectively, various federal and state laws govern the questions you can ask applicants. The following list outlines major areas of concern and specifies whether the related questions can or cannot be asked. This applies not only to the interview but also to questions on an application form or questions asked when checking references.

Although the civil rights laws vary somewhat from state to state, federal law governs all organizations doing business in the United States. The following list of "lawful and unlawful" questions is presented as a general guideline that is applicable under federal law and the strictest states. However, to ensure that you are in compliance with legal requirements and interpretations in any specific state, check with local authorities or an attorney specializing in this field. The items listed as "unlawful" represent commonly asked questions in the category but are not the only unlawful questions.

An asterisk (*) indicates inquiries that otherwise would be deemed lawful, but in certain circumstances might be seen as evidence of unlawful discrimination. These items will be deemed unlawful when the questions are used to get information about a candidate that is not job related, and which has a disproportionate burdensome effect upon the members of a minority group and cannot be justified as business necessity.

List of Lawful and Unlawful Questions

SUBJECT: Race or color
LAWFUL*: None
UNLAWFUL: Questions about complexion, color of skin, or coloring.

SUBJECT: Religion or creed
LAWFUL*: None
UNLAWFUL: Inquiry into applicant's religious denomination, religious affiliations, church, parish, pastor, or religious holidays observed. Applicant may not be told "This is a Catholic, Protestant, or Jewish" organization.

SUBJECT: National origin
LAWFUL*: None
UNLAWFUL: Inquiry into applicant's lineage, ancestry, national origin, descent, parentage, nationality, or nationality of applicant's parents or spouse. Applicant may not be asked, "What is your native tongue?"

SUBJECT: Gender
LAWFUL*: None
UNLAWFUL: Inquiry about gender

SUBJECT: Marital status
LAWFUL*: None
UNLAWFUL: Asking for a name or other information about a spouse. Applicant may not be asked, "Are you married, single, divorced, or separated?" "Where does your spouse work?" or "Do you wish to be addressed as Mr., Miss, Mrs., or Ms.?"

SUBJECT: Birth control
LAWFUL*: None
UNLAWFUL: Inquiry about capacity to reproduce, advocacy of any form of birth control, or family planning. Applicant may not be asked, "What are the ages of your children, if any?"

SUBJECT: Age
LAWFUL*: Applicant may be asked, "Are you 18 years or older? If not, state your age."
UNLAWFUL: Applicants may not be asked, "How old are you?" "What is your date of birth?" "What year did you graduate from high school?"

SUBJECT: Disability
LAWFUL*: Applicant may be asked, "Do you have any impairment, physical, mental, or medical, which would interfere with your ability to perform the job for which you have applied?"
UNLAWFUL: Applicant may not be asked, "Do you have a disability? Have you ever been treated for any of the following diseases ...?"

SUBECT: Arrest record
LAWFUL*: Applicant may be asked, "Have you been convicted of a crime?" and may be asked to provide details.
UNLAWFUL: Applicant may not be asked, "Have you ever been arrested?"

SUBJECT: Name
LAWFUL*: Applicant may be asked, "Have you ever worked for this company under a different name?" "Is any additional information relative to change of name, use of an assumed name or nickname necessary to enable a check on your work record? If yes, explain."
UNLAWFUL: Applicant may not be asked his or her original name if name has been changed by court order or otherwise; asked for a maiden name if a married woman; or, "If you have ever worked under a different name, state name and dates."

SUBJECT: Address or duration of residence
LAWFUL*: Applicant's place of residence or length of time the applicant has been a resident of this state or city.
UNLAWFUL: None

SUBJECT: Birthplace
LAWFUL*: None
UNLAWFUL: Birthplace of applicant; birthplace of applicant's parents, spouse, or other close relatives.

SUBJECT: Birth date
LAWFUL*: None
UNLAWFUL: To require that applicant submit birth certificate, naturalization, or baptismal record as proof of age.

SUBJECT: Photograph
LAWFUL: None
UNLAWFUL: Requirement or option that applicant affix a photograph to employment form at any time before hiring.

SUBJECT: Citizenship
LAWFUL: An applicant may be asked any of the following: Are you a citizen of the United States? If not a citizen of the United States, do you intend to become a citizen of the United States? If you are not a United States citizen, have you the legal right to remain permanently in the United States? Do you intend to remain permanently in the United States? (Proof of citizenship or legal right to work in the U.S. can be required only after applicant has been hired; see the section "The Immigration Reform and Control Act of 1986" in Chapter 3.)
UNLAWFUL: An applicant may not be asked if he or she is a naturalized or a native-born citizen, or the date when the applicant acquired citizenship. Applicant may not be required to produce naturalization papers or first papers; be asked whether applicant's parents or spouse are naturalized or native-born citizens of the United States, or the date when such parents or spouse acquired citizenship. An applicant may not be asked, "Of what country are you a citizen?"

SUBJECT: Language
LAWFUL: Inquiry into languages applicant speaks and writes fluently
UNLAWFUL: Inquiry into how applicant acquired ability to read, write, or speak a foreign language. An applicant may not be asked, "What is your native language?"

SUBJECT: Education
LAWFUL: Inquiry into applicant's academic, vocational, or professional education and the public and private schools attended
UNLAWFUL: Dates attended or graduated

SUBJECT: Experience
LAWFUL: Inquiry into work experience
UNLAWFUL: None

SUBJECT: Relatives
LAWFUL: Names of applicant's relatives, other than spouse, already employed by this company
UNLAWFUL: Names, addresses, ages, number, or other information concerning applicant's spouse, children, or other relatives not employed by this company

SUBJECT: Notify in case of emergency
LAWFUL: None
UNLAWFUL: Name and address of person to be notified in case of an emergency. (This may be asked only after employment begins.)

SUBJECT: Military experience
LAWFUL*: Inquiry into an applicant's military experience in the Armed Forces of the United States or in a state militia. Inquiry into an applicant's service in a particular branch of United States Army, Navy, and so on.
UNLAWFUL: Inquiry into applicant's military experience in a country other than the U.S.

SUBJECT: Organizations
LAWFUL*: Inquiry into applicant's memberships in organizations that the applicant considers relevant to his or her ability to perform the job.
UNLAWFUL: Requirement to list all clubs, societies, and lodges to which he or she belongs.

SUBJECT: Driver's license
LAWFUL*: Do you possess a valid driver's license?
UNLAWFUL: Requirement that applicant produce a driver's license prior to employment.

The Structured Interview

Most good interviews have a definite structure. If not, they result in a chaotic exchange of questions and answers with little possibility of either side making reasonable decisions. However, some companies use specially prepared *structured interview* forms that interviewers must follow virtually line by line.

Meanings and Gleanings

Structured interviews are conducted using a list of questions that must be asked in exactly the same way in exactly the same order with every candidate. They also are called *patterned interviews, diagnostic interviews,* and *guided interviews.*

One reason for this type of interview is legal; another, psychological. Some labor lawyers assert that asking each applicant exactly the same questions in exactly the same order will be a defense against charges of discrimination.

Whether the reason is legal, or just pragmatic, there are some advantages of using some form of structured interview. For example, by asking questions that are printed on a form, you won't miss asking an important question. The structured interview form provides space next to the questions to record answers. And, as all applicants are asked the same questions, it's easy to compare applicants when making the final decision.

The negative side of a formal structured interview is that it stifles creativity and flexibility in both parties. In the formal structured interview, you are not allowed to deviate from the form.

Using a Less Formalized Structure

To enable you to be flexible, the structured interview should be used as a guide. This cannot be done if the format you use is one in which the psychologist requires the interviewer to phrase questions exactly as printed and to ask them in the same order each time. However, most structured interviews are not of this nature; variations and flexibility can be built into them.

The *Personalized Personnel Profile,* shown in the following, is an example of a modified structured interview form. It is designed to serve as a guide and gives the interviewer freedom to be flexible. Feel free to adapt this for your own use. Follow the instructions at the beginning of the form.

INSTRUCTIONS: To use this profile effectively, it must be personalized for each specific job and for each applicant. The printed questions are to be used only as guidelines. They may or may not be asked of each applicant depending upon pertinence.

MOST IMPORTANT: Specific questions relating to job requirements should be developed for each job based on *your* job description, company needs, and interviewer's follow-up to responses given by the applicant.

Write only brief phrases in the space provided for answers—just enough to help you remember the applicant's responses.

*****Complete this section before the interview begins*****

Name of applicant:

Address:

Phone: FAX: E-MAIL:

Position: Department:

Interviewed by: Date:

Note: In designing the form to use in your company, leave space between questions to note answers.

EDUCATION: Ask questions in PART A of applicants who did **not attend college.** Use questions in PART B for college graduates or those who have had same college. **For applicants who have been out of college 5 years or more** omit PART A or PART B and ask only questions in PART C.

PART A. For applicants who did **not attend college:**

1. What was highest level of schooling completed?
2. Why did you decide not to continue your formal education?
3. How were your overall grades?
4. In what extracurricular activities did you participate?
5. Tell me about the class or club offices held?

6. If you worked, how many hours per week? Summers? What kind of jobs?

7. What steps have you taken to acquire additional education since leaving school?

8. What training have you had in high or other schools that helped in your career?

9. What was the first significant job you held after leaving high school?

10. How did this lead to your present career?

PART B. For **college graduates** or those **with some college:**

1. I see that you attended (name of college). Why did you select that school?

2. What was your major? Why did you choose it?

3. What were your overall college grades? How did they compare with your high school grades?

4. What courses did you start in college and later drop? Why?

5. In what types of extracurricular activities did you participate in college? What offices did you hold?

6. How did you finance your college education?

7. If you worked in high school or college, how many hours per week? Summers? Kind of jobs?

8. What were your vocational plans when you were in college?

9. If they are different now, when did you change your thinking? Why?

10. What additional education have you had since college?

11. How do you think college contributed to your career?

12. (If college was not completed.) When did you leave college? Why? Do you plan to complete your degree? (If so, ask about plans.)

13. What was the first significant job you held after leaving (graduating from) college?

14. How did this lead to your current career?

PART C. For persons **out of school 5 years or longer:**

1. What educational background have you had that has contributed to success in your career?

2. What courses or seminars have you taken recently? (If job-related, how did you apply them to your job?)

3. What are you doing now to keep up with the state of the art in your field?

4. What are your plans at present to continue your education?

5. Other than job-related programs, what else are you doing in self-development?

6. What magazines do you read regularly?

7. What books have you read recently?

WORK EXPERIENCE: Ask these questions for each job held.

1. On your application you indicated you worked for (name of company). Are you still there? (Or: When were you there?)

2. Describe your duties and responsibilities in each of your assignments with this company?

3. What were some of the things you particularly enjoyed about that job?

4. What were some of the things you least enjoyed in that position?

5. What do you consider your major accomplishment in that assignment?

6. Tell me about some of your disappointments or setbacks in that job.

7. Tell me about the progress you made in that company.

8. (If progress was significant, ask: To what do you attribute this fine progress? If not, ask: Were you satisfied with this progress? If not satisfied, ask: How did you attempt to overcome this?)

9. What was the most valuable experience you obtained in that position?

10. Why did you leave (or: why do you want to leave) that company?

SPECIFIC QUESTIONS: On a separate sheet of paper, list specific questions to be asked—based on the job description. (Refer to the section "Preparing Specific Job-Related Questions" later in this chapter.)

INTANGIBLE FACTORS:

1. What are you seeking in this job that you are not getting in your present job?

2. Tell me about your career goals—long term? Short term?

3. In what way could a job with our company meet your career objectives?

4. What goals have you set in previous jobs or school? What have you done to accomplish them? What results?

5. What are your criteria for your own success?

6. What factors have contributed most to your own growth?

7. What factors have handicapped you from moving ahead more rapidly?

8. If you had to do it over again, what changes would you make in your life and your career?

9. What aspects of a job are most important to you?

10. Think of a supervisor you particularly respected. Describe his/her management style? Describe your least effective supervisor?

11. What have supervisors complimented you for? For what have they criticized you?

12. Tell me about some of the significant problems encountered? How did you solve them?

13. If hired for this position, what can you bring to it that will rapidly make you productive?

14. In what areas could we help you become even more productive?

When using a structured interview form, don't fall into the trap of reading the question as if it were a questionnaire. Present the questions in a conversational tone and rephrase where necessary to put the question into the context of the conversation. In addition, read your job specs carefully. Discuss the job with the department head or team leader. Frame questions that will enable you to get the information needed to determine whether this applicant is best for the open position.

Preparing Specific Job-Related Questions

The responses to the general questions will give you enough information to determine if the candidate is basically qualified for your job. However, in every job there are certain very specific areas of knowledge, experience, and expertise that the applicant must demonstrate to become productive rapidly. To determine this, you also should prepare a list of questions that will probe for these details.

Management Miscellany

Lists of specific questions to ask applicants for more than 70 different jobs can be found in the book *Be A Better Employment Interviewer*, by Dr. Arthur R. Pell (Personnel Publications).

As the questions differ from job to job—even jobs with the same or similar titles might require different specific factors—you must develop appropriate questions for each job. To do this study not just the job specification, which lists the qualifications required, but also the job description, which gives details of job functions.

For example, if your opening is for a medical technician, prepare questions about the types of medical equipment the applicant learned to operate in school, experience in operating the equipment, and the venues in which the person worked (at a hospital? clinic? physician's office?). If you are not fully knowledgeable about the job, have the person to whom the position reports design these questions for you—and, of course, the desired answers.

Getting Started

Tense applicants don't respond fully to your questions. To obtain the best results from an interview, the interviewer must put the applicant at ease. To do this takes a little time, but even in a brief interview it's well worth it. Here are a few suggestions that will make your interview go more smoothly and provide you with the information you need to make good hiring decisions.

Establish Rapport

To make the applicant feel at ease, the interviewer must be at ease and feel comfortable about the interviewing process. An ideal setting for an interview is a private room, comfortably furnished with a minimum of distracting papers on the desk. To avoid telephone interruptions, turn on your voicemail or have somebody else answer your phone.

Go out and greet the applicant. It's much better to personally go to the reception area than to send a secretary to fetch him or her; so get up from your chair and get out there. Introduce yourself and escort the applicant to the interviewing room.

When greeting the applicant, use his or her full name: "David Livingston, hi, I'm Henry Stanley." By using both the first and the last name in addressing the applicant and introducing yourself, you put both of you on equal footing. If you call yourself Mr. or Ms., and call the applicant "Dave," it sounds condescending. This also makes the applicant feel you identify him or her as an individual; not just another candidate. Dale Carnegie said, "Remember, a person's name is to that person the sweetest and most important sound in any language."

The opening should be related to the interview, but should not make the applicant defensive or upset. Don't start with such questions as, "What makes you think that you could handle this job?" or "Why were you fired from your last job?" A better approach would be to select an innocuous area from the application and comment on it. It might be based on something in the background that you relate to. For example, "I see you went to Lincoln High School. Did you know Mr. Salkin, the drama teacher?" or "I see you live in Chelsea. That neighborhood is growing rapidly."

Guidelines for Better Interviewing

How you frame the question is important. Choose your words carefully. Remember, your objective is to get the applicant to give you meaningful information. To get the most out of the interview, here are some guidelines to follow when asking questions:

➤ Don't ask questions that can be answered "Yes" or "No." This stifles information. Instead of asking, "Have you any experience in budgeting?" say "Tell me about your experience in budgeting."

➤ Don't put words in the applicant's mouth. Instead of asking, "You've called on discount stores, haven't you?" ask, "What discount stores have you called on?"

➤ Don't ask questions that are unrelated to your objectives. It might be interesting to follow up on certain tidbits of gossip the applicant volunteers, but it rarely leads to pertinent information.

➤ Do ask questions that develop information about the applicant's experience ("What were your responsibilities regarding the purchasing of equipment?"), knowledge ("How did you, or would you cope with this problem?"), and attitudes ("How do you feel about heavy travel?" or "Why do you wish to change jobs now?").

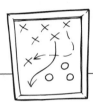

Tactical Tips

An important objective of the interview is to create a favorable image of the company in the eyes of the applicant. The reputation of the firm might be improved or harmed by the manner in which applicants are treated. You want a successful applicant to accept a job offer—and even unsuccessful applicants are potential customers.

An effective way of probing for full information is to use the "W" questions: what, when, where, who, and why. With the addition of "how," you can draw out most of the information needed. For example:

"What computer software did you use?"

"When did you design that program?"

"Where was the program installed?"

"Who was responsible for supervising that project?"

"Why did you make that decision?"

"How did you implement the new system?"

Ask Situational Questions

Give the applicant a hypothetical situation and ask how he or she would handle it. The situations should be reasonably close to actual problems found on the job. Judge the response by knowledge of the subject, approach to the solution, value of the suggestions, and clarity in communicating the answer. Glib applicants might come up with high-sounding solutions to situations, but they might not be really practical. Follow through by asking what problems might be encountered if the idea were implemented.

Summary Questions

When you have finished questioning the applicant about a phase of his or her background, ask a question that will summarize what has been presented. For example,

"You certainly have an extensive background in quality control; can you briefly summarize what you can contribute to make our company more effective in that area?" This will enable you to put what has been said thus far in perspective.

Using Nondirective Techniques

It's not always possible to obtain necessary information by direct questioning. *Nondirective* approaches might help in these cases. Nondirective questioning uses open-ended questions such as, "Tell me about …." The applicant then tells whatever he or she feels is important. Instead of commenting about the response, you nod your head say "uh-huh," "yes," and "I see." This encourages the applicant to keep talking without you giving any hint of what you are seeking.

Another way of using the nondirective approach is to remain silent for several seconds after the applicant stops talking. Most people can't tolerate silence. If you don't respond instantly, the applicant is likely to continue talking and provide additional information.

By using nondirective approaches applicants are likely to bring up matters that may indicate problems, personality factors, attitudes, or weaknesses that might not have been uncovered directly. On the other hand, it might bring out some positive factors and strengths that were missed by direct questioning.

Tactical Tips

Try this: After the applicant responds to your question, count to five slowly (to yourself, of course) before asking the next question. By waiting five seconds, you'll be surprised how often an applicant adds something—positive or negative—to his or her response.

Giving Information to the Applicant

An important part of the interview is giving the applicant information about the company and the job. All the work and expense to get good employees is lost if the applicant you want doesn't accept your offer. By giving applicants a positive picture of the job at the interview, you're likely to have a higher rate of acceptances.

When and What to Tell About the Job

Some interviewers start the interview by describing the job duties. Some give the applicant a copy of the job description in advance of the interview. These are serious errors. If an applicant knows too much about a job too soon, he or she is likely to tailor his or her answers to all of your questions to fit the job.

For example, you tell a prospect that the job calls for selling to department store chains. Even if the applicant has only limited experience in this area, when you ask, "What types of markets did you call on?" guess which one will be emphasized. In this way you won't feed the applicant information that may influence the answers to your questions.

The best way to give information about duties and responsibilities is to feed it to the applicant throughout the interview. However, you'll want to do this only after you have ascertained the background of the applicant in that phase of the work. For example:

> **Interviewer:** What types of markets did you call on?
>
> **Applicant:** Drug store chains, discount stores, department stores, and mail-order houses.

The interviewer then should ask specific questions about the applicant's experience in each of these markets. If the department store background is satisfactory, the interviewer might then say, "I'm glad you have such a fine background in dealing with department store chains as they represent about 40 percent of our customer list. If you should be hired, you'd be working closely with those chains." If the background in this area was weak, the interviewer might say, "As a great deal of our business is with department store chains, if you should be hired, we would have to give you added training in this area."

At the end of the first interview, the interviewer should have a fairly complete knowledge of the applicant's background and the applicant should have a good idea of the nature of the job. At subsequent interviews, the emphasis will be on obtaining more specific details about the applicant and giving the applicant more specific data about the job.

Answering Applicants' Questions

Most interviewers give the applicant an opportunity to ask questions about the job and the company at some point (usually at the end) of the interview. The questions asked can give some insight into the applicant's personality and help you in your evaluation. Are the questions primarily of a personal nature (such as vacations, time off, raises, and similar queries)? Or, are they about the job? People who are concerned only about personal aspects are less likely to be as highly motivated as job-oriented applicants.

An applicant's questions also can be clues to his or her real interest in the job. If based on these questions you feel that a prospective candidate is not too enthusiastic about the job, it gives you another chance to sell him or her on the advantages of joining your company. You are always "selling" when you interview. It's important that you present your company and the job in a positive and enthusiastic manner.

However, this doesn't mean you should exaggerate or mislead the applicant. Tell the applicant the negatives at the interview—but show how the positive aspects outweigh them. Every job has its negative aspects; if you hide them, the applicant will find out sooner or later. This could lead to rejection of the job offer—or worse, acceptance and early resignation.

Closing the Interview

Once the interviewer has all the information needed, and the applicant has been told about the job and has had the opportunity to ask questions, you can bring the interview to a close. All interviews should end on a positive note. The applicant should be told what the next step will be: another interview, testing, or perhaps a final decision.

Telling the Decision to the Applicant

If, based on the interview, you have decided that the applicant is not to be considered, it's only fair to tell him or her. In most cases, the reason might be obvious. Perhaps during the interview, it became clear to both of you that the applicant was not qualified. Just say, "As you don't have experience in area X and Y, which are essential to being able to do this job, we cannot consider you for it."

If the reason is not directly job related, such as lacking personal characteristics or your reaction to the applicant, rather than reject him or her outright, say, "We have several more applicants to interview. Once we've seen them all, we'll make a decision." After a reasonable period, let the person know he or she was rejected.

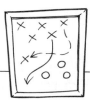

Tactical Tips

Don't keep applicants on a string waiting to hear from you. If you are not interested in a candidate, write or phone him or her no later than one week after the interview. If the applicant is still being considered but the decision is delayed, keep the applicant advised of the status.

Remembering the Applicant

You've evaluated a dozen applicants for the open position. Unless you've kept good records of the interviews, it's unlikely that you'll remember what each one has told you and your reactions to each candidate. By taking, and later rereading, notes rather than depending on your memory, it's easier to compare candidates and you are more likely to make sound judgments. When several people interview the same candidate, a consistent system of recording information will facilitate an in-depth analysis of the applicant's qualifications. See the following figure for a sample summary form to use when interviewing candidates.

Interview Summary Sheet

Applicant: _____ Date: _____

Position applied for: _____ Interviewer: _____

Job factors[1]: _____

Applicant's background[2]: _____ Qualification rating[3]: _____

Duties: _____
_____
_____

Responsibilities: _____
_____
_____

Skills required: _____
_____
_____

Education required[4] (level): _____

   Specific types: _____
_____
_____

   Educational achievement: _____
_____
_____

Other job factors: _____
_____

[1]*Job factors should be listed from job specifications for position applicant applies for.*
[2]*Interviewer should note aspects of applicant's background that apply to each factor in this column.*
[3]*Rate applicant on a scale of 1 to 5 for how closely background fits specifications.*
[4]*Level of education means how much schooling completed; type represents subjects related to job taken; achievement represents grades or standing.*

Interview Summary Sheet.

Personal factors	Comments	Qualification rating
Growth in career		
Accomplishments		
Intangibles		
Appearance		
Motivation		
Resourcefulness		
Stability		
Leadership		
Creativity		
Mental alertness		
Energy level		
Communications skills		
Self-confidence		

Comments

Applicant's strengths: _____

Applicant's limitations: _____

[   ]   Applicant should be hired.

Recommendations for additional training: _____

[   ]   Applicant should NOT be hired.

Reasons: _____

Additional comments: _____

_____

_____

Interview Summary Sheet (continued).

Good Notes Keep You Out of Trouble

Good records help if you face legal problems. In case of an investigation by government agencies such as the EEOC or state civil rights divisions, good records of the interview can be your most important defense. Where no records or inadequate records have been kept, the opinion of the hearing officer is dependent on the company's word against the applicant's. Good, consistent records provide solid evidence.

Taking Notes

Taking notes during an interview often has a negative effect on applicants. Some get very nervous when they see you write down everything they say. They might be inhibited from talking feely and hold back on important matters. In addition, taking notes might have a negative effect on you as the interviewer. You're so busy writing what the applicant just said that you don't listen to what is now being said.

Write brief notes during the interview. Immediately after the interview review them and write a summary while the interview is still fresh in your mind. Succinct reasons for acceptance or rejection should be stated; this will discourage you from making an intuitive decision based on some vague like or dislike. Interviewers must keep in mind that the reason might be challenged by the EEOC or other agencies.

Some companies have special forms designed for interview record keeping. Others suggest you make notes on the application form or attach a page of notes to the form after the interview. In any case a summary form should be completed immediately after the close of the interview.

The Least You Need to Know

➤ Before conducting an interview, review the job specs and description as well as the applicant's resumé and application form.

➤ Prepare a list of key questions. A good interview should be structured, but flexible enough so that follow-up questions can be asked.

➤ Put the applicant at ease by asking nonthreatening questions at the start of the interview.

➤ To get full information, use the "W" questions: what, when, where, who, and why. With the addition of "how," you can draw out most of the information needed.

➤ Use nondirective approaches to elicit information not directly asked about.

➤ Make brief but pertinent notes during the interview. Write a summary report immediately after the interview.

Chapter 9

Making the Hiring Decision

In This Chapter

➤ Employment tests—a boon or a bane?

➤ Making meaningful reference checks

➤ Determining if the applicant can do the job

➤ Comparing applicants

➤ Making a job offer that will be accepted

➤ Countering the counteroffer

The interviews are over and now you have to decide which candidate to hire. This can be one of the most important decisions you are required to make as a manager. It is even more significant today because the old hierarchical structure in which top management makes all the decisions is gone. In its place are more collaborative, team-based, cross-functional organizations in which important decisions are made at all levels. This means that no matter the level of job, choosing the right person is key to the success of your organization. In this chapter we'll look at the steps that lead to making the hiring decision.

Employment Testing

In the effort to minimize subjectivity in hiring decisions, companies use a variety of tests to help assess applicants. These tests vary from gimmicky quizzes that are supposed to predict success or failure on a job to well-designed, carefully validated instruments. Do these tests really help? Some companies swear by tests; others swear at them.

In companies in which tests are used extensively as part of the screening process, the human resources department or an independent testing organization does the testing. In other firms, applicants are sent to a testing organization or an industrial psychologist. Let's look at the most frequently used pre-employment tests.

Intelligence Tests

Like the IQ tests used in schools, these tests measure the ability to learn. Some are simple exercises that can be administered by people with minimal training, such as the Wunderlic tests, a simple 50-question inventory. Others are sophisticated tests that must be administered by specialists with a Ph.D. in psychology.

The major flaw in using general intelligence tests is that two individuals who receive the same score can earn it in very different ways. One might be high in reasoning, low in numerical skills, and average in verbal skills. The other might be high in numerical skills, low in reasoning, and high in verbal skills. They display entirely different intelligence profiles. Judging them by the total score can be misleading. To get the true picture, the test has to be evaluated by the scores of its components.

Another problem is that some tests violate the equal opportunity laws. To ensure that a test is in compliance, it must be validated to be free from cultural bias, and the score on the test must be directly related to the ability to do the job. The Equal Employment Opportunity Commission has issued guidelines on how you can validate the tests you use. These guidelines can be obtained directly from the EEOC office in your area. Most test publishers have taken steps to eliminate cultural bias, but it is up to the company itself to prove that the test has relevance to job success.

Aptitude Tests

Aptitude tests are designed to determine the potential of candidates in specific areas such as mechanical ability, clerical skills, and sales potential. Such tests are helpful in screening inexperienced people to determine whether they have the aptitude in the type of work for which they are applying.

Performance Tests

Performance tests measure how well applicants can do the job for which they apply. Examples include operating specific machinery, entering data into a computer, writing advertising copy, or proofreading manuscripts. Such tests usually are not controversial, and in most instances give the employer a realistic way of determining the ability of the applicant to do the job.

Designing performance tests for more complex jobs is not easy. There are no performance tests for managerial ability or for most advanced jobs. Some companies, as part of the screening process, have asked applicants for such jobs to develop programs or projects for them. This makes sense. Asking an applicant for a marketing position to develop a marketing program for a new product can provide insight into his or her methods of operation, creativity, and practicality.

However, such tests can be carried too far. One company asked an applicant for a training director's position to create a leadership-training program for team leaders. He worked on it for several days and submitted it, but didn't get the job. Some months later, he learned that the company was using his plan to train team leaders. He billed the company for providing consulting services. When the company ignored his bill, he sued and won the case.

Personality Tests

Personality tests are designed to identify personality characteristics. They vary from quickie questionnaires to highly sophisticated psychological evaluations. A great deal of controversy exists over the value of these types of tests. Supervisors and team leaders should be cautioned by management against making decisions based on the results of personality tests. Persons who have been trained to understand their implications should only interpret such tests.

Selecting tests or similar assessment tools must be done very carefully. When buying a published test, ascertain the legitimacy of the publisher and the test by checking with the American Psychological Association. You also can contact current and, if possible, past users of the test for their opinions.

Personnel Perils

If performance tests are used, the exact same test, under the same circumstances must be used for all applicants. For example, in a recent case, a company testing applicants for a clerical job gave each candidate a spelling test. However, black applicants were given words that were much more difficult than those given to white applicants, which, of course, is not legal.

Management Miscellany

A large number of personality tests are available. You can obtain information about tests that are approved by the American Psychological Association, from that organization at 750 First St, Washington, DC, 20002 (202-336-5500).

Managers should always remember that the administration of one or more personality tests is not the same thing as a comprehensive pre-employment assessment by an industrial psychologist. These assessments include ability and personality measures, plus an extensive interview. These assessments typically cost in the neighborhood of $500–$1,000 per candidate.

Are these tests worth the cost? It depends on whom you speak to. Most of the companies that use some form of testing report mixed results. As many factors—not just the test results—are considered before making a hiring decision, it's difficult to determine just how valuable the tests are. In some cases they show that persons who do not do well in the tests—but are hired anyway—fail in the job. However, there also are people who don't test well but become very successful once hired.

"Wow! What a Background!" But Is It True?

Applicants can tell you anything they want about their experiences. But how do you know whether they're telling the truth? A reference check is one of the oldest approaches to verifying a background, but is it reliable? Unfortunately, former employers don't always tell the whole truth about candidates. They might be reluctant to make negative statements, either because they don't want to prevent the person from working—so long as it's not for them—or because they fear being sued. Still, a reference check is virtually your only source of verification.

Unless your company policy requires that the human resources department make reference checks, it's better for you, the supervisor to do it. You have more insight into your group's needs and can react to the responses with follow-up questions. The answers to those questions will help you determine whether the applicant's background fits your needs. Be careful to follow the same guidelines in asking questions of the reference as you do in interviewing applicants. For example, just as you can't ask an applicant whether she has young children, you can't attempt to get this type of information from the reference.

Getting Useful Information from a Reference

Most reference checks are made by telephone. To make the best of a difficult situation, you must carefully plan the reference check and use diplomacy in conducting it. The following are some tips for making a reference check:

➤ Call the applicant's immediate supervisor. Try to avoid speaking to the company's HR staff members. The only information they usually have is what's on file. An immediate supervisor can give you details about exactly how that person worked, his or her personality factors, and other significant traits.

➤ Begin your conversation with a friendly greeting; then ask whether the employer can verify some information about the applicant. Most people don't mind verifying data. Ask a few verification questions about date of employment, job title, and other items from the application.

➤ Diplomatically shift to a question that requires a substantive answer, but not one that calls for an opinion. Respond with a comment about the answer, as in this example:

You: Tell me about her duties in dealing with customers.

Supervisor: Gives details of the applicant's work.

You: That's very important in the job she is seeking because she'll be on the phone with customers much of the time.

Personnel Perils

Never tell an applicant that he or she is hired "subject to a reference check." If the references are good but you choose another candidate, an applicant will assume that you received a poor reference. Also, never tell a person that the reason for rejection is a poor reference. Reference information should be treated as confidential.

By commenting about what you have learned, you make the interchange a conversation—not an interrogation. You're making telephone friends with the former supervisor. You're building up a relationship that will make him or her more likely to give opinions about the applicant's work performance, attitudes, and other valuable information. The few extra minutes it takes to make a little conversation pays off in obtaining much better information.

"All I Can Tell You Is That She Worked Here"

If a former employer refuses outright to answer a question, don't push. Point out that you understand any reluctance. Make the comment, "I'm sure that you would want to have as much information as possible about a candidate if you were considering someone." Then ask another question (but don't repeat the same one). Once the responses come more freely, you can return to the original question, preferably using different words. See the following telephone reference worksheet for questions to ask and information to gather.

Telephone Reference Worksheet

Name of applicant _____

Position applied for _____ Department _____

Company contacted _____

Person spoken to _____ Title _____

Suggested introduction: Hello, I'm _____(your name)_____ from _____(company)_____ .
We are considering one of your former employees, _____(name of applicant)_____ for a
position as ____(job title)____ . I'd appreciate a few minutes of your time to verify some
facts about his/her background.

1. ____(state applicant's name)____ said that he/she was employed as from _(start date)_
to _(end date)_ . Is this correct? _____ (If not, insert correct dates:
_____.)

2. He/she stated her salary was $ _____ per _____ . Is this correct? (If not, indi-
cate correct figure: _____.)

Activity Comments

3. He/she stated that his/her work included: _____ (List a few major activities from resumé, application form, and interview notes.) _____
_____ Is this correct? _____

4. Can you tell me some of the other activities in which he/she was engaged?
_____

5. In which of these activities did he/she perform most effectively?
_____

6. List here additional specific questions related to your job specs or other facets of
background you wish to explore. _____
_____

7. In which of these activities did you have to give him/her added support?
_____
_____

8. What were some of his/her greatest accomplishments in this job?
_____
_____

9. Over the time worked in your company, what progress did he/she make in terms of
being given added responsibilities, promotions, and salary increases other than routine cost of living raises? _____
_____

10. How did (applicant's name) get along with co-workers? _____
_____

11. Can you comment on:

Attendance _____

Dependability _____

Ability to take on responsibility _____

Potential for advancement _____

Degree of supervision needed _____

Overall attitude _____

12. Why did he/she leave the company? _____
_____

13. If there were an opening in your company for a person with (applicant's name)'s background, would you consider him/her for that position? _____
(If not, why?) _____
_____

14. Is there anything else we should know about (applicant's name) in order for us to make our hiring decision? _____
_____

Notes and Comments

Reference check conducted by _____ Date _____

What happens if you believe the person you're speaking to is holding something back? What if you sense from the person's voice that he or she is hesitating in providing answers? Maybe you detect a vagueness that says that you're not getting the full story. Now what?

Here's one way to handle this situation: "Mr. Controller, I appreciate your taking the time to talk to me about Alice Accountant. The job we have is very important to our firm, and we cannot afford to make a mistake. Are there any special problems we might face if we hire Alice?" Here's another approach: "Ivan will need some special training for this job. Can you point out any areas to which we should give particular attention?" From the answer you receive, you might pick up some information about Ivan's weaknesses.

The great paradox in reference checking is that companies want full information about prospective employees from former employers—but clam up when asked for information about their own former employees. Because of their fear of being sued for defamation, when asked for information about former employees companies often give little more than basic information—dates of employment and job title.

Determining Whether the Applicant Can Do the Job

When it's time to make a decision, all of those under consideration probably are basically qualified to do the job. Your responsibility is to select the best one. Although all the surviving applicants meet the basic specs, they all offer different degrees of expertise in the key areas as well as additional qualifications.

For example, Betty and Sue both have been operating room nurses. Betty's experience has been in a hospital in a small community. She hasn't worked with the sophisticated equipment that Sue, who worked in a large hospital, has. Your hospital doesn't have this equipment at this time, but is planning to install it. Your decision between Betty and Sue should depend on their total backgrounds. Sue's experience is an asset, but perhaps Betty is a better overall candidate with the potential to learn to use the new equipment when it is installed.

Meeting the job specs is just part of the decision-making process. Equally important is having those intangible factors that make the difference between just doing a job and doing it well. Let's look at a few of these factors and how to evaluate them when interviewing the candidates.

Personnel Perils

Some applicants can talk a good game, but can they perform? To determine whether an applicant is a talker or a doer, ask in-depth questions and probe for specific examples of his or her work. Glib phonies cannot come up with meaningful answers. "Why" questions are more useful for this than "what" questions.

Self-Confidence

When Jeremy was interviewed he exuded self-confidence. He was not afraid to talk about his failures; unlike people who try to impress interviewers by bragging about their accomplishments, Jeremy was matter-of-fact about his successes. He projected an image of being totally secure in his feelings about his capabilities. It is likely that Jeremy will manifest this self-confidence on the job, enabling him to adapt readily to the new situation.

Fluency of Expression

Laura was able to discuss her background easily and fluently. She did not hesitate or grasp for words. When the interviewer probed for details, she was ready with statistics, examples, and specific applications. Not only does this indicate her expertise, but her ability to communicate.

Maturity

Maturity cannot be measured by the chronological age of a person. Young people can be very mature and older people might still harbor childlike emotions. Mature applicants are not hostile or defensive. They do not interpret questions as barbs by a "prosecutor out to catch them." They do not show self-pity or have excuses for past failures or inadequacies. They can discuss their weaknesses as readily as their strengths.

Intelligence

Although some aspects of intelligence can be measured by tests, we can pick up a great deal about the type of intelligence a person has at an interview. If the job calls for rapid reaction to situations as they develop (such as a sales rep) a person who responds to questions rapidly and sensibly probably has the kind of intelligence needed for the job. However, if the person is applying for a job in which it is important to ponder over a question before coming up with an answer (such as a research engineer), a slow, but well-thought-out response might indicate the type of intelligence required.

Growth Potential

The job for which you are hiring can lead to rapid advancement into more responsible positions. In making your decision, keep in mind the potential of the candidate. Does he or she have what it takes to move up the ladder? Potential for growth is an important factor in choosing the best candidate for this opening.

Choosing Among Several Top-Level Applicants

In a tight job market, you might have only one viable candidate, in which case your choice is easy: Hire or don't hire. However, in most cases, you do have several good people from which to make your final selection. To make the decision systematically, compare applicants by placing their backgrounds side by side. One way of doing this is to use a grid like the one that follows.

Final Selection Spreadsheet

Job Specs	Applicant #1 Name:	Applicant #2 Name:	Applicant #3 Name:	Applicant #4 Name:
Education				
Experience				
Intangibles				
Other				

Often candidates are very close in their qualifications for the job. You have to make a choice among relatively equally competent people. Now it is a matter of your judgment. Choosing a candidate purely on gut feeling without systematically analyzing each prospect's background in relation to the job specs is a mistake. However, when the decision is choosing the best among equals, you have to trust your gut feelings. As we said, hiring is both a science and an art. When you've exhausted the science—the systematic comparison of candidates, the art—your gut feeling—takes over.

Making the Offer

Once you've decided on the person you want to hire, you are ready to make a job offer. All through the interviewing process, you have been getting feedback from the applicants about their interest in the job. Any applicant who has not expressed serious interest in the job should not have reached this point, but this does not necessarily mean that he or she will automatically accept your offer.

Before making the formal offer, there should be a clear understanding by the applicant and the company about what the job entails. This includes what the company expects from the applicant and what the applicant expects from the company. You also must be sure not only that the applicant is qualified for the job, but that it fits his or her career goals.

Review the Job Specs

Don't take anything for granted. During the entire process, the candidate has been enthusiastic about the job, has expressed sincere interest, and seems anxious to start work. However, before making the offer, it's important to review the job and make sure both you and the applicant are on the same track.

Go over the job description point by point. Although the candidate might have read it already, most job descriptions are not comprehensive; often, many facets are not specified. Discuss each aspect of the job to ensure that it is what the applicant has understood.

What the Company Expects

In addition to the job duties expected of a staff member, most companies have policies and practices that should be made clear to an applicant before making a job offer. If the job requires travel, overtime, weekend work, or unusual working conditions this should be made clear to the applicant. Indeed, this should have been brought up early in the process, so if there is a problem in complying, the applicant could withdraw before reaching this point.

In today's competitive market, the applicant often has to be sold on accepting your job offer. Often, it isn't money that will make the difference between acceptance and rejection. Learn about the applicant's goals, aspirations, special needs, and anything else that might affect his or her job satisfaction.

The Compensation Package

When negotiating salary, keep in mind what you pay currently employed people for doing similar work. Offering a new person considerably more than that amount can cause serious morale problems. Of course, there are exceptions to this rule. Some applicants have capabilities that you believe would be of great value to your company; to attract these people, you might have to pay considerably more than your current top rate. Some companies create special job categories to accommodate this situation.

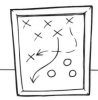

Tactical Tips

Most companies have a clearly defined compensation program. Before making an offer, check all the arrangements with the HR department and your boss to avoid misunderstandings.

A salary alone does not comprise a total compensation package. It includes vacations, benefits, frequency of salary reviews, and incentive programs. All these items should be clearly explained to the applicant. Even if the salary you offer is less than an applicant wants, you might persuade that person to take your offer by pointing out how the job will enable him or her to use creativity, engage in work of special interest, and reach a career goal.

Overcoming Obstacles

What do you do if at the time you make the offer, the applicant brings up new objections? Just as a salesperson must be prepared to overcome last-minute reservations to buy a product, you must be ready to face and overcome these objections. Let's look at some common problems.

"The Salary Is Too Low"

Your first choice is Hillary. Early in the interview process, you explored her salary requirements, and your offer is in line—at least that's what you thought. Now Hillary demurs, "If I stay where I am, I'll get a raise in a few months that will bring me above that salary. You'll have to do better."

Having received approval of the hire at the salary offered, you have to either reject her, persuade her to take the job by selling her on other advantages, or go back to your boss for approval of the higher rate. What you do depends on many factors. Do you have other viable candidates for the job? If not, how urgent is it to fill the job? Determine whether you can legitimately offer other benefits, such as a salary review

Personnel Perils

Don't let your anxiety over losing a desirable candidate tempt you to make an informal offer—promising a higher salary or other condition of employment that hasn't been approved—with the hope that you can persuade management to agree to it. Failure to get this agreement will not only cause the applicant to reject the offer but also can lead to legal action against your company.

in six months, opportunity for special training in an area in which she is particularly interested, or other perks. Think over the situation carefully, and discuss it with your manager. Caution: Don't make commitments you don't have the authority to honor.

If you and your boss agree that Hillary should still be considered for the position, determine how much you're willing to increase your offer and any additional compensation. With this in mind, you can negotiate with her and try to reach an acceptable arrangement. If this new negotiation doesn't lead to agreement, discontinue the discussion and seek another candidate. Once you have set a ceiling on what can be paid, continuing to haggle over terms of employment will be a waste of both your time and that of the applicant.

"I Need Flexible Hours"

Some companies have an established policy on flextime. If the job for which the candidate is being considered is compatible with this policy, there's no problem. All that has to be worked out are the hours. However, if there is no policy, granting this request depends on a variety of circumstances. If you give a new employee flexible hours, will the current staff also want their hours changed? There are some jobs in which flexible hours are more appropriate than in others. Is filling this job so difficult that it pays to bend the rules?

"What Are My Opportunities for Advancement?"

Of course, you can't promise automatic advancement in most jobs. Employees have to earn promotions. You should point out that the company conducts periodic performance reviews and that advancement is based on these reviews. If the company has a career pathing program, take this opportunity to describe how it works.

"I'm Considering Other Offers"

It's not unusual for a good applicant to be looking at several possibilities. All through the interviewing process, you should be feeling the applicant out to determine what he or she is really seeking in the new job. Keep a record of this. Does she seek rapid advancement? Does he want special training? Has she commented on a particular type of job interest? Has he expressed concern about health benefits? Here is where you can use that information to persuade your best candidate to accept your offer.

One way to counteract this is to ask the prospect to write down all the advantages of joining the other company or staying on the present job. Meanwhile, you list all the advantages of joining your team. Be prepared to show how your job—which might even pay less or have fewer benefits than other offers—is still the best bet. Use all the information gleaned at the interviews about what the candidate desires, and show how your job will help the prospect meet the goals he or she has set for the future. If this prospect is the one you really feel will be the best for your team, it's worthwhile to make this effort.

Countering the Counteroffer

You've knocked yourself out reading resumés, interviewing applicants, and comparing candidates. You make the decision that you'll hire Barbara, and she accepts your offer. A week later she calls to tell you that she has changed her mind—when she told her boss that she was leaving, her boss made a counteroffer. Frustrating? You bet. To minimize the possibility of a counteroffer, assume that any currently employed candidate will get one. At the time you make your offer, bring it up and make these points:

➤ You know that she has done a great job in her present company. You also realize that when she notifies her company that she's planning to leave, it will undoubtedly make a counteroffer. Why? Because they need her now.

➤ If the company truly appreciated her work, it wouldn't have waited until she got another job offer to give her a raise; it would have given it to her long ago.

➤ Many people who have accepted counteroffers from a current employer find out that, after the pressure is off the company, it will train or hire someone else and let her go.

➤ From now on, she will always be looked on as a disloyal person who threatened to leave just to get more money.

➤ When the time for a raise comes around again, guess whose salary has already been "adjusted"?

When these arguments are used, the number of people who accept counteroffers decreases significantly.

The Least You Need to Know

➤ Well-selected employment tests might provide valuable information about the applicant that interviewing might miss.

➤ In checking references, speak to the applicant's direct supervisor.

➤ To make the decision systematically, compare applicants by placing their backgrounds side by side. Use a candidate comparison spreadsheet to make this comparison easier.

➤ To ensure that a job offer will be accepted, learn what the applicant really wants and fit your offer as close to this as possible.

Part 3

Building a Collaborative Team

You've staffed your organization. Now comes the hard part: getting your employees to work. Sure, some of the men and women you hired have good experience in the type of work they'll do in their new jobs, but others have little background and have to be brought up to snuff fast. Even the experienced people need training. They have to be assimilated into your company.

This starts with a good orientation to make newcomers feel comfortable in the new job; and it's followed by training them in the actual work they'll do.

Once they're settled into the job, you still have lots to do to meld them into the groups or teams in which they'll work. The best-managed companies recognize that to run a successful company requires a collaborative, cooperative workforce.

In these chapters you'll see how to establish first-rate orientation, training, and development programs. You'll also learn how to improve communications, whether they are downward, upward, lateral, or external—an essential ingredient to teamwork.

Chapter 10

Getting Started on the Right Foot

In This Chapter

➤ Orienting the new employee to the job

➤ On-boarding—a comprehensive orientation process

➤ Selecting the "critical few objectives" that lead to success

➤ Mentors—the people that make on-boarding work

➤ More tips on effective orientation

➤ What you shouldn't do when breaking in new people

You've done everything right in attracting, screening, and finally hiring the person for the open job. A starting date has been set and at last, the new employee reports to work. What you do those first few days might determine whether that person becomes a loyal, dedicated, enthusiastic staff member or a halfhearted worker already on the way to disillusionment and potential problems.

In this chapter we'll look at some steps organizations can take to minimize the trauma faced by an employee in those critical first weeks on the job.

What the New Employee Is Thinking

Let's look at this from the viewpoint of the new employee. Starting a new job is both exciting and scary. The new person doesn't know what to expect. During the period of

Management Miscellany

Recent studies have shown that a failure to properly introduce and assimilate newly hired employees into the new culture is one of the key reasons a whopping 55 percent of them don't make the grade, or voluntarily leave within the first two years.

interviews and pre-employment discussions, the employee developed some impressions and expectations—now comes the reality check. Does the job live up to what was expected?

When the company hired Ken, he was told the job would involve creative approaches to the work, but from day one, he was told not to deviate from what the manual specified. When Dorothy was interviewed, she was given the impression that the company believed strongly in employee participation in making decisions affecting the work. After she was hired, she found that her boss usually ignored suggestions from employees.

In many cases these problems are due to poor leadership by the immediate supervisors. However, often the problems can be alleviated if the new workers are properly oriented to fully understand the company's policies, the true nature of their jobs, and what they might expect over time.

The Orientation Program

Orientation programs help new employees get a better start on the job by making them feel that they are part of the group from the beginning. Most companies have some type of orientation program for new employees. The human resources department usually conducts these on the day the new employee reports to work, before they are sent to the department in which they will work.

Employees might be shown videos, be given a tour of the facilities, receive literature, or attend a lecture. They learn the history of the organization, the benefits are explained, and the rules and regulations are outlined. This is a good start—but not enough. The team leader or supervisor must augment this with an orientation to the team or department. This should include a discussion of the nature of the specific job and details of how the supervisor plans to train and assist the employee in becoming productive.

Lack of adequate orientation is one reason employees quit during the first few months of starting a job. Often, new employees are just thrust into the job without really feeling welcomed. They might have only a vague concept of the company's culture, mission, and goals. They just don't feel that they "belong."

What Makes a Good Orientation Program?

As the manager of the department or leader of the team, you are a key person in making the new employee feel part of the team. Here are some things you can do to make him or her feel welcome:

➤ Acquaint him or her with the background and history of the team. Tell about past projects and challenging assignments.

➤ Discuss the department's mission and what is being done to accomplish it.

➤ Describe the functions of the other members of the group so that when you introduce them, the new person will have a head start in remembering who does what.

➤ Introduce the new person to the others. When making the introduction, comment about both parties. For example, "Alice, this is Carla, our expert in state taxes. Carla's been with the company for 10 years and in our group for the past 3 years. Carla, Alice will be working on developing systems for our new project."

➤ Give the new person a chance to chat with each member. Make a practice of having each member spend break time or lunchtime with the new associate during the first few weeks.

➤ Choose one of the members of the group to mentor the new associate. He or she will take a special interest in the newcomer; show him or her the "ropes"; answer questions about the work, the company culture, and the other staffers; and in general be there to help the new person get started properly (more on this later in the chapter).

➤ You, the manager, should make a point to check with the mentor every day to learn about the new associate's progress and to determine how you can be of help.

➤ Most important, speak to the new member; take a personal interest in how he or she is doing. Visit his or her work station—not as a boss checking the work, but as a colleague who is sincerely interested in making that person feel comfortable in the new job. It's tough for most people starting a new job. Take the time to make him or her feel comfortable and meld into the team as quickly as possible.

On-Boarding

A relatively new approach companies are using is known as *on-boarding*. This process supplements traditional orientation programs and makes them more effective. Originally, on-boarding was designed to rapidly and thoroughly bring newly hired executives into the mainstream. Now it is being extended to technical, professional, and administrative personnel and in some companies, to all new hires. Let's look at how a successful on-boarding process works.

Meanings and Gleanings

On-boarding is a comprehensive program to assist a new employee in adapting to the new company, the new job, and his or her new colleagues.

Establish a Plan

The single most important aspect of successful on-boarding is the development of a comprehensive plan to shepherd the new employee through the first several months. Companies that successfully transition new employees into happy, productive, well-integrated members of the culture take the time to think through the key goals and objectives for the first year. They prepare a written set of guidelines for the orientation process to avoid any misunderstanding and to gauge progress.

Specify a Statement of Purpose

Indicating a clear sense of what your organization is trying to accomplish is very important to the on-boarding effort, and serves as insurance against some future misunderstanding. In many cases, the purpose statement is no more than a sentence or two. However, the objective is always the same: to clarify the reason a successful on-boarding effort is important to the company and the new employee. Rather than using a boilerplate plan for all new employees, the most effective on-boarding plans are tailored to the special needs of the new employee and the organization.

Assess the Current Environment

Every company culture has positive and negative qualities, and every new employee is likely to experience both. The best, most successful on-boarding plans carefully evaluate both the forces that tend to work in favor of a new employee (or increase the likelihood of a successful introduction) and those that work against it. Being sure of which is which and to what extent they operate can contribute to success or failure as much as anything else.

When a company hires a new employee, it is most likely to emphasize all of the positive points about the job and the company and to either hide or minimize the negatives. New employees will find out those negatives—often during the first days or weeks on the job—and this can affect their attitudes toward the company. To avoid this, any negatives should be brought up before the final offer is made, while pointing out that the positives of the job far outweigh the negatives. This will prevent potential disillusionment.

Often, new employees have a misconception of the true nature of a situation when they move into a new job. For example, Jason expected to take over an ongoing collections program that "needed a little sharpening up." When he started the job, he found that the system was in shambles and collections were well behind schedule. Had he been given the true picture, he would have been far better prepared for the work he had to do.

Identify the Critical Few Objectives (CFOs)

All aspects of a job are not equal—some are far more important than others. Too often companies fail to understand that most failure on the job can be traced to the inadequate accomplishment of just a handful of objectives. However, if these objectives are identified and a plan is prepared to help ensure that they're accomplished, the probability of success increases dramatically.

Dr. Raymond Harrison, a management consultant, asserts that every new job has at least two or three *critical few objectives*. These are the handful of objectives that must be achieved if the new employee is to succeed. It's essential to identify and clarify, in the first 90 days of employment, these three or four (seldom more) objectives. They mean so much that even if a new person does a hundred other things superbly and these few things poorly, the result will be a failure.

Identifying Goals with Timetables

Once the critical few objectives have been identified, good on-boarding plans also specify a series of key goals and the dates by which they'll be achieved. These are very specific, quantifiable goals, with clearly indicated timetables; for example, short-term, intermediate, and long-term goals.

Assigning a Mentor

Another major step in successfully on-boarding a new employee is selecting and recruiting a *mentor*. Obviously, it's important that this person be intimately familiar with the internal workings of the firm, including the key political players and the informal—leaders—the people in every organization, who may not have a title or official position, but have considerable influence among the employees.

Meanings and Gleanings

A **mentor** is an employee assigned to act as counselor, trainer, "big brother or sister" to a new member of the organization.

Mentors provide important advice for new employees on a range of topics. A mentor's overall mission is to "pave the way" for the new person, introduce him or her to the right people, and run interference should the going get tough.

The most valuable qualities and characteristics of a good mentor include the following:

➤ A reputation for honesty and effectiveness within the firm.

➤ The respect of senior-most management and the rank-and-file.

➤ Strong communications skills, especially good listening skills.

➤ A counseling background or skills.

➤ A willingness to invest the necessary time.

➤ A personal stake in the success of the new employee.

➤ A results-oriented, "can-do" attitude.

➤ A likable personality with a good sense of humor.

Mentors are not only useful in the on-boarding process; with proper support, they can be valuable aids in training and motivating employees, and dealing with on-the-job problems. Because the on-boarding process is so important to the longer-range success and assimilation of the new employee, the mentor should always be someone with both a thorough knowledge of the organization and a good measure of clout. Partnering with this type of person also sends a signal to the rest of the organization that the new hire is important, worthy of the personal attention of one of the company's heavy-hitters, and not to be taken lightly.

Mentoring is serious business and, according to recent research, often can be the most important difference between the successful retention of a new employee and a decision to leave. When done well, it provides not only a platform for the ready and enthusiastic acceptance of a new hire, but also a much-needed reference guide to the dangers and subtleties of the organizational culture.

Management Miscellany

Few things are more helpful to a new employee, and contribute more to a successful assimilation, than the development of a well-conceived job description. The majority of successful organizations make a practice of using *job results descriptions* (JRDs), which focus on the results expected and how they will be measured. This was discussed in Chapter 5, "Starting the Search."

Arrange for Some Early Successes

One of the biggest problems new employees face in assimilating with the culture of a new company is a lack of initial focus. One method that helps new hires get off on the right foot is to help them achieve some significant successes during the first couple of weeks on the job. As the old saying goes "nothing succeeds more than success."

Let's see how this worked in one company. As part of the on-boarding process for Ben, an assistant marketing manager, he was given an assignment to study the possibility of using e-marketing outlets for the company's products. As Ben had worked with e-markets in his previous job, he had a good deal of knowledge in this area. By enabling him to use his expertise immediately, the company gave him the opportunity to demonstrate his value to the organization early on. This not only was a benefit to the company, but also made Ben feel a part of a winning team from the beginning. It also enabled his colleagues and teammates to observe their new team member at his very best—ensuring his acceptance by the group.

Overcome Resentment of "Bypassed" Employees

When outsiders are hired for higher-level jobs, it's not uncommon for jealousy or resentment of the new hire to occur within the team. Current employees might feel they were unfairly "overlooked" for the job. In some cases, it might lead to flagrant attempts to undermine the new person through whispering campaigns, unjustified criticisms, rumor mongering, and subtle refusals to cooperate. Of course all of these things can lead to diminished morale in the department and perhaps the company itself.

Here are some ways to keep these issues from coming up:

➤ Eliminate emphasis on promotion from within. All employees should know what is required for the positions above theirs and what they must do to qualify for them. Longevity, seniority, and good performance are important factors, but these alone will not ensure promotion. Help employees gain the skills they need for that promotion. If the purchasing assistants had worked to acquire the needed skills and knowledge, one of them likely would have qualified for the promotion.

➤ Once the decision is made not to promote, let the employees know in advance that an outsider will be hired. Explain the reasons for the decision.

➤ Don't seek the new employee secretly. Post the job. Announce that it will be advertised or an executive recruiter has been retained. Be open about your search.

When companies make the effort to be frank with employees about their opportunities for advancement, it is much more likely that they will understand and accept your hiring decisions.

Provide Unwavering Support

There is little question that the single most valuable contribution company executives can make to the assimilation of a new hire is unwavering support. Too many organizations underestimate the importance of this. As a result they encourage—however unintentionally—resentment from the new employee to their decision.

There is no surer way to ensure the failure of a new hire than to make a decision on that person's value or effectiveness in the first few months. Worse yet is allowing the person to be put "on trial" by coworkers. The results of practices like this are almost always negative and destructive. They remain a leading cause of failed assimilations, and the early

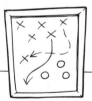

Tactical Tips

Providing the new employee with full support, training, and encouragement over the first few months will maximize the chances of developing a productive and loyal staff member.

exit of those who otherwise might have made important contributions. Obviously, it's the job of those with authority to be sure things like this simply don't happen.

125

A good example of this is giving the new employee a "baptism of fire." This happened to Carlos on the first day on his new job as a systems engineer. He was given a tough, major assignment that required him to work day and night for a week to identify the problems and come up with solutions. When he complained to his boss, the response was, "If you can't stand the heat, get out of the kitchen." Carlos quit. When the human resources manager asked his boss why Carlos left so soon, he was told, "I give the new guys tough problems to solve, so I can test their mettle. He didn't make it." This doesn't really make sense. Had Carlos been properly broken in; given a thorough orientation and an initial assignment he could readily accomplish, he most likely would have developed into a highly productive employee.

Poor Orientation Practices

Many executives don't recognize the importance of a good orientation, and often pay little attention to how new employees are treated during those first critical days on the job. They not only ignore good on-boarding procedures, but use approaches that are self defeating. Let's look at some of these.

Who's In Charge of the Orientation?

Delegating the orientation of new hires to clerical and administrative employees can give the wrong impression. This is particularly true when the new employee is at the management, higher technical, or specialized levels. Allowing people well below the level of the new employee to be responsible for the orientation sends a signal that senior management doesn't value the assimilation of new employees enough.

Please don't misunderstand: It's not at all uncommon for members of the clerical or administrative team to play a very important role in the success or failure of a new hire. Often they know more—even much more—about the real inner workings and culture of the company than the heavy-hitters. That said, it's also important to remember that the perception of unconditional support from senior-most management is the single most important determiner of a successful assimilation. Without it, the orientation is much more difficult.

Survival of the Fittest

Some managers over-delegate because they believe that remaining detached from the day-to-day details is the best way to encourage leadership and a "take charge" attitude among workers. Although that might be true in some cases, it does appear that managers of this type have more difficulty retaining outstanding workers than those with a more involved management style. One of the reasons for this evidently is the increased likelihood that new hires will come to feel "abandoned" or "tossed to the wolves" by their perhaps well-intentioned but still ill-advised managers.

To get the best results in managing, carefully balance a hands-off style, in which you expect people to work independently with *micromanagement*, in which the manager makes all the decisions. Find the happy medium.

This doesn't mean that the boss should micromanage the new employee, but he or she also shouldn't tell the person, "Here's what I expect of you—go do it" with no other guidelines. Even highly experienced and self-confident new employees need guidance when starting in a new position. They don't know the culture, history, working style, or inner soul of the company; the varying personality quirks of co-workers; or the management philosophy of their new bosses. It's worth the time and effort it takes to provide new hires with a set of guidelines on all of these facets and to work closely with them over the first weeks and months to monitor their progress.

Meanings and Gleanings

Micromanaging is supervising every phase of an assignment. The manager makes all the decisions and looks over the employee's shoulder to check that every *i* is dotted and every *t* is crossed. This stifles creativity and prevents employees from working at their full potential.

Expecting Significant Results Too Soon

In the last decades of the twentieth century, in a desire to cut costs, many managers have overly downsized their organizations. This often has resulted in workers who survived the layoffs working longer and harder. When business picked up in the late 1990s, these same companies began to rebuild their workforces. However, due to the emphasis placed on maintaining a favorable bottom line, they often had lofty expectations of their new hires. To get them productive as soon as possible, on-boardings were minimized, often lasting less than a day before they expected the new hire to start "pitching in" and demonstrating his or her value. The results of this practice—asking too much too soon from a new hire are almost always negative—and almost always increase the likelihood of an early exit.

Poor Recruiting Practices

Few things contribute more to the loss of good people—and sometimes to expensive lawsuits—than evidence of dishonesty or deceptive business practices in the upper reaches of an organization. With increasing regularity this includes deceptive hiring practices. No doubt this has been driven largely by extremely low unemployment rates in the United States and elsewhere.

According to a survey of new hires by Dr. Frank Ashby, President of Leadership Capital Group, HR consultants, a surprising 50 percent said they felt misled or intentionally deceived by some aspect of their interviewing process. Among new hires who left their new companies within 60 days, claims of deceptive or misleading hiring practices were reported by nearly 80 percent. Among the most common were misrepresentations about the nature of the job. At one company, applicants were told that there would be "occasional overtime." After they were on the job, they found they were expected to work many hours overtime and, as exempt employees, were not compensated for this.

Another company boasted about its "generous" health insurance plan, only to offer an HMO that had a reputation for denying benefits for trivial reasons. Other frequent complaints were that special training that was promised was never given, salary readjustments that had been promised were not made, and "moderate travel" turned into long assignments away from home.

The Least You Need to Know

➤ Successful on-boarding plans should include a statement of purpose and specific goals and timetables.

➤ Identify the critical few objectives (CFOs), objectives that are critical to the success of the new colleague, within the first 90 days.

➤ Assign a mentor with some level of prestige within the organization. This is particularly important when assimilating someone in the more senior ranks of the organization.

➤ Few things are more helpful to a new employee, and contribute more to a successful assimilation, than the development of a well-conceived job results description.

➤ Give new employees, particularly in the management and technical areas, up to three months (and even more in some instances) to settle into their jobs and "learn the ropes" before assuming major responsibilities.

➤ The single most valuable contribution company executives can make to the assimilation of a new hire is unwavering support.

Chapter 11

Training for Today's Job and Tomorrow's Advancement

In This Chapter

➤ Learning what areas of training are needed

➤ Keeping up to date on training techniques

➤ Using outside trainers

➤ The "ready-set-go" approach to training

➤ Tools and techniques

➤ Measuring whether the training works

Properly developed training programs can have a dramatic, lasting, invigorating effect on a business. These effects can show an enormous return on investment as employees increase current skills and develop new ones. This development results in an increase in innovative ideas and creative problem solving, and is a major factor in the retention of good workers. In this chapter we will examine how to establish and implement effective training programs, and explore some techniques to help you develop training for your organization.

Who Needs to Be Trained—And to Do What?

As important as training is, it is only cost effective if the areas in which people will be trained are selected carefully. Too often companies waste time and money on

Meanings and Gleanings

Determining just what types of training are worth spending your company's dollars on is called a **needs assessment.**

programs that may be pet projects of some manager, but are not of real value. Training programs should truly reflect what is needed to attain higher productivity and a better bottom line.

Many companies can only guess what type of training is needed. Sure, training in the specific skills required to do the work is obvious, but skills alone do not ensure productivity. Too often, companies implement unnecessary training programs, ignoring more valuable, significant areas in which people actually would benefit from some training. Before choosing any training program, the company should conduct a *needs assessment.* Professional training experts apply systematic approaches to needs assessment, but you can make some basic assessments on your own.

To make valid needs assessments, here are some questions that should be asked and answered:

1. What is the gap between desired and actual performance?
2. Is the problem caused by lack of technical skills?
3. Is the problem caused by attitudes of employees?
4. Can the gap be closed through supervisory attention or is special training needed?
5. If training is needed, which employees need the training?
6. Is the capability to provide the training available within the company? If so, who will do it and when? If not, what other sources are available?
7. What performance results should be expected as a result of the training?
8. What will the training cost?
9. What financial benefits will result?

Once you have the answers to these questions, you can determine the type of program to institute.

Keeping Up with the Latest Developments in Training

Basic skills training still has its place in the business world. The fundamentals of a job must be acquired as a start, but we can't stop there. Continued training must be an ongoing concern. Training in new technologies is already in place in most companies, but even that's not enough. Here are five ways to bring your training and development up to date:

1. Emphasize ways to identify and solve problems rather than presenting specific problems and teaching trainees how to deal with them.

2. Place the ultimate responsibility for learning on the individual (or, in team learning, on the team). The person who conducts the training is a facilitator: Rather than spoon-feeding information to trainees, he or she guides them through the process, and summarizes and reinforces the resulting insights.

3. Make sure that people who will learn together share a common vocabulary, are trained to use the same analytical tools, and have communication channels such as an intranet or internet available so that they can work together and with other people or teams within an organization.

4. To learn to solve problems, trainees should be encouraged to tap resources in other departments or from sources outside the company such as customers, suppliers, and trade or professional associations.

5. Avoid allowing professional trainers to do all the training. Let people from all job categories (managers, team leaders, HR specialists—technicians in all fields) be the facilitators. This technique not only expands a company's training resources; it helps develop future leaders.

You have a wealth of talent within your organization. Use it well and not only will you get better results from the training, you will increase the value of each person involved in the organization.

Using Outside Trainers

Immediate supervisors or others in the company who are specialists in the field usually do the most training. However, in some areas, outside training organizations can do a better job. For example, manufacturers of technical equipment usually will train customers' employees in how to use their products. Generally they also will provide continuing training for new employees at either no cost or for a reasonable fee. There are also training organizations with expertise in specialized areas such as sales, leadership, and technical matters.

Don't get stuck with a third-rate training organization. Before selecting a training organization, study the backgrounds of its principals, check with companies that have used its services, and interview the trainers. It is important that you get as much information as possible to ensure the organization can provide what you need.

Using Local Schools and Colleges

All training need not be done in-house or by retaining expensive consultants. Some training can be provided inexpensively through local schools. These facilities are especially helpful in training employees in skills such as English as a second language, basic computer skills, typing, and business practices.

Many community colleges develop special programs to meet the needs of the companies in their communities. For example, in South Carolina several community colleges offer courses to develop skills geared toward the textile industry. In New York City, there is a community college located near La Guardia Airport that offers training in various skills used by the aviation industry.

Many universities not only offer degree programs at the undergraduate and graduate levels; they also have nondegree courses in their continuing education divisions. These courses are designed for people who either don't have a degree or who have a degree in one field and want to acquire knowledge of other areas. Companies can encourage employees to participate in such programs by paying or reimbursing tuition.

The Ready-Set-Go Approach to Training

Training is not a haphazard activity. It takes planning and careful execution. One such time-tested approach is job instruction training (JIT), a systematic approach to training people to perform tasks. JIT involves four steps: preparation (ready), presentation (set), performance (go), and follow-up (check it out). Each will be discussed in the following sections.

Ready

Before the training begins, you must prepare the trainee and the training environment. This is both physical and psychological. All physical equipment and facilities necessary for training should be in place before you begin. For example, if you're training someone in a computer process, you should have a computer, the software, a training manual, the data, and any other necessary materials on hand. You don't want to be interrupted while training by having to look for items you need.

Psychological readiness starts by telling the trainee—before the training begins—what will be taught, why it's performed, and how it fits into the overall picture. When people can see the entire picture—not just their small part in it—they learn faster and understand more clearly, and they're more likely to remember what they've been taught.

Set

To get set, you present the job to the trainee. It won't work to just say, "Watch me and do what I do." It's not that simple. Work today is much too complex to learn just by observation. The following four steps can guide you in showing someone how to perform a task:

1. Describe the task you're going to do.
2. Demonstrate the task step by step. As you demonstrate, explain each step and explain why it's done. For example, "Notice that I entered the order number on the top-right side of the form to make it easy to locate."

3. Have the trainee perform the task and explain to you the method and reason for each step.

4. If the trainee doesn't perform to your satisfaction, have him or her repeat the task; if he or she performs well, reinforce the behavior with praise or positive comments.

Go!

After you're satisfied that a trainee can do a job, leave him or her alone to do it. The trainee needs an opportunity to try out what he or she has learned. Mistakes are to be expected; from time to time, check out how things are going and make necessary corrections.

Check It Out

After the trainee has been doing the job for a short period of time, check it out. Follow-up is important because people tend to change what they have been taught. Careless people might skip some steps in a procedure, causing errors or complications. Smart people might make changes that they believe are better than what they were taught.

Managers must be alert to such changes. To ensure that employees stay on track, schedule follow-up discussions of new assignments three to four weeks after the presentation step. At that time, review what the associate has been doing and, if changes have been made intentionally or inadvertently, bring the person back on track.

Personnel Perils

Encourage your associates to find more effective approaches to their jobs, but caution them not to make any changes until they have discussed them with you. They might not be aware of the ramifications of their changes.

Training Tools

Managers have a variety of aids and techniques available to facilitate their training efforts. Some have been around for years; others have been developed more recently. Some of the most important are discussed in the following.

Training Manuals

Training manuals, or "do it by the numbers" handbooks, are helpful for teaching routine tasks. They make the training process easy for both the trainer and the trainees; you can always refer to them when you're in doubt about what to do. Unfortunately, some training manuals are poorly written and as confusing as the instructions that come with "assemble-it-yourself" products made in some faraway country. Others are laced with technical terminology that is intelligible only to the engineers who wrote it.

Because today's jobs are becoming less and less routine, training manuals often are inadequate—to the point that they might even stifle creativity. Don't rely on a book because it's easy rather than thinking out new and possibly better approaches to training. Make sure that any training manual you write or approve is written so that it is clear, concise, and complete; thus, easily understood by the trainees.

Management Miscellany

Training people should not be a one-way process—the teacher presents information; the student absorbs it (you hope). Just presenting information is not enough. The emphasis should be on developing the trainee's ability to identify and solve problems, seek knowledge, and take the initiative to continue self-development.

Interactive Computer Training

Many companies have developed interactive computer programs to train employees in a variety of areas. Such programs initially were designed for use in schools to enable students to learn at their own pace. Slower learners could take their time and repeat unclear sections until they understood them. Fast learners or students who had more background in an area could move quickly ahead, and students could test themselves as they progressed.

Because each company has its own ways of doing things, generic programs such as the ones used by schools haven't been of much value. Some larger organizations have customized programs to suit their own needs; usually these programs are proprietary and aren't made available outside the companies that developed them. Perhaps you also can customize programs to meet your own requirements.

Computer-Based Training

Walk into any computer store and you will find a variety of standard courses on CD-ROM. These can be used at the workplace or given to employees to use at home. Among those are courses in mathematics, from basic algebra through calculus; courses to teach almost all foreign languages and English as a second language; programs to increase vocabulary; a variety of science subjects; and even entire programs to prepare students for taking high school equivalency exams. In addition, you'll find courses for training employees in all types of functions on the computer such as typing, general office skills, accounting, marketing, business planning, and general management.

The Internet—The School of the Future

The Internet has moved training from the classroom to the desk, the kitchen table, and even the laps of individuals. Universities and private organizations offer courses and less formal individual study programs on hundreds of subjects online. You can study a foreign language, learn basic or advanced math, acquire technical know-how, and even obtain a college degree through the Internet.

Teleconferencing

Classroom training is still one of the most common ways to train or retrain employees. In large organizations employees from several locations can be brought together for the training. However, this kind of training is expensive. Not only are the participants taken away from their regular work for the training sessions; there is the high cost of travel, hotels, and meals; and often the cost of renting the training facility (for example, a conference center).

One way to reduce the cost and time involved is *teleconferencing*. Using specially designed computer and TV equipment, participants can see, hear, and interact with the instructor and each other without going far from their respective bases. Larger organizations might have teleconferencing technology available on site in each of their facilities. Smaller companies can use the services of teleconferencing firms, which can set up such conferences wherever needed.

> **Meanings and Gleanings**
>
> **Teleconferencing** *is a means of bringing together via satellite employees from various units of an organization for the purpose of training or other business meetings. People at diverse locations can see, hear, and interact with each other by sophisticated electronic technology.*

Case Studies

A case study is a description of a real or simulated business situation presented to trainees for analysis, discussion, and solution. Case studies provide realistic simulations of the types of situations that will be faced after the training is completed. The experience of working out these types of problems in a classroom instead of learning by trial and error on the job pays off in fewer trials and less costly errors.

A significant advantage of using case studies in management development is that trainees work on the cases collaboratively. They learn how to organize and use teams to solve issues. To make case studies most effective, design cases that are related to the job. Make them complex and challenging, and make sure their solutions require collaboration and teamwork to attain the best solutions.

Role-Playing

Most jobs today require interaction with other people. One of the best ways to train people for this type of interaction is through role-playing. As in case studies, role-play should be based on realistic situations similar to what a trainee might face on the job. Some good examples are dealing with a customer, resolving a dispute among team members, or conducting a performance review. Role-play should be fun, but if it's not also a learning experience you're wasting your time.

Video as a Training Tool

Probably the most dramatic innovation in training and development in recent years is the use of video as a training tool. Video catalogs list tapes for training people in a variety of types of work. Videotapes, like training manuals, are most appropriate for training people to do routine jobs. For situations in which flexibility and initiative are necessary, tapes (like training manuals) can impede creativity. People tend to accept what they see on video as the one correct approach.

In such cases, customizing videotapes to meet your own needs is a more effective option. Here are some ways to use customized video to enhance the effectiveness of your training programs:

➤ **Tape demonstrations** For work of a physical nature (most factory or maintenance jobs and some clerical jobs), a good demonstration is an important part of the training. No matter how good a live demonstration is, it can be done only in real time. If the demonstration is videotaped, it can be shown in real time to demonstrate the pace at which a job should be carried out and in slow motion to better explain each of the steps. You can tape yourself or one of your best workers performing the job. Once you have a good demonstration on tape, it's available to show to any trainees at any time.

➤ **Tape job performance** One of the best ways to help people recognize exactly what they're doing on the job is to videotape them at work. Instead of verbalizing your trainees' strengths and weaknesses, let them view the tapes. This enables them to see for themselves what they are doing well and what needs improvement.

➤ **Tape team meetings** In one company, a team leader videotaped several team meetings. By studying the tapes, she noticed that she tended to dominate group discussions. She pushed her ideas across, shut off opposing arguments, and sometimes was rude to other team members. She had considered herself a good leader, but until she saw the tape she didn't realize the way she came across to others. She agreed to attend a human-relations training course.

➤ **Tape role-playing** Role-playing is an excellent way to develop interpersonal relationships. By videotaping role-playing and then reviewing the tapes, this technique becomes an even more effective training tool. Watching their own performance makes participants much more aware of their actions than just being told about them by the trainer.

Audiotaping

Tape recording your telephone conversations is one of the best ways to train people who use the telephone as a major part of their jobs. This technique is most useful in training telemarketers, customer service representatives, order clerks, credit checkers, and similar personnel. Tape several conversations; then, review them with the employee. Listen to what is said and how it's said. Pay close attention to the way the employee reacts to what the other party says—and how that person reacts to the employee.

Personnel Perils

Some states have laws that restrict the taping of telephone conversations without notifying the other party who is being recorded. (Remember Linda Tripp!) Check your state laws.

Preparing for Advancement

Training isn't limited to teaching job skills. Training employees to move up the ranks is an important aspect of organizational development. It enables individuals to prepare for advancement and at the same time provides a continuing source of talent to meet the company's future needs.

Management Trainee Programs

For many years, training for management positions was limited to people who were on a special management track. They usually were hired as management trainees after graduating from college, and completed a series of management training programs within an organization. These programs often were supplemented by seminars, courses, and residencies at universities or special training schools.

One technique included in these programs was job rotation. After basic orientation the trainees were assigned to work for a short period in each of several departments. The ostensible objective was to give them an overview of the company so that when they moved into a regular position, they would have a good concept of the entire operation. Make sense? Only sometimes.

In many companies, the time spent in each training assignment was not long enough to give the trainees any more than superficial knowledge. They never really got their feet wet. They wasted the time of the department heads, who had to divert their energies from working with their own teams. The regular team members, knowing that the trainees would be gone shortly, often resented their intrusion. Their real training began when they were finally given regular assignments.

Everybody Is a Potential Manager

In recent years the special management track has been replaced by team development, in which training for management is open to any employee. And why not?

Even the military has learned that graduation from military academies isn't essential for top leadership. (Two of the recent chairmen of the Joint Chiefs of Staff—Colin Powell and John Shalikashvili—weren't West Pointers.) Companies have recognized that latent leadership talent exists—and can be developed—in most people.

Mentoring

As pointed out in Chapter 10, "Getting Started on the Right Foot," mentors are valuable resources in developing the skills of their protégés—and equally important in orienting them to the organizational culture. Most organizations don't have a formal program to encourage mentoring. Some managers want to share their knowledge and experience with newcomers; others take a special liking to a new employee and become his or her mentor. Some young people take the initiative and ask managers they admire to become their mentors. It is a symbiotic relationship as both the mentor and the person who is mentored benefit from it.

Coaching

Not only must trainers utilize the most effective techniques of instructing; they also must be good coaches. A coach has the ability to recognize each trainee's strengths and limitations and work with each to maximize his or her potential. Some of the qualities that good coaches possess are as follows:

➤ They are expert motivators. They bring out the best in others.

➤ They instill self-confidence by reinforcing the strengths of the people they coach and their determination to succeed.

➤ They provide the tools, plans, and techniques that enable people to achieve their individual goals and the goals of the team.

➤ They're role models. They practice what they preach.

Coaches do not have to be skilled in every aspect of the jobs they supervise. Some workers on a job might be better performers than their supervisors. The ability of the coach lies not in his or her ability to excel in every aspect of a job but in bringing out the best in the people he or she coaches.

Does Training Pay Off?

Training is expensive. Are companies getting their money's worth from the tremendous outlay of funds? Many companies swear by their training experience; others swear at it. Is there any way to assess whether the training you paid for has really worked?

Measuring Results

Donald L. Kirkpatrick, now professor emeritus at the University of Wisconsin, developed a model for measuring the effectiveness of training programs that many companies use today. He set up four levels of measurement; they are as follows:

➤ **Level 1: The traditional trainee evaluation forms**   If you've ever attended a training meeting or seminar, you probably were asked to fill out an evaluation form at the end of the session. Although not very sophisticated, this immediate feedback by class members describes their reactions to the program including such important aspects as feelings about course content, instructor effectiveness, and whether the course met the trainees' expectations.

➤ **Level 2: Determination of what the trainee learned**   Just as schools have always tested students on what they learned in class, trainees can be given a written or oral examination, or asked to demonstrate the skills acquired.

➤ **Level 3: Evaluation of behavioral changes and application of learning on the job**   This can be a significant tool in determining the value of training. Have the training objectives been applied on the job? This is easy to measure in such areas as reduction of products or parts rejected for poor quality, increase in productivity, or similar tangible factors. However, it is much more difficult to measure such skills as leadership, interpersonal relations, and communications.

➤ **Level 4: Tying training to organizational impact**   Assessing whether the training resulted in a measurable improvement in business achievements is important to determining the value of the training. Once the program objectives have been met successfully, this level focuses on the actual results the program attains in the organization.

To these four levels Dr. Jack J. Phillips, a leading consultant in training program evaluation, has added:

➤ **Level 5: Return on Investment (ROI)**   This focuses attention on whether the monetary value of the results exceeds the cost of the program. Dr. Phillips cautions that most organizations conduct evaluations to measure satisfaction; few conduct evaluations on ROI level. Both are desirable. Evidence shows that if measurements aren't taken at each level, it's difficult to show that any improvement can be attributed to the training.

Tactical Tips

To measure the effectiveness of your training activities, it's best to retain a training consultant with special expertise in this area.

A company's training investment is most likely to pay off when training is held accountable for results, used only when it is the appropriate tool, and linked to the company goals. By using the Kirkpatrick and Phillips measurement techniques, a company can obtain a comprehensive picture of the results of its training programs. Ongoing, well-organized, and carefully implemented training programs keep employees at the cutting edge of effectiveness. This reduces overall turnover and helps to retain your best employees.

The Least You Need to Know

➤ Before choosing any training programs, the company should conduct a needs analysis to determine whether the training is worth the investment.

➤ Basic skills training still has its place in the business world. The fundamentals of a job must be acquired as a start, but we can't stop there: Continued training must be an ongoing concern.

➤ The immediate supervisors or others in the company who are specialists in the field usually conduct most of the training. However, there are many areas of training in which outside training organizations can do a better job.

➤ A systematic approach to training people to perform tasks involves four steps: ready (preparation), set (presentation), go (performance), and check it out (follow-up).

➤ Helpful training tools include training manuals, CD-ROMs, the Internet, teleconferencing, using case studies, role-playing, and audio- or videotaping.

➤ Training isn't limited to teaching job skills. Training team members to move up the ranks is an important aspect of organizational development.

➤ A company's training investment is most likely to pay off when the training is held accountable for results.

Chapter 12

Getting Ideas Across

In This Chapter

➤ Tips on improving communications with your staff

➤ What you say and how you say it

➤ Overcoming bad speech habits

➤ Your body also speaks

➤ Become a better listener

➤ Running effective meetings

It has been said that communication is the lifeblood of organizations. If this is true, the blood vessels in most organizations are clogged with cholesterol. For ideas, data, instructions, and other essential information to flow smoothly, those conduits must be cleared out.

Communication takes place when people or groups exchange information, ideas, and concepts. Everybody in the organization is a communicator. Whether you are a top executive, a middle manager, a team leader or supervisor, or a rank-and-file employee, you can do your part in making communications more effective. In this chapter you will learn some strategies to reduce the clots that block your communications to the people you supervise. Equally important is to unclog communications from your staff to you—a major step in applying the human resources approach to your management style.

Communications: A Two-Way Process

Communication between people is like a two-way radio conversation. A person sends a message from one radio to a person on the second radio. Of course, at any time the roles can be reversed. The receiver becomes the sender and the sender the receiver; they talk back and forth.

Effective communication requires that the receiver get that message clearly and understand it. As with a radio, interference might distort the communication, causing the receiver to misunderstand what is being sent. To compound it, the sender might not realize that the message is not being received as intended. The source of the interference might lie with the sender or with the receiver, or maybe between the two. Just as in radio transmission, the interference is referred to as "static" or "noise." Let's explore the messages and how this static can be overcome.

What You Say

Suppose you call a meeting to discuss a new project. Or you sit down with an associate for a serious discussion about performance. Or perhaps you're called upon to present a progress report to the executive committee. In all these situations, the words you choose and how you say them might determine your success or failure.

Personnel Perils

Unless your audience is familiar with it, don't use jargon—those special initials, acronyms, or words that are used only in your field or perhaps just in your company, and nowhere else. On the other hand, if an audience consists of people who use this jargon regularly in their work, the terms will be familiar to them and might even add to their understanding of your message.

Whether you're addressing a group or having a one-on-one conversation, you should think out your message and prepare in advance what you intend to say. There are situations when there is little time to prepare and you'll have to think on your feet. Even under these circumstances, take a few minutes before you open your mouth to plan what you will say.

Know Your Subject

On the job, usually you'll communicate with others about subjects you're thoroughly familiar with; you'll talk about the work you're doing, matters in your own area of expertise, or company-related issues. Still, you should review the facts to be sure you have a handle on all the available information before speaking.

Occasionally you might be asked to report on matters with which you are unfamiliar. Doing your homework will pay off in a presentation; you will be easily understood and earn credit as a good communicator. For example, your company might be considering purchasing a new type of computer software and ask you to check it out. Here's how you should tackle the assignment:

➤ Learn as much as possible about the subject.

➤ Know 10 times more than you think you ought to know for the presentation.

➤ Prepare notes about the pluses and minuses of the proposed purchase.

➤ Whether you will make this report to one person (your boss, for example) or to a group of managers or technical specialists, be prepared to answer questions about any subject that might come up.

Know Your Audience

Understanding your audience is a key ingredient of good communication. Choose words that your listeners will easily comprehend. If the people you're addressing all come from a technical background, you can use technical terminology. But if you talk about a technical subject matter to an audience that is unfamiliar with it, drop the technical language. If your listeners don't work in the same technical field and can't understand your vocabulary, your message will be lost.

For example, suppose you're an engineer whose work primarily involves dealing with other engineers. You're accustomed to using technical terms all the time. Now you're about to make a presentation to your company's finance department to arrange funding for a new engineering project. It's your responsibility—not your audience's—to ensure that your message gets across. If you can explain the technical matter in layperson's terms, do so. When it is necessary to use technical language, take the time to explain the term the first time you use it and at least once again if you feel it needs reinforcement.

How You Say It

No matter how well-thought-out your message is, no one will understand it unless you express it clearly and distinctly. Make a point to learn how you come across to others and if there are problems, do all you can to correct them. Following are some common problems in speaking clearly:

➤ **Mumbling**   Do you swallow word endings? Do you speak with your mouth almost closed? Practice in front of a mirror. Open up those lips.

➤ **Speaking too fast**   Whoa! Give people a chance to absorb what you're saying.

➤ **Speaking too slowly**   If you speak too slowly you'll lose your audience; while you're plodding through your message their minds will wander to other matters.

➤ **Mispronouncing words**   Not sure how a word is pronounced? Look it up or ask someone who does know. Some of the online dictionaries now provide pronunciation help.

➤ **Speaking in a monotone**   Vary the inflection of the tone and pitch of your voice; otherwise, you'll put your listeners to sleep.

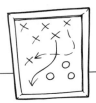

Tactical Tips

All voicemail programs give you the opportunity to listen to your outgoing message; some enable you to listen to the message you leave for someone else before making it final. Listen. By listening to your own voice, you hear how you sound to others.

➤ **"Word whiskers"** These are the extra sounds, words, or phrases intermingled in a speech, such as "er," "uhhhh," "uh-huh," "y'know," "right," and "okay." They distract and annoy your audience. Listen to yourself—and shave off those "whiskers."

You don't hear yourself as others hear you. Listen to yourself. Get a voice-activated tape recorder, place it on your desk, and turn it on so you can record your voice when you talk to others in person or on the phone. Listen to the tape. You'll hear whether you're mumbling, speaking too fast (or perhaps too slowly), or speaking in a monotone.

All you need to do to correct most of these problems is to be aware. If you're aware that you mumble, you'll make an effort to avoid mumbling. If you're aware that you speak too fast, you'll make an effort to slow down. If you're aware that you speak in a monotone, you'll make the effort to speak in a more interesting tone.

Watch That Body Language

People communicate not only through words but also through their facial expressions and body movements. According to a recent study by speech pathologists, listeners get at least 65 percent of a message through body language? Body language can cancel or reinforce what words say. Great communicators pay special attention to their gestures, facial expressions, and body movements when they speak. If only there were a dictionary of body language, we could easily interpret what those signs signify. But because body language isn't standardized like verbal language, no such dictionary could be written.

Our cultural or ethnic backgrounds, the way our parents expressed themselves nonverbally, and other individual experiences influence the way we use our bodies. Body language differs from one person to another. Some gestures, such as a nod or a smile, might seem universal, but not everyone uses body language in the same way. It's easy to misinterpret a listener's body language.

For example, the woman to whom you are talking is nodding. Good; you assume she's agreeing with you. Not necessarily. There are some people who nod just to acknowledge that they're listening. Another listener folds his arms as you speak. You might interpret this as a subconscious show of disagreement, but it could simply be that he's cold. There is danger in misreading nonverbal cues.

Study the body language of people with whom you work. You might notice that when John smiles in a certain way, it has one meaning—a different smile, a different meaning. Or maybe when Jane doesn't agree, she wrinkles her forehead. Make a conscious effort to study and remember the body language of each person with whom you have regular interaction.

Learn to Listen

Listening is hard work. It's more than just keeping your ears open. Let's say one of your colleagues brings a problem to you and asks for help. At first you listen attentively. But it's not long before your mind begins to wander. Instead of listening to the problem, you're thinking about other things: the pile of work on your desk, the meeting you have scheduled with the company vice president, the problems one of your children is having at school. You hear your colleague's words—but you're not really listening.

One way to improve your listening skill is to take an active role. Instead of just sitting or standing with your ears open, follow these guidelines to becoming an active listener:

➤ Look at the speaker. Eye contact is one way of showing interest, but don't overdo it. Look at the whole person; don't just stare into his or her eyes.

➤ Show interest by your facial expressions. Smile or show concern when appropriate.

➤ Indicate that you are following the conversation by nods or gestures.

➤ Ask questions about what's being said. You can paraphrase "So the way I understand it is …" or ask specific questions about specific points. This technique not only enables you to clarify points that might be unclear; it also keeps you alert and paying full attention.

➤ Don't interrupt. A pause should not be a signal for you to start talking. Wait. The other person might have more to say.

➤ Be an empathic listener. Listen with your heart as well as your head. Try to feel what other people are feeling when they speak. In other words, put yourself in the speaker's shoes.

You can become a better listener by stopping some of the main causes of ineffective listening before they begin. All you have to do is make a few changes in your work environment and in your approach to listening—a small effort with a big return. Try the following strategies to make you a better listener:

➤ **Shut off the telephone.** The greatest distraction probably is the telephone. You want to give the speaker your full attention. The phone rings. Answering the call not only interrupts your discussion but also disrupts the flow of your

145

thoughts—and those of the speaker's. Even after you've hung up, your mind might still be pondering the call. If you know you'll be having a lengthy discussion at your desk, arrange for someone else to handle your calls or set your voicemail to pick up all calls right away. If this isn't possible, get away from the telephone. Try an empty conference room—no one knows you're there so the phone in that room probably won't ring.

➤ **Hide the papers.** If your desk is strewn with papers, you'll probably sit there skimming them until you realize too late that you're reading a letter or memo instead of listening. If you go to a conference room, take only the papers that are related to the discussion. If you must stay at your desk, put the papers in a drawer so you won't be tempted to read them.

➤ **Don't get too comfortable.** Some years ago I was discussing a situation with another manager. As was my custom, I sat in my comfortable executive chair with my hands behind my head. Maybe I rocked a little, but fortunately, I caught myself before I dozed off. Ever since then, rather than taking a relaxing position—leaning backward—when I engage in discussions, I've made a point of sitting on the edge of my chair and leaning forward. This position not only brings me physically closer to the other person; it makes me more attentive and helps me to maintain eye contact. It also shows the other person that I'm truly interested in getting the full story he or she is relating and that I take seriously what is being said. And because I'm not quite so comfortable, there's less of a tendency to daydream.

➤ **Don't think about your rebuttal.** It's tempting to pick up one or two points that the speaker is making and plan how you will respond to them. Do this and you'll probably miss much of the balance of what is being said—often the really important parts. Concentrate on what is said throughout the entire process.

➤ **Take notes.** It's impossible to remember everything that's said in a lengthy discussion. Jot down key words or phrases. Write down figures or important facts, just enough to help you remember. Immediately after a meeting, while the information is still fresh in your mind, write a detailed summary. Dictate it into a recorder, enter it into your computer, or write it in your notebook—whichever is best for you.

State of Mind

Some of the major statics that impede communication are psychological rather than physical. You might have perfect articulation and choose your words wisely—but static develops in intangible areas: assumptions, attitudes, and the emotional baggage each of us carries. All of these influence the way what we say is interpreted by our listeners.

You've seen this situation repeatedly. Let's say you have a pretty good idea about what causes a particular problem and how to solve it. In discussing it with others, you assume that they know as much about it as you do, so what you say is based on the assumption that they have knowledge that they really don't have. The result is that you don't give them adequate information to deal with the situation. Static! Equally confusing is when the other party assumes you know his or her limitations and will help overcome them. More static!

Another barrier to communication are the attitudes of the sender and the receiver. A manager who is arrogant will convey this feeling in the way directions and information are given. He or she might appear to be talking down to members of the group. This causes resentment, which blocks communication. For the message to be received, not only must it be understood, it must be accepted by the receiver. When resentment develops, acceptance is unlikely.

Personnel Perils

People who resent the supervisor's attitude do not really hear what's being said. Consciously or subconsciously, they close their ears. Good leaders avoid attitudes that cause resentment such as arrogance, sarcasm, and "pulling rank" when communicating with staff.

Keep an Open Mind

People tend to hear what they expect to hear. The message you receive is distorted by any information you have already heard about the subject. If the new information is different from what's expected, you might reject it as being incorrect. Rather than actually hearing the new message, you might be hearing what your mind is telling you. What does this mean to you? Keep your mind open. When someone tells you something, make an extra effort to listen. Evaluate the new information objectively instead of blocking it out because it differs from your preconceptions.

When communicating with others, also try to learn their preconceptions. If they are people you work with regularly, you probably know how they view many of the matters you discuss. When you present your views to them, take into consideration what they already believe. If their beliefs differ from yours, be prepared to make the effort to jump over those hurdles.

We All Have Biases

Your biases for or against a person influence the way you receive their messages. We listen more attentively and are more likely to accept ideas from somebody we like and respect. Conversely, we tend to block out and reject the ideas of people we don't like.

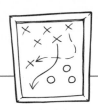

Tactical Tips

Perception is reality in the mind of the perceiver. Unless yours and your associate's perceptions of a situation are congruent, each of you will be working with different premises and come to different conclusions.

Tactical Tips

Often, when two teams or groups are working on a project together, much time and trouble can be saved if, on routine matters, members bypass team leaders and deal directly with their counterparts in the other team or group.

Biases also affect the way subject matter is received. People turn a deaf ear to opposing viewpoints concerning matters about which they have strong feelings. Carol is a good example of such a person. As company controller, she is fixated on reducing costs. She won't even listen to any discussion that might increase costs no matter what the long-term benefits might be.

Be Aware of Your Emotional State

Did you ever have a bad day? Of course; we all do. And on one of those bad days, one of your staff members comes to you all excited about a new idea. How do you react? Probably you think, "I have enough on my platter now, who needs this?" Your mind is closed and the message doesn't come through.

Channels: The Static Between Sender and Receiver

In communication, another source of interference and distortion is the path the message takes from sender to receiver. In many large organizations, communications must flow through set channels. The more extensive the channels, the more likely that distortion will occur.

This can be illustrated in the popular party game telephone, in which one person tells an incident to his or her neighbor, who repeats it to the next person, and so on, around the room. By the time it is retold to the originator, the story is completely different. It is not unusual for a piece of information passed orally "through channels" to be distorted at each station, so that what the receiver receives is not at all what the sender sent.

One way to alleviate this difficulty is to use written communications. Writing is more difficult to distort, although interpretation of what is written might vary from station to station. However, writing has certain disadvantages: Many matters can't or shouldn't be communicated in writing. Writing is time consuming. For rush matters and matters of transient interest, writing is not appropriate.

A more effective way is to shorten channels and allow for bypassing where feasible. The fewer stations along the way, the less chance there is for distortion. The main reason for channels is to ensure that people who are responsible for a project are kept aware of everything that applies to it. This makes sense, but usually it is overdone. If a matter involves policy decisions or major areas of activity, channels are important. But a great portion of the communications in companies concern routine matters. Using channels for these not only might distort the message, it will slow down the work.

Get Feedback

The sender must always be sensitive to how the receiver receives and accepts the message. One way feedback can be obtained is by asking questions. However, you have to ask the right questions. The most commonly asked question is, "Do you understand?" That's not a good question because the answer can be misleading. Many people will say "Yes"; but this doesn't mean the receiver really does understand. He or she might be ashamed to say, "No" for fear of being considered stupid. Or, the receiver might honestly *think* he or she understands but actually comprehends only part of the message, or interprets it quite differently from how it was intended.

A better approach is to be more specific. Ask, "So that we both understand what you are going to do, let's go over it again" or "Tell me how you view this." Another approach is to ask questions about the key points to ensure that the receiver fully understands. It's essential that both parties are in agreement as to what actions are to be taken.

Conducting Effective Meetings

Meetings are another frequently used means of both giving and exchanging information. However, meetings can be a big waste of time if they're not organized properly. You often might have left a meeting thinking, "What a waste of time. I could have accomplished so much more if I had been at my desk during this past hour." In a recent survey, more than 70 percent of people interviewed felt that many meetings they had attended were a waste of time.

There is hope. Meetings can be made productive. The following sections contain some suggestions you can use when conducting meetings in your company.

Keep Meetings Small

Invite only appropriate participants. Some managers hold staff meetings on a regular basis—sometime weekly or even daily. Quite often, many of the people who attend are not involved in the matters that are discussed. By inviting only the people who you know can contribute to the meeting or will be affected by what is discussed, you can avoid wasting the time of others and keep the meetings short.

Set the Meeting Agenda

Prepare an agenda. An agenda is the key to the success or failure of a meeting. It should be planned carefully, covering all matters that are to be discussed. By determining in advance the subjects that will be addressed and the order in which they will be covered, the meeting will run more smoothly.

When establishing the sequence of topics at a meeting, put the most complex ones at the beginning of the program. People come to meetings with clear minds and are able to approach deeper matters more effectively early on. If you schedule the important issues for later, not only are participants likely to be less attentive; they might be distracted by what was discussed earlier.

Stick rigidly to the agenda. Don't allow anyone to bring up any topics not on the agenda. If this should be attempted, point out that unless it's an emergency, it cannot be discussed at this meeting. Suggest that it be placed on the agenda for the next meeting.

Personnel Perils

When people who usually are invited to meetings are not invited, they might worry, "Why wasn't I asked? Is the boss giving me a hidden message? Am I on the way out?" Avoid this concern by explaining the new policy of limiting the number of meeting attendees and why you've instituted it.

Get Everyone Involved in the Meeting

Attendees should be encouraged to study the agenda and be prepared to discuss each item. If specific data is needed to make a point, organize it into easy-to-follow visuals. Such data should be prepared in a way that is easily presented such as charts, other visuals, and handouts. Create an atmosphere in which disagreements can be brought out without fear of ridicule or retaliation.

If you are the leader, ask questions that stimulate discussion. Be open to questions and dissention. It's better to have people butt heads at the meeting than have unresolved matters fester in the minds of the participants.

Ending the Meeting

At the end of the meeting, after all the items on the agenda have been covered, the leader should summarize what has been accomplished. If any participants were given assignments during the course of the meeting, ask them to reiterate their understanding of the expectations and the deadline.

Take Meeting Minutes

So that there is no misunderstanding of what has been decided at a meeting, notes should be taken. These need not be detailed transcripts of the entire discussion, but a summary of the decisions made on each issue. After the meeting, copies of the minutes should be distributed—not only to the attendees; to all people who might be affected by the determinations.

The Least You Need to Know

➤ Effective communication requires that the receiver clearly gets the message.

➤ Doing your homework will pay off in a presentation that will be easily understood and earn you credit as a good communicator.

➤ No matter how well-thought-out your message is, no one will understand it, unless you express it clearly and distinctly.

➤ People communicate not only through words but also through their facial expressions and body movements.

➤ Be an active listener. Pay close attention to what the other party says. Ask questions, makes comments, and react verbally and nonverbally to what is said.

➤ Some of the major statics that impede communication are assumptions, attitudes, and the emotional baggage each of us has.

➤ The sender must always be sensitive to how the receiver receives and accepts the message. One way feedback can be obtained is by asking good questions.

➤ To make the best use of time in meetings prepare and follow an agenda, encourage participation, and stimulate discussion.

Chapter 13

Put It in Writing

In This Chapter

➤ Preparing what you plan to write

➤ Spelling and grammar do count

➤ What to say and how to say it

➤ The e-mail revolution

➤ The advantages and dangers of e-mail

Most communications between managers and staff are oral. This is logical; in most cases managers and employees are in the same location. In these circumstances it's easy to maintain continuous contact with each other—to give directions, exchange ideas, and interact. The telephone, which is an extension of oral communication, also is a useful tool.

However, there are many occasions when communication must be in writing. For years this has been done through interoffice memos and letters; however, increasingly in the twenty-first century, written communication is done by e-mail. This is particularly useful when managers are required to supervise people in several locations. Indeed, some people even use e-mail when communicating with people in the same building—even in an adjacent cubicle.

Clear writing is essential no matter what medium is used: memos, letters, e-mail, or instant messages. In this chapter you'll learn how to make all your written communications a dynamic tool in your interpersonal relations. As managers also write to customers, vendors, and others outside the company, the suggestions for improving writing also can be very helpful in that aspect of your work.

Getting It Down

How often have you sat down to write something (a memo, a letter, an e-mail, or a fax), knowing exactly what you wanted to say, but the right words just wouldn't come? A simple process to help you plan your written correspondence can be summarized in the acronym TAB. This process provides clues to help you think clearly about what you want to write before starting to write it:

Think about the situation: Why am I writing this?

Action: What do I want to accomplish?

Benefit: How will this be of value to the recipient of this communication?

Ask yourself these questions. Jot down the answers on a scratch pad. By "TABing" your thoughts before you do the writing, you'll get a clear idea of what you want to convey. The notes will help you organize all the information concerning your subject matter. It will indicate what you want done, how to deal with it, and how those actions will benefit your readers.

The Three C's

Once you've thought out the message you can formulate the way you'll write it. Keep in mind the three C's of good communication. Anything you put in should be ...

➤ **Clear.** Is easy to read and understand.

➤ **Complete.** Covers all the points.

➤ **Concise.** Is brief and to the point.

For example, if you're writing a memo concerning the status of an order, also be sure to respond to any specific questions your recipient might have about the order. Include the order number, date of the order, identification of materials, and other pertinent information; and avoid going into extraneous details.

Management Miscellany

Lincoln's Gettysburg Address contained only 272 words—each word a gem.

Get to the Point

Steer clear of complex sentence constructions or extravagant phraseology. Keep it as brief as possible, but make it punchy. One way to make your points stand out is to write the item in the form of a bulletin; here are some suggestions:

➤ Headline your main point—use **bold** print.

➤ Break the body of the letter or memo into separate sections; one for each subsidiary point.

➤ Use an asterisk (*) or bullet (•) to highlight key points.

➤ Where appropriate use graphs, charts, diagrams, or other visual aids to augment the impact of your words.

Watch Your Grammar and Spelling

You can't always depend on a secretary to correct your grammar, sentence structure, and spelling errors. Today, most supervisors or team leaders don't have secretaries or administrative assistants; they write their own correspondence. Even if you're one of the lucky few who has an assistant, you still should check everything that goes out with your signature on it. If you are weak in grammar or spelling, seek out a colleague to be your in-company "editor" for constructive review and suggestions.

Some help can come from the spelling and grammar checks in your word processing program, but this is not enough. Remember, the computer is a machine that will highlight only a word that is obviously wrong; however, if you write "brake" instead of its homonym, "break" the spell check won't pick it up. You have to reread what you've written to ensure it's written in proper style.

Write the Way You Speak

As the old saying goes, "Keep it simple, stupid!" When you sit down to write a letter or memo, pretend you're talking face-to-face or on the phone with the person who will read the letter. Relax. Be informal. Speak your thoughts in your usual manner, with the vocabulary, accents, idioms, and expressions you usually use. You wouldn't normally say, "Please be advised that because of the fire in our plant there will be a 10-day delay in shipping your order." Instead you'd get right into the message, "Because of the fire in our plant, shipping your order will be delayed 10 days." So why not write just that?

Use Contractions

When speaking to somebody, you rarely use full phrases such as "I do not want this" or "I will not be able to go." More likely, you say "I don't" or "I won't." It's okay to use these commonly used contractions in your writing. It makes your letter come across in a sincere and personal manner. Naturally, avoid slangy contractions such as "ain't"; of course, you shouldn't use such language when speaking, either.

Ask Questions

Oral conversation isn't one-sided. First, one person speaks; then, the other comments or asks a question such as, "If we do that, how will it affect sales to the fast-food chains?" Do this in your writing. By interjecting questions in your letter, you focus the reader's attention on specific points. For example, instead of writing "If you desire, we can incorporate additional applications in this software" write, "What additional applications would you like to have incorporated in this software?" This gives the reader a chance to reflect on your message in terms that are specific to his or her needs.

Personalize Your Letter

When we speak we use the pronouns "I," "we," and "you" all the time. They're part of the normal give and take of conversation. However, when we write as representatives of our company we tend to use the passive voice. We rarely write "we," never write "I," and even avoid the straightforward "you." Instead we use such phrases as: "It is assumed …," "It is recommended …," or sentences such as, "An investigation will be made and upon its completion a report will be furnished to your organization." Try clearly stating, "We're investigating the matter and when we obtain the information we'll let you know."

Tactical Tips

Give your letters a human touch. Express your natural feelings. Be courteous, polite, and interested. A friendly writing style will please—and a cold one might annoy—the reader.

When writing for an organization, usually there isn't too much opportunity to be personal and write "I." However, you should use "I" when you express feelings or thoughts that are your own. It's better to say, "I'm sorry" or "I'm pleased" rather than "we're sorry" or "we're pleased."

Another way to personalize a letter is to use the addressee's name in the text. If you're friends, use the first name—if just business acquaintances, the last name. Instead of writing, "This will result in benefits for your organization," write, "So you see, Beth (or Ms. Smith), how this will benefit you."

Break Some "Rules"

You can use a preposition to end a sentence. The rule you learned in grade school about not ending sentences with a preposition is passé. In speaking, we don't even think about such things. However, when we're writing we restructure sentences to fit this rule. Don't. It makes the sentence—therefore the letter—sound awkward. Put the preposition at the end whenever it sounds right to do so. Instead of writing, "Our health plan does not cover the treatment for which you applied," it's okay to write, "Our health plan doesn't cover the treatment you applied for."

Another grammatical superstition tells us to avoid split infinitives. "To successfully reduce costs in our department, we should take the following steps," sounds more powerful than, "To reduce costs in our department successfully, we should take the following steps." It usually is quite clear where one idea leaves off and another begins.

156

Keep sentences short and uncomplicated. If a sentence has too many words, chances are the full meaning will be missed. The ordinary reader can take in only so many words before his or her eyes come to a brief rest at a period. Studies show that sentences of no more than 20 to 25 words are easiest to read and absorb.

Limit each sentence to one idea. Remember, your objective is to get the idea across to the reader—not to create undying prose. It's also helpful to use short rather than long words. Of course, in writing on technical matters to technically trained people, technical language is appropriate. However, when writing to people who might not have the background that you have in a specific area, avoid language and jargon that they are unlikely to possess.

Avoid Business Clichés

Instead of using overused and often meaningless business terminology, use simple terms. Even in this day and age of increased casualness in the world of work, business letters still are loaded with overly formal language, overly used phrases, and stilted phraseology. The following is a list of some commonly used clichés and better ways to express the thoughts:

Instead of Writing:	Write:
At a later date	Later (or exact time)
At the present time	Now
Despite the fact	Although
For the period of a year	For a year
In accordance with your request	As requested
In the near future	Soon (or in May)
Is of the opinion that	Believes
Made an adjustment	Adjusted
The undersigned or the writer	I
We are herewith enclosing	Enclosed is
We are not in a position to	We cannot
With the exception of	Except

Give your letters just the right human touch. Express your natural feelings. If it's good news, say you're glad; if it's bad news, say you're sorry. Be as courteous, polite, and interested as you'd be if the addressee sat in front of you.

The E-Mail Explosion

Give as much attention to composing e-mail as you do to the composition of standard letters and memos. Remember that e-mail is a form of written communication.

157

Management Miscellany

More and more inter- and intra-office communication is now done through e-mail. According to a poll conducted by Ernst & Young, 36 percent of respondents use e-mail more than any other communication tool, including the telephone.

Many people think of it as a substitute for a phone call rather than a letter, so they dash off their messages with little or no consideration of style or even content. Unlike the phone call, e-mail can be kept either electronically or as a printout, so it should be carefully planned and composed.

Make Your E-Mail Exciting, Expressive, Even Engaging

Too many people think of e-mail as a form of oral communication—sort of a written telephone call. Not so. E-mail is a brief letter. Unlike a telephone call, it can be printed out, filed, stored in memory and retrieved for future use. Take as much care in writing an e-mail as a memo. Here are some tips to help you write better e-mail:

➤ Think carefully about what you write. If the message is more than just casual chitchat, plan it as carefully as you would a formal letter. Put yourself in the place of the reader. If you're giving instructions, make sure the reader knows just exactly what action you're requesting. If you're answering an inquiry, make sure you've gathered all the information necessary to respond appropriately to the questions.

➤ Use a meaningful subject line. Your correspondent might receive dozens, even hundreds, of e-mail messages each day. To ensure that your message will be read promptly, use a subject heading that will be meaningful to the addressee. For example, instead of "RE your e-mail of 6/25," use the subject line to refer to the information you provide in your message (for instance, "Sales figures for June").

➤ Follow the suggestions given earlier in this chapter on writing letters and memos. Use the three C's and the TAB approach. Use short, punchy sentences. Keep to the point and be brief.

➤ If you attach files to the e-mail, specify in the text which files are attached so the reader can check to make sure they all came through.

➤ Read the message carefully and spell-check it before you click "Send now." If you are not happy with the message, don't send it. Postpone the transmission. Review it and rewrite it. Make sure it's okay before it is sent. You can always save it as a draft and come back to it later.

Also keep in mind that the numerous e-mails that co-workers receive can result in your message being ignored or inadvertently deleted. Ask the receiver to acknowledge receipt of your e-mail. If the matters involved are very important, follow up with a telephone call to ensure that the message was received and understood. Many e-mail programs include a "return-receipt" function. By using this, you can determine if your message was received.

E-Mail Versus Phone Calls or Visits

Many people tend to resort to e-mail rather than making a phone call or a personal visit. Using e-mail often is an easy way out. You don't have to leave your desk and it's less time consuming than a telephone call. There's no time wasted in small talk or lengthy discussion about a project. All that's sent is the basic message. Often, though, that small talk and pro-and-con discussion are important. In addition, the phone call allows for instant feedback. It not only helps clarify the message; it ensures that both you and the other person understand the matters involved in the same way.

Tactical Tips

When immediate response or a discussion of a situation is needed, you can use the IM (Instant Message) function, available in most Internet programs. This provides an ongoing, real-time conversation with a colleague, customer, vendor, or any other party.

Charles Wang, CEO of Computer Associates, found that e-mail's alleged efficiencies were ruining the interpersonal dynamics that had made his company so successful in the first place. People stopped having face-to-face meetings and stopped speaking to each other altogether. His simple but shocking solution: Turn the whole system off for most of the day and force people to communicate in person. He follows this himself. When he wants a staff member, he goes down the hall and finds that person.

"Who's Reading My E-Mail?"

How private is your e-mail? Not very. Sure, you might have a password and assume that it ensures privacy, but hackers have shown that they can easily break through even sophisticated systems. Assume anything you e-mail can be intercepted. If confidentiality is required, maybe e-mail is not the medium to use.

Remember that any e-mail sent through the company computer can be read by anybody in the company. Over the past few years there have been cases in which employees were fired because of e-mails they sent that violated company rules. The courts threw out employee claims of invasion of privacy.

Personnel Perils

E-mail is not private. It can be accessed easily by anybody. Don't use company e-mail for gossip, off-color jokes, or any matter that can embarrass you or the company.

More serious are the cases of people who have made comments or sent jokes in their e-mail that were considered sexually or racially harassing or threatening. Printouts of such e-mail have been entered as evidence in suits against employees' companies, even though company officials weren't aware of the messages. This has led to termination of the senders and legal action against both the senders and the companies.

Some E-Mail Do's and Don'ts

E-mail can be a valuable addition to your communication tools; however, it also can become a nuisance and a time-waster. Learn to master e-mail before it begins to master you. The following are some useful guidelines:

➤ **Do** carefully plan your e-mails.

➤ **Do** read and reread your messages before clicking "Send now."

➤ **Do** inform recipients when your e-mail doesn't require a reply. It will save both of you time and clutter.

➤ **Do** use bullets instead of paragraphs. It makes it easier to read and grasp key points.

➤ **Do** respond promptly to e-mail you receive, especially when immediate attention is required. Speed of communication is the chief advantage of this medium.

➤ **Do** check whether important e-mail has been received by asking the respondent to acknowledge it or by following up with a phone call.

➤ **Do** indicate whether the e-mail message is sent just for the recipient's information or if it requires action or a reply. This will save your time and that of your recipient's.

➤ **Don't** use e-mail to replace telephone or personal contacts. It is important to maintain voice-to-voice and face-to-face relationships with the people you deal with.

➤ **Don't** play e-mail games, or send or respond to chain letters or similar time-wasters on company time and company computers.

➤ **Don't** download pornographic material or items that are derogatory to any racial or ethnic groups on company computers. Remember that your e-mails can be read by anybody and could offend other people in the organization. It could lead to embarrassment, charges of sexual or racial harassment, termination, or all of these.

➤ **Don't** spread gossip or rumors through e-mail. It's bad enough when gossip is repeated on the telephone or in person, but e-mail exponentially expands the number of people receiving such information.

➤ **Don't** send a message to your entire list unless the message applies to everyone on it.

➤ **Don't** send off-color jokes or stories via company e-mail.

E-mail has replaced "snail mail" and even telephone conversations in many organizations. It can be a blessing or a curse. By using it wisely, it can make your job easier and more efficient, but resorting to e-mail for all your communication can lead to the loss of personal interaction with colleagues that's so important to a company's culture.

The Least You Need to Know

➤ Whether the person you write to is a member of your own team or an outsider, choose words that the reader will easily understand.

➤ Use the TAB approach before writing, and the three C's when you write.

➤ Watch your grammar! Watch your spelling! Your writing style reflects your intelligence, personality, and authority.

➤ Talk to your reader. Pretend the person who will read the letter or report is sitting across from you or you are on the telephone with him or her. Be informal. Relax. Write it as you would say it.

➤ Give as much attention to writing e-mail as you do to standard letters or memos.

Part 4

Money, Money, Money

"Show me the money." That's the line that most people remember from the movie Jerry Maguire. Let's not kid ourselves. That's why most of us work—for the money. We need money to survive.

But money isn't just the salary we're paid. There's a lot more to the total compensation package: incentive pay, benefits, and perks.

In this part of the book you'll look at various aspects of compensation packages including how salaries are determined, salary adjustments, incentive pay systems, and various types of benefits and perks.

Yes, you have to "show the money," but it might not be the best way to motivate people. Read on to find out why.

Chapter 14

The Compensation Conundrum

In This Chapter

➤ Determining the right salary for a job

➤ Raising salaries—when and how

➤ Money as a motivator

➤ A look at financial incentive programs

➤ Stock options and profit-sharing plans

➤ Objectives as incentives

As discussed in Chapter 5, "Starting the Search," the first step in creating a new job or refilling an old one is to conduct a job analysis. One part of job analysis involves determining the pay scale for the job. Most organizations have a formal job classification system in which various factors are weighed to determine the value of a job. These factors include level of responsibility, contribution of a job to a company's bottom line, type of education, and training and experience necessary to perform the job. This becomes the basis for the compensation assigned to that job. Notice that the classification applies to the job—not to the person performing the job.

A well-thought-out compensation program leads to an equitable determination of what people will be paid and is a bulwark against claims of unfair treatment. In this chapter you'll learn how salaries are determined. You'll also explore various aspects of compensation such as giving raises, using money as an incentive, and various other types of incentive programs.

Determining the Pay Package

In smaller organizations the pricing of a job often is done haphazardly: You pay what you have to pay to hire the person you want. However, you must have some guidelines about what a job is worth so that you don't pay more than necessary or offer too little. You have to determine the "going rate" for a job you want to fill.

Management Miscellany

Seeking salary information? Two books that provide general information on salaries, listed by occupation are *The American Almanac of Jobs and Salaries* by John W. Wright (Avon Books, published annually) and *Occupational Outlook Handbook* (U.S. Department of Labor, published annually). For specific salary information by region, check the Web site for the city in which you are interested. Most major cities and many small communities provide this information on their Web sites.

Determining the "Going Rate"

Research the market to find out what the going rate is. In a competitive job market in which the available employees outnumber the available jobs, you might have to pay more—sometimes much more—than the going rate to attract good applicants. Following are some sources for obtaining information about the salary scales in your community or industry:

➤ **Trade and professional associations**   Many of these groups conduct and publish periodic salary surveys that enable you to compare your pay scales with other companies in your field or geographic area. These surveys are most useful when you seek salary information for specialists in your industry or profession.

➤ **Chambers of commerce**   Some chambers of commerce publish salary surveys for their locations. Because these surveys include several industries, you can obtain salary information about jobs that exist in a variety of companies such as computer operators and clerical personnel.

➤ **Employment agencies**   These agencies can inform you about the going rate for any type of position in which they place employees.

➤ **Networking**   Ask managers you know in other companies in your community or industry. They often are willing to share information about going rates.

➤ **The Internet**   Look for Web sites for trade associations, local governments, or chambers of commerce in the industry or geographic area in which you are interested. They often provide salary information.

Setting the Salary Range

Once you have a clear understanding of what the job is worth you are in a position to discuss the specific starting salary with the candidate. In some cases there is no negotiation; you make an offer and the candidate takes it or leaves it. However, if you or the candidate—or both—are flexible with the salary, there might be some give and take.

Usually the salary is set within a range. Jobs are classified according to a set procedure; the range is specified based on a survey of salaries paid for similar jobs in your industry and locality. For example, a company might have six salary grades. The lowest might be basic clerical workers, the next more skilled office jobs, then technical specialists, line supervisors … all the way up to senior managers.

The salary you offer within the range depends on the person who will be performing the job. Usually new employees start at the low end of the range; however, managers might have flexibility to offer a higher amount to more qualified people. When promoted, employees move into a higher classification—thus, a higher salary range.

When hired for a new job, most people are offered a moderate increase over their current or most recent salary. Occasionally, a higher increment is warranted for improved credentials, an advanced degree, or a professional license that the candidate has received since starting the previous job. For example, in the current market, IT personnel are in very short supply. To attract a candidate, you might have to offer him or her a significant increase over what is currently earned. Sometimes companies are so desperate to fill jobs that they have to create new job classifications with higher salary ranges to reach out to qualified people.

Raises, Cost of Living Increases, and Other Adjustments

In most companies pay raises are given as part of the performance review system (see Chapter 22, "Evaluating Performance"). It's only under unusual circumstances that an employee is given a raise at other times. Unless specified in a union or personal contract, there's no legal obligation to give employees raises at all. The amount of an increase and how and when it's given depend on each company's policy.

Many companies have given employees who meet minimum performance standards an annual raise based on increases in the cost of living. However, as cost of living has not increased significantly in recent years, the usual annual raises given by companies have been very small or eliminated entirely.

Personnel Perils

Don't make promises that are beyond your power to keep such as promising that a freeze on salary increases will soon be lifted. It's better to be honest about bad situations. If the company is in financial trouble and this is unlikely to change in the near future, say so, and point out the necessity of everybody working together to overcome the problems.

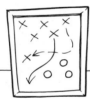

Tactical Tips

Supervisors and team leaders rarely have control over the basic satisfiers: working conditions, salary scale, employee benefits, and the like. These factors are set by company policy. However, managers can use the real motivators: job satisfaction, recognition, and the opportunity for team members to achieve professional successes.

When people don't get the raise they expect—or no raise at all—it leads to low morale. It's not easy for managers to keep people motivated if an expected raise is not granted—and you can't ignore the issue of a salary increase. Encourage any dissatisfied person to express his or her concerns. In most companies whether or not an employee gets a raise and how much the raise will be is based on the performance appraisal. If an employee is denied an increase because of poor performance, discuss it with the employee. Help him or her improve performance so that the next review will warrant a raise. If the reason is a company freeze on pay increases, explain this to the entire group; let them know that by working hard to improve the profitability of the company, the company will be in a position to renew salary increments.

Does Money Motivate?

Money has been the major form of incentive used by companies since the Industrial Revolution. Its use as a motivator is based on the belief that everybody wants to make as much money as possible and will knock himself or herself out to do so. But is this necessarily true? A team of behavioral scientists led by Frederick Herzberg studied what people want from their jobs and classified the results into two categories:

➤ **Satisfiers**   Also called *maintenance factors,* this is what people require from a job to justify expending even a minimum effort in that job. Some of these satisfiers are working conditions, money, and benefits. However, after employees are satisfied, just giving them more of the same factors won't motivate them to work harder. Often, what most people consider to be motivators really are just satisfiers.

➤ **Motivators**   These are the things that really stimulate people to put out more energy, effort, and enthusiasm in their jobs. These include recognition, control over one's own work, and obtaining satisfaction from the job.

You might assume that offering more money generates higher productivity. For many people you're probably right—but not for everyone. People have different needs, different priorities, and different ways of being motivated. The following sections discuss various kinds of employee motivators.

Incentives for Sales Staff

The sales department is a good example of the difficulties in using money as a motivator. Because salespeople usually work on a commission—or incentive—basis, they're in the enviable position of rarely having to ask for a raise. If salespeople want to earn more money, all they have to do is work harder or smarter and make as much money as they want. Therefore, all salespeople are very rich. Right? Wrong!

Why doesn't this logic work? Sales managers have complained about this problem from the beginning of time. They say, "We have an excellent incentive program, and the money is there for our sales staff. All they have to do is reach out, but they don't." Why not? To understand this problem you have to delve deep into the human psyche.

We all set personal salary levels, consciously or subconsciously, at which we are satisfied. Until we reach that point, money does motivate us; once it is reached it's no longer a motivator. This level varies significantly from person to person. Some people set this point very high; money is a major motivator to them. Others are content at lower levels. This doesn't mean they don't want their annual raise or bonus; but if obtaining the extra money requires special effort or inconvenience, you can forget it. Other things might be more important to them—time with their children or hobbies, for example.

Another adverse result of sales incentives is that it encourages salespeople to concentrate on getting new business, often at the expense of established customers. Effective sales incentive programs should present challenges to the sales reps. Perhaps the goals will vary from one period to another, depending on what the company wants to emphasize at any one time. Using one or more variations instead of the traditional commission plan stimulates creativity and leads to increased sales.

Here are some examples of variations on sales incentive programs:

➤ Number of new accounts opened

➤ Increase in volume of sales to current accounts

➤ Sales of specific items that the company is pushing

➤ Introduction of new markets (for instance, the company has sold primarily to drug stores and now is promoting sales to food outlets)

Learn as much as you can about your employees: their interests, goals, lifestyles, and the level of income at which they're satisfied. To offer the opportunity to make more money as an incentive to people who don't care about it is futile. You have to find other ways to motivate them. You'll learn more about motivating people in Chapters 17 and 18, "Motivating Your Staff for Peak Performance" and "Building Motivation into the Job," respectively.

Incentive Pay

Even with its limitations, money has some value as a motivator and companies still use financial incentives as part or all of their compensation programs. Frederic Taylor, the founder of scientific management, and his followers believed that people could be motivated by wages based on productivity. Indeed, many compensation programs have financial incentives built into them. The following is a description of some of these plans.

Piecework and Quotas

Wages based solely on the number of units produced once was the primary pay plan in some industries. The harder you worked, the more money you received. In the early days of scientific management, speed of production was the primary factor in determining wages, and this method worked well.

Meanings and Gleanings

Piecework is a system of compensation in which workers' pay is based exclusively on how much that person produces.

However, administrative abuse of the *piecework* system was rampant. Often, when workers mastered their work and produced more quotas than required, companies reduced the price paid per piece to keep their overall costs down. This practice led to demotivation. Workers set their own top limits and would do only a fixed amount of work. This defeated the purpose of the incentive program.

Industrial engineers in the age of scientific management (the 1920s and 1930s) introduced a variation of piecework. Instead of being paid by the piece, workers were paid on an hourly basis. To provide an incentive, quotas were established based on time-and-motion studies, and people who exceeded quotas received extra pay. These types of programs still exist and, properly designed and administered, succeed in motivating some people.

However, even the best of these programs have problems. For example, Arthur was young and energetic and wanted to make money to pay college expenses. He quickly mastered the work and soon exceeded his quota. One of his co-workers pulled him aside and said, "Hey, you're working too fast. You're making it bad for the rest of us." His tone of voice expressed that if Arthur didn't slow down, he would break his arm.

As work became more complex, paying by the piece often was no longer practical. Because of pressure from unions and later, minimum wage laws, hourly rates replaced piecework rates in most industries. Today, in an economy that is rapidly moving away from mass production and manufacturing-based businesses into custom-engineered production and service-type industries, those methods have little value. New types of incentive programs have been developed to meet the changing needs of industry. However, the straight piecework system lives on. In 1995, government agents raided illegal garment factories in which undocumented aliens worked in sweatshops for 12 or more hours a day at piece rates that netted them earnings well below minimum wage.

Stock Options

Stock option programs provide opportunity for employees to benefit from an increase in the company's stock value. Employees are given rights to purchase company stock at a price lower than the market price. Let's say the stock currently is selling for $25 per share. Employees are given options to buy the stock at $22 per share. If they exercise the options immediately, they make a $3 per share profit. However, the incentive is to keep the options until the stock rises in value. A year later, the stock is selling at $40 per share. They can still purchase it at $22 and sell it immediately for a profit of $18. The incentive is to help the companies grow through their efforts, which will result in higher stock prices.

Personnel Perils

The benefits and incentive pay area is complex and regulated by federal and state laws. Few companies have the expertise to institute effective programs without professional help. Some of the top consultants in this field are Towers Perrin (245 Park Avenue, New York, NY 10167); Hay Group (229 S. 18th Street, Philadelphia, PA 19103); and Hewitt Associates (40 Highland Avenue, Rowayton, CT 06853).

The downside is that stock price does not necessarily reflect the company's profitability. Other market factors might influence the stock price. If the stock falls below the option price, the rights are worthless. Stock options usually are not offered to lower-level employees, but often are a major part of executives' compensation packages.

Hiring Bonuses

If you follow sports, you know all about sign-on bonuses. The sports pages are always reporting about fabulous amounts of money paid not only to top players, but also to promising rookies just out of high school or college. To attract hard-to-find specialists such as computer whizzes or financial geniuses, and sometimes just to get people who qualify for high-demand positions, companies have paid hundreds and sometimes thousands of dollars in signing bonuses.

Some New Twists in Incentive Programs

In our tough, competitive economy, businesses need incentive plans that really motivate their employees. As was pointed out earlier in this chapter, money is not necessarily the best motivator, but money combined with other types of motivation makes an effective motivational package. These programs might be based on exceeding predetermined expectations or the special achievements of employees, and can result in sharing the company's profits.

Management by Objective (MBO) as a Monetary Incentive

Management by objective is used in many companies as both a management tool and an incentive program. Although there are many variations, the basic idea is that managers and associates together determine the objectives and results expected for that period. After a time period is agreed on, associates work with minimum supervision to achieve the specified goals. At the end of the period, the manager and the associates compare what has been accomplished with the objectives that have been set. To make MBO an incentive to greater productivity, bonuses are awarded for meeting or exceeding expectations.

Meanings and Gleanings

Management by objective (MBO) is a philosophy of management in which employees are rewarded for achieving objectives that have been jointly established with their superiors.

Special Awards for Special Achievement

One way a company that wants to promote a special product, service, or activity can motivate its staff to put out extra effort is a special awards program. For example, the Footloose Shoe Store chain instituted periodic campaigns to emphasize various aspects of its work. One campaign centered on increasing sales of "add-ons" (accessories for customers in addition to the shoes they just purchased). The campaign, which lasted four weeks, began with rallies at a banquet hall in each region in which the chain operates. Staff members from all the stores in the region assembled in a party atmosphere where food, balloons, door prizes, and music set the mood as the program was kicked off.

Footloose announced that prizes would be awarded, including $2,000 to be divided among all the staff members in the contest-winning store. The sales clerk who made the most personal add-on sales in the region would receive $500, and the sales clerk who made the most add-on sales in each store would receive $100. The campaign was reinforced by weekly reports on the progress of each store and each sales clerk.

This resulted not only in a significant increase in accessory sales for that period; it also resulted in an increase in regular sales. These gains could be attributed to the excitement and enthusiasm generated by the campaign. Another party was held to present the awards and recognize the winners. Footloose runs three or four campaigns every year (too many parties would diminish the novelty).

Xerox is another company that adds financial reward for recognition. To encourage team participation, special bonuses are given to teams that contribute ideas that lead to gains in production, quality, cost savings, or profits.

Make sure you tailor your incentive plan to what your company wants to accomplish. Create innovative programs that will motivate workers to help the company meet its goals. There are many varieties of incentive plans other than those directly tied to a person's individual productivity. The following are some widely used plans.

Profit Sharing

Companies use many variations of profit-sharing programs—plans in which a portion of the profits the company earns is distributed to its employees. Many of these plans are informal. At the end of the fiscal year the executive committee or board of directors sets aside a certain portion of profits to be distributed among employees.

Meanings and Gleanings

An **employee stock owner-ship program (ESOP)** is a program in which the major portion of the company stock is sold or given to employees so that they actually own the company.

In some organizations only managerial employees are included in a profit-sharing plan. In others, all employees who have been with the company for at least a certain number of years also are included; the entire workforce gets a piece of the profits. Some union contracts mandate profit-sharing plans.

Another way to establish a profit-sharing program is to base it on employee stock ownership. Various types of stock ownership plans are used, including giving stock as a bonus, giving employees the option to buy company stock at below-market rates, and *employee stock ownership programs* (*ESOPs*), in which employees own their company.

Open Book Management

Open book management is a relatively new financial incentive approach that is revolutionizing the traditional compensation system. In the old approach, bosses ran a company and employees did what they were told (or what they could get away with). This system is being replaced by open-book companies, in which every employee has access to numbers and facts that are critical to tracking the company's performance. Employees are given the training and tools to understand these company dynamics, ensuring that they recognize their stake in their company's success. They're rewarded for their successes and accept the risks of failure—if the business is profitable, they share in the profits; if it isn't, there are no profits to share.

This changes employee attitudes toward the company and the job. Rather than complaining and griping, they pitch in to solve problems. Rather than evading assignments with the plaintive excuse "It's not my job," employees seek out areas in which they can contribute. They understand the reason that raises are frozen, that some of their actions have curtailed productivity rather than enhanced it, and what steps they can take to save their company and their jobs.

The Least You Need to Know

➤ Determine the "going rate." Research the market to find out what other companies are paying for similar jobs.

➤ Herzberg divided what people seek from their jobs into satisfiers—basic needs such as good working conditions and adequate compensation—and motivators, which inspire people to extend themselves on the job.

➤ To offer the opportunity to make more money as an incentive to people who don't care about it is futile. You have to find some other ways to motivate them.

➤ Using one or more variations on incentive plans instead of just one standard plan stimulates creativity and leads to increased productivity.

➤ In management by objective (MBO) programs, managers and associates determine together the objectives and results expected for that period. Bonuses are awarded for meeting or exceeding expectations.

➤ In employee stock ownership programs (ESOPs), the major portion of the company stock is sold or given to employees so that they actually own the company.

Chapter 15

Benefits: They're Not Fringes Anymore

In This Chapter

➤ Social Security, unemployment insurance, and workers' comp

➤ Vacations and holidays

➤ How many sick days do I get?

➤ Health insurance versus HMOs—what's best?

➤ Accruing money for retirement

In most companies employees receive a wide variety of compensations in addition to the paycheck. These compensations used to be called "fringe benefits" because they were little extras given either voluntarily by a benevolent employer or negotiated as part of a union-management agreement. Today in almost all large organizations and in a good number of smaller firms, benefits are an integral part of the compensation package and in many cases, add up to a whopping portion of payroll costs. In the early 1940s, benefits accounted for about 4 percent of total compensation. Today, benefits account for about 33 percent of payroll outlays.

In addition, the benefits that a company offers play a major role in attracting qualified people and retaining employees. Administering the benefits programs has evolved from a minor clerical activity of the accounting department to a separate department or an HR function headed by a senior executive. In this chapter we'll examine some of the benefits provided by most companies—and a few unusual ones as well.

Are Benefits Required by Law?

Some people assume that when they take a job, the company will provide them with a variety of benefits including paid vacations, holidays, health care, life insurance, and pensions. It's not so! Except for a few mandatory benefits that we'll discuss in this section, companies have no legal obligation to provide many of the benefits that often are taken for granted. In this section we'll examine those benefits required by federal law.

Social Security

Before Social Security laws were passed, older employees who worked for firms with no pension plan (the great majority of organizations) either had to work indefinitely or they were terminated when the boss considered them too old. The Social Security Act of 1935 was passed to help these people.

The Social Security Act provides retirement benefits for persons 62 years and older. It also covers loss of earnings due to disability and provides insurance for dependents of deceased workers who were covered by the law. Even if an employee is eligible for full Social Security benefits, it is illegal to terminate him or her because of age—no matter how old that person is.

Tactical Tips

Managers should know the Social Security rules. A worker may retire with partial benefits at age 62. Retirement with full benefits starts at 65 for persons who were born in 1937 and earlier. Persons born after 1938 can retire with full benefits at age 65 and two months. The eligibility ages increase by two months per year of birth for people born in subsequent years until it reaches a maximum of 67 for people born in 1960 and later. People taking earlier retirement face similar changes in eligibility ages.

The employer and the employee share the cost of the premiums for Social Security on a 50/50 basis. You see it listed on your paycheck as FICA deduction. This is an obligatory benefit. All workers must be enrolled in the program and all companies must comply with the law. Neither a company nor an individual can choose to decline coverage.

There are some jobs or areas of employment that are not covered by Social Security. For example, railroad workers, federal employees, and some state employees are covered by their own programs and are exempt from Social Security coverage. People who are self-employed are covered by Social Security; however, as they are their own employers, they must pay the full premium.

Unemployment Insurance

In addition to the old age, disability, and survivor's insurance, employees covered by the Social Security Act are eligible for up to 26 weeks of unemployment insurance. Unlike the Social Security benefits, unemployment insurance is administered by the states—not the federal government. To qualify, the worker must have been laid off for lack of work or for reasons other than misconduct. Each state's laws determine the amount of unemployment compensation for workers in that state.

Workers' Compensation Insurance

Workers' compensation insurance covers the cost of treatment and loss of income due to work-related accidents and illnesses. In all states except New Jersey, South Carolina, and Texas, all employers are required to provide workers' compensation insurance. Companies can purchase this insurance from private insurance companies or, in most states, from a state-owned insurance facility.

Leaves Without Pay

As pointed out in Chapter 3, "Still More Laws," the Family and Medical Leave Act (FMLA) requires companies with 50 or more employees to provide to eligible employees as much as 12 weeks of unpaid leave in any 12-month period. Note that the company has no obligation to pay employees who take advantage of this act. However, some firms will give employees the option of using vacation, personal days, and in some cases, sick days for which they are paid before starting the unpaid leave period.

Time Off

As you read through the required benefits, you might have been surprised to notice what was not mentioned. Nothing was said about vacations, holidays, health care, and other benefits that most companies give. That's because, although most firms do provide them, they are not legally mandated. Let's look at some of these.

Vacations

There is no federal law that requires a company to offer vacations, either paid or unpaid—other than the FMLA discussed in the previous section. However, most companies do give paid vacations. There usually is a minimum amount of time on

Management Miscellany

The United States is one of the few industrial countries that does not mandate paid vacations. In Canada, the legal minimum vacation time is 10 days; in Japan, 19 days; in France, 25 days; and in Sweden, 30 days.

the job before a person is eligible for a vacation. This might range from a few months to a full year. One common method of determining the number of vacation days is a simple incremental policy; for example, one week of vacation after six months of employment, two weeks after one year, three weeks after five years, and so on.

More complex policies require employees to earn vacation days based on number of months employed the first year and then a set amount, such as ten days per year, after that. Often, additional vacation time is given to longer-term employees.

Paid Holidays

There are no required paid holidays for employees in the private sector under federal law (not the Fourth of July, Thanksgiving, or Christmas). There are laws that require paid holidays for employees of the federal and state governments. Banks are required to observe certain holidays—but for the rest of us, observing a holiday is either a voluntary decision by management or is the result of a labor-management agreement.

From a practical viewpoint, most companies do pay their employees for most or all of these standard holidays: New Year's Day, Labor Day, Martin Luther King Day, President's Day, Memorial Day, Independence Day, Columbus Day, Veteran's Day, Thanksgiving, and Christmas. Many union contracts add paid holidays such as the Friday after Thanksgiving; Good Friday; or, in older contracts, both Lincoln's and Washington's birthdays instead of President's Day.

Most companies have a policy that if a holiday falls on a Saturday or Sunday, it will be observed on the preceding Friday or the following Monday. Some companies have "floating holidays" to create long weekends when a holiday falls on a Tuesday or Thursday. Sometimes unions may negotiate to substitute a floating holiday for one that is specified in the contract. For example, the day after Thanksgiving instead of Veterans' Day.

There is no law requiring a company to pay a premium to employees who work on a holiday. However, to maintain employee morale, usually they either pay them regular pay plus a premium or give them another day off. Some union contracts require that people working on holidays be paid double their regular rate for those days.

Sick Days

Sick leave is a short-term salary continuation program for employees for nonjob-related illness or injury. To qualify for sick leave, the employee must be sick or injured.

Many companies ask for a physician's statement for absences longer than a few days. It's important that the sick leave policy be clearly understood by all employees.

There is no federal law requiring companies to provide paid sick leave for employees. However, most employers do have some form of sick leave policy. Most employers require that the employee be on the payroll for between three and six months to be eligible for sick leave. Generally, employers determine the number of sick days on an accrual basis; employees accrue sick days based on the number of days worked per month up to an annual maximum.

Most union contracts specify the number of sick days to be allowed employees. If there is no formal contract, the number of sick days is entirely up to management. Many companies use the accrual method similar to that used in setting vacation days. The average number of sick days offered in the private sector is between 6 and 12 days per year.

Several states require employers to provide *short-term disability insurance,* which pays 50 percent of the employee's salary during the period of disability (in New York State, maximum $170 per week) for 26 weeks per year. There are no laws requiring coverage for *long-term disability.*

Oh!

Meanings and Gleanings

Short-term disability insurance provides coverage by partially paying employees for loss of income due to nonjob-related illness or accident. Most policies begin coverage after the sick days are used up and expire after six months. **Long-term disability insurance** provides payment to partially cover loss of income for catastrophic illness or accident. Coverage commences at a specified time after the onset of the illness or accident and is continued until the time specified in the policy.

Suppose an employee doesn't get sick. What happens to his or her sick leave? In some companies, if the sick leave isn't used in the calendar or fiscal year, it's lost. Such a policy encourages workers to take every possible sick day. More enlightened organizations allow sick time to be accrued. If it's not used during the year it's added to the next year's allowance. In such cases, employees whose illness requires longer absences in a later year will have coverage when it is needed.

Another alternative is for companies to pay employees for unused sick leave at the end of a specified number of years or at retirement. This is a common practice in some government agencies. We often read of government employees getting several months of accumulated sick leave pay when they retire.

Personal Days

In addition to vacation and sick leave, some companies give employees additional paid time off to deal with personal matters. Employees need not explain the reason, but must give reasonable notice that they will not report on those days. Depending on the company, personal days might be accrued in the same way sick leave days are.

Health Care

As the cost of medical treatment, hospitalization, and prescription drugs keeps rising, health care is the one benefit that most people seek. From the employers' view, the cost of providing this benefit has increased so much that companies are constantly looking for ways to reduce this expense. For many years, companies have provided health care plans that cover medical, hospital, and surgical expenses. Today there are pressures from both unions and individual employees to add prescription drugs, dental, optical, and mental health benefits to the health care package.

According to the U.S. Chamber of Commerce, the employers' share of health care benefits represents 11.1 percent of payroll costs. This cost is increasing at more than twice the rate of increase in the cost of living index. This has become a major political issue and there is pressure in Congress for government to provide or help pay for health care policies.

Medical Indemnity Insurance

The typical health care policy is *medical indemnity insurance.* The premiums may be paid entirely by the company, or paid partially by the employer and partially by the employee. Employees are advised in writing just what is and is not covered by the policy. When an illness or accident occurs, the patient goes to his or her own physician. After the doctor visit, surgery, or hospitalization is completed the health care provider submits an invoice to the company. The company then refers it to the insurance carrier. Neither the company nor the insurance carrier has any control over the amount of money charged for the services performed. These costs have accelerated to an alarming degree over the past few years.

Meanings and Gleanings

Medical indemnity insurance is a policy that pays all or part of medical expenses incurred by a covered employee directly to the health care provider or by reimbursing the patient. **Health maintenance organizations (HMOs)** are organizations of physicians and other health care professionals that provide health care on a prepaid basis. HMOs generally emphasize preventive care and early intervention.

Health Maintenance Organizations (HMOs)

To reduce the cost of medical benefits, increasingly companies are turning to *health maintenance organizations* (*HMOs*) to handle health care. HMOs are organizations of physicians and other health care professionals that provide health care on a prepaid basis. HMOs generally emphasize preventive care and early intervention.

HMOs differ from medical indemnity insurance because it is the health provider that agrees to provide care rather than the insurance company. Theoretically, this eliminates the "middle man" and cuts costs.

However, as HMOs grew in the 1990s, insurance companies formed their own HMOs or purchased established organizations. Today most HMOs are owned or controlled by insurance companies.

In most HMOs the employee is required to use the services of doctors affiliated with the plan, go to hospitals or clinics that are associated with the group, and purchase drugs from affiliated pharmacies.

There are many advantages of companies using an HMO:

➤ Because HMO services are prepaid, employees of the company can receive regular medical care without concern about the cost. This can result in early detection of medical problems and should alleviate expensive treatment at a later time.

➤ HMOs have an incentive to encourage good health habits by providing members with exercise, nutrition, and stop-smoking programs.

➤ The administrative work, such as filing claims and other red tape is handled by the HMO.

➤ As most HMO doctors have evening and weekend hours, employees don't have to take time off from work for medical appointments.

However, there has been a good deal of criticism of HMOs, particularly since insurance companies have taken them over:

➤ Cost control often is a major factor in making medical decisions. Patients might not get proper care because the doctors often are rated by the HMO on their cost effectiveness rather than the medical effectiveness of their treatments.

➤ Patients may use only health care professionals that are members of the HMO. If they are not satisfied with the treatment, they can see other doctors in the group, including specialists—but only with a referral from their primary care physicians. No payments will be made by the HMO or the company for medical treatment (except in emergencies) to nonmember hospitals or physicians.

➤ Because of pressures to keep costs down, doctors delegate much of the examination to medical aides or nurses and spend minimal time with the patient.

All HMOs are not alike. Before a company chooses to use an HMO, it should check it out carefully. Speak to the managers of some of its clients, speak to patients who have used it, and visit the hospitals with which it is associated. Most important,

Management Miscellany

There are some variations to HMOs. For example, PPOs or preferred provider organizations are similar to HMOs, but members can select the physician from a loose confederation of health care professionals that are approved by the plan.

visit its offices and speak at length with doctors, nurses, and administrators about your company's needs, desires, and concerns.

Other Health Care Benefits

One of the rapidly growing additions to health care benefits has~~ ~~ dental care. Until the early 1990s, very few companies covered ~~ ~~ Even Medicare, which pays for most medical costs for older pe~~ ~~ cost of dental treatment. However, over the past decade, most~~ ~~ health care agreements have added dental coverage and many~~ ~~ tarily included it in their health indemnity policies or with th~~ ~~

Another innovation is coverage for optical care. Many policies ~~ ~~ exams and some payment for eyeglasses or contact lenses. Oth~~ ~~ added to many programs are audiological examinations and th~~ ~~

Shared Costs

In most health care policies the employee must pay a portion ~~of the cost~~ down between employer and employee charges varies considerably. In some compa~~ ~~ nies, the entire premium is paid by the organization for the employee and his or her family. In others, the company pays the premium for the employee, but the premiums for family members are shared with the employee. Most policies require co-payments by the patient—usually a small payment for each visit to the doctor or hospital, or for prescription drugs.

Life Insurance

Probably the oldest employee benefit is life insurance. Companies provide group life insurance policies to employees after they have been employed for a specific time period (usually six months). These policies often include coverage for accidents and permanent disabilities such as loss of limbs, eyesight, or hearing.

Retirement

As noted earlier in this chapter, most Americans can look forward to receiving Social Security benefits when they retire at age 62 or later. Many companies provide additional retirement benefits for their employees. There are several ways of providing retirement income; some of these follow.

Types of Pension Plans

Each company must determine the type of retirement coverage it wishes to provide for its employees and how it will be financed. Pension plans can be divided into contributory and noncontributory plans:

➤ In contributory plans the premiums are paid by both employers and employees on a basis determined by the plan. Often it's a 50/50 split; in others the company picks up most of the cost.

➤ In noncontributory plans the company pays the total premium. Until recently, most plans in the private sector were noncontributory but this is changing, particularly when the plans are replaced with 401(k) programs (to be discussed in the next section).

Another way to categorize plans is by method of payment:

➤ In a defined benefits plan the amount the employee is to receive as a pension is specifically stated. This amount usually is based on the employee's age at time of retirement, years of service, and average earnings during a specific period of time. The amount of his or her pension can be calculated from a formula that incorporates these factors.

➤ Defined contribution plans are based on the amount the employer will contribute to the pension fund. Unlike the defined benefits plans, the amount the employee receives on retirement is not a pre-established figure. It is based on the funds accumulated in the account at the time of retirement and the type of retirement benefits the fund will purchase. The retiree receives the amount accumulated in the fund and can choose to invest the proceeds in an annuity, buy mutual funds, or invest it some other way.

401(k): The Fast-Growing Pension Option

Recently, the most significant option offered for pension coverage is the tax-deferred savings plan named after Section 401(k) of the Internal Revenue code. More and more firms are offering this option. The 401(k) allows employees to save through payroll deductions. Employers might (but are not required to) match this amount. The amount employees save is not included in their taxable income. These earnings are deferred until after retirement. In most cases, full *vesting* comes after five

Meanings and Gleanings

Vesting refers to the percentage of an employee's benefit account that he or she is entitled to retain after leaving the company.

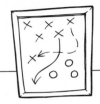

Tactical Tips

It's essential to retain professional help when setting up a 401(k) plan for your company. To do it right requires expertise in tax law and pension planning.

years. Once vested, if the employee leaves the company, he or she can roll over the account into another qualified plan—either another company's 401(k) or an IRA.

Many companies have changed their pension plans to 401(k)s or created 401(k) plans where no pension plan previously existed. It's cheaper to administer than standard pension plans, and as companies do not have to match the employees' contribution, might not cost anything other than administrative expenses.

Protecting Pension Rights

Unfortunately, there have been companies that have misused pension funds (either deliberately or because of poor management); their employees lost part or all of their pensions. There also have been cases of workers who were fired after many years of employment just before they became eligible for their pension. Some employees have lost their pensions when the companies they worked for went out of business.

To deal with such situations, Congress passed the Employee Retirement Income Security Act (ERISA). This act sets standards and controls for pension plans. It requires minimum funding standards to ensure that benefits will be available when an employee retires. It also protects employees by requiring provisions for vesting their funds.

Under ERISA, an employee is fully vested in a pension plan, 401(k), or other profit sharing or retirement income after five years; or may have the option of vesting 20 percent after three years, plus 20 percent per year thereafter. If an employee leaves the company before being vested, he or she is entitled to receive only the money he or she has contributed to the fund; not any matching funds. Once vested, employees must be paid the entire balance of the fund upon leaving the company.

The Least You Need to Know

➤ Social Security is an obligatory benefit. All workers must be enrolled in the program and all companies must comply with the law. Neither a company nor an individual can choose to decline coverage.

➤ Other obligatory benefits are unemployment insurance, workers' compensation, and unpaid time off for family emergencies.

➤ There usually is a minimum amount of time on the job before a person is eligible for vacation time. This might be from a few months to a full year.

➤ For an employee to be eligible for sick leave, most employers require that they be on the payroll for between three and six months. Most employers determine the number of sick days based on the number of days worked per month up to an annual maximum.

➤ Health care plans cover medical, hospital, and surgical expenses. Some plans also cover prescription drugs, dental, optical, and mental health benefits.

➤ To reduce the cost of medical benefits, more and more companies are turning to HMOs to handle health care. Before choosing an HMO, check it out carefully.

➤ Defined benefits plans are pension plans in which the amount of retirement pay is specifically stated and the amount the employer will contribute to the pension fund is established.

➤ A 401(k) plan allows employees to save through payroll deductions. Employers might (but are not required to) match this amount.

Personalizing the Benefits Package

In the previous chapter we discussed the several types of benefits that are provided by most large companies and many smaller ones. In addition to these, a variety of special benefits or "perks" are offered to meet the special needs of employees.

You might expect employees to know the benefits to which they are entitled. On the contrary, HR managers have found that many people assume they have benefits they do not have—and often they are not aware of those they do have. In this chapter we'll look at some additional benefits companies provide and some ways to communicate the benefits programs to employees.

Pensions

One area in which there is much misunderstanding is retirement benefits. When most companies had defined benefits plans, workers could easily figure out how much they would get when they retired. Now, with more and more companies using defined contribution plans and 401(k)s, this is much more confusing.

Management Miscellany

Information on employee benefits plans and methods of communicating them can be obtained from the International Foundation of Employee Benefits Plans, PO Box 69, Brookfield, WI 53008-0069; telephone 262-786-6700; fax 262-786-8670; Web site www.ifebp.org.

Meanings and Gleanings

There are two parts to **Medicare.** Part A covers hospital care and all persons who are covered by Medicare receive this benefit. Part B covers payment to doctors and other health care providers. This is optional and a fee is charged for this. (As of 2001, it is $600 per year.) As some people have this coverage through their employer's policies, and retain this after retirement, they may opt to decline Part B coverage.

The Employee Retirement Income Security Act (ERISA) requires that all companies inform their employees about their pensions and other benefits. This information must be provided in language that can be clearly understood by the average worker. This means it should be free from the legalistic gobbledygook that often is printed in insurance policies and pension documents.

One way of doing this is writing special benefits booklets, publishing articles in the company newsletter, or posting the information to the company intranet. New employees should be given careful orientation about the benefits and have the opportunity to have their questions answered clearly. It's also a good idea to give each employee periodic statements of the current status of his or her benefits. A member of the HR Department or a benefits specialist should be available to counsel employees and explain benefits.

Health Plans

With the climbing costs of health care, many companies are reexamining their health care benefit plans. This close examination often results in changing of carriers, affiliating with an HMO, or in some cases dropping the plans altogether. These changes must be clarified to employees in adequate time for them to make decisions based on the changes. For example, when Irving's company moved from a medical indemnity plan to an HMO, he was required to pay an additional premium to cover his children. Because he was informed of this change he could arrange for his wife to put the children on her company's plan.

Another common change affects coverage after retirement. Many plans provided continuing coverage for all retired employees, even though they were eligible for *Medicare.* As many of these plans provided for drugs, dental, and other benefits, it was better for the retiree to keep this policy as primary coverage, rather than enroll in Part B of Medicare. To save costs, many companies no longer cover retirees once they become eligible for Medicare. It's imperative that this be made clear to employees before retirement so they can take the necessary steps to make Medicare their primary coverage.

Cafeteria Plans

One growing trend is to give employees a choice of benefits. For example, a young, unmarried worker has different needs from those of a 40-year-old father of a large family, a single mother, or an older person close to retirement. By placing a dollar value on the benefits package, the employee can choose among several options to create the best package for himself or herself. This often is referred to as a "cafeteria plan."

Typically, workers are offered a core benefits package of life and health insurance, sick leave, personal and vacation days, plus a set amount of credits that can be applied to other benefits. For example, Mary chose a day-care program for her daughter, Sam used his credits for additional personal days, Sandra used hers for tuition reimbursement, and so on.

Employee Assistance Programs

Although not usually listed among the benefits or perks, an employee assistance program, or EAP, can be a very helpful benefit for employees. An EAP is a company-sponsored counseling service. Many companies have instituted these programs to help employees deal with personal problems that interfere with productivity. The counselors aren't company employees; they are outside experts retained by the company on an as-needed basis.

Management Miscellany

Today, 66 percent of companies surveyed by the Society for Human Resource Management have employee assistance programs, many of which are expanding their services to handle a wider range of issues than ever before.

What EAPs Cover

Employees with problems that interfere with their work should be encouraged to use the facilities of the EAP to help them cope. EAPs offer a variety of services. Experts in various areas are available as resources so that if an employee needs additional help, he or she can be referred to a qualified specialist.

Some of these areas are ...

➤ **Legal services** These usually cover such things as preparing legal documents—wills, real estate transactions, routine legal matters, and so forth. They also might provide legal advice on divorce, civil, or criminal cases. They do not usually represent employees in litigation.

➤ **Financial counseling** They help employees who are in debt to work out payment plans with their creditors, develop budgets, and live within their income.

➤ **Marriage and family counseling**   Psychologists or social workers are able to help employees work out personal problems. This type of situation is one of those most frequently brought to EAPs.

➤ **Alcohol and drug problems**   EAP counselors are trained to help employees deal with addiction. They may refer employees to special counselors, suggest that they participate in Alcoholics Anonymous, or other rehabilitation programs.

Working with the EAP

Use of the EAP can be initiated in one of two ways. In the first option the company informs its employees about the program through e-mail, bulletins, announcements in the company newsletter, meetings, and letters to their homes. Often, a hotline telephone number also is provided. Knowing that he or she has access to this program, the employee initiates contact with the company's EAP to address a problem.

For instance, let's say one of your employees, Greta, believes she needs help. Constant squabbling with her teenage daughter has made her tense, angry, and frustrated. In a brief telephone interview with her company's EAP, the screening counselor identifies Greta's problem and refers her to a family counselor. Greta makes her own appointment on her own time. Because the entire procedure is confidential, no report is made to the company about the counseling (in most cases, not even the names of people who undertake counseling are divulged).

In the other option the supervisor or team leader suggests to the employee that he or she contact the EAP. For instance, suppose the work performance of one of your top performers has recently declined. You often see him sitting idly at his desk, his thoughts obviously far from his job. You ask him what's going on, but he shrugs off your question by saying, "I'm okay, just tired." After several conversations, he finally tells you about a family problem, and you suggest that he contact the company's EAP.

Management Miscellany

EAPs aren't new. They began in the 1940s as alcohol rehabilitation programs, created by companies to protect large investments in skilled employees whose work suffered because of alcohol addiction. The success of these programs led to their expansion to the present-day function of dealing with a variety of personal problems.

Even though you've suggested the referral and the employee has followed through, don't expect progress reports. From now on, the matter is handled confidentially. Your feedback comes from seeing improvement in the employee's work as the counseling helps with the problem.

Employee assistance programs are expensive to maintain, but organizations that have used them for several years report that they pay off. Good employees are hard to find and well worth keeping. EAPs salvage skilled and experienced workers who, without help, might leave a company.

Those "Little" Extras—Perks

In many companies employees are given perks—those little extras that might not seem like much, but often are significant additions to the traditional compensation package. Why do perks motivate people? Why not give the employees cash bonuses and let them purchase or lease their own car, pay their own dues to the country club, or buy what they wish?

Companies have found that most employees like receiving perks. If they did get a cash equivalent, they probably would use it to pay bills or fritter it away. Perks keep reminding them that the company is giving them something. Every time they step into the company car, it reinforces their loyalty to the company. Every time they pass the day-care bill to the accounting department, they thank the company for taking that burden off them.

Perks should not be confused with benefits. Benefits such as pensions, health care, and life insurance are part of the compensation package. Today almost all large companies provide these standard benefits. Perks usually are add-ons to make life more pleasant for employees. Here are some of the more commonly provided perks:

➤ Coffee/snacks and subsidized lunchrooms

➤ Memberships in professional associations

➤ Subscriptions to professional and technical journals

➤ Membership in social clubs and company cars

➤ Child care and elder care

➤ Tuition and scholarships and charter schools

➤ Flextime and casual dress days

➤ Birthday celebrations and pets at work

➤ Exercise and recreation rooms

➤ Financial counseling and banking

➤ Laundry facilities and concierge services

Management Miscellany

Some of the more unusual chores reported by some companies include bringing employees' cars to be serviced, arranging pet care, waiting at an employee's home for a repairman to come, making arrangements for weddings and parties, and locating hard-to-find collectibles.

There's nothing unusual about these perks. Most of them have been used for some time. To meet and beat the competition for top-level employees, some companies have stretched their imaginations and developed innovative perks. Don't just copy what other companies do to add perks to your buffet; talk with your employees to determine their real interests. What might work for one group might not be effective in another.

Do keep in mind, though, that when business goes bad and companies look for cost savings, one of the first things to go are the perks. If you must cut perks, don't eliminate them entirely. Survey your people to see which perks are most important to them and which you can eliminate with the least amount of discontent. Make your decisions accordingly.

The Least You Need to Know

➤ ERISA requires that all companies inform employees about their pensions and other benefits in easily understood language.

➤ In "cafeteria benefits plans," employees can choose among several options to select the package that is best for them.

➤ Employee assistance programs, or EAPs, are company-sponsored counseling services created to help employees deal with personal, family, and financial problems.

➤ Just as benefits add to the compensation package, perks provide financial advantages and convenience that express the company's concern for its employees. Learn what your employees find helpful. Create your own perk buffet.

Part 5

Day to Day on the Job

As a manager, you have to face the daily tasks of seeing that your staff performs at optimum capacity. To do this you must be a leader. A good leader is a person who inspires his or her team members to do the very best to meet shared objectives on the job.

Good leaders motivate their people. Having a motivated staff might seem to be an ideal situation—but it is achievable. Doing this should be the primary goal of all managers, team leaders, and supervisors.

However, motivating people is just one step in running a successful department. No matter how good a leader you are, you'll probably have to deal with employee problems such as absenteeism and tardiness, and employees who are stressed or have difficult personalities. You might be faced with complaints of sexual or racial harassment. You also are responsible for seeing that the working environment meets the standards of safety and health laws. All these and more will be discussed in the following chapters.

Chapter 17

Incorrect.

Motivating Your Staff for Peak Performance

In This Chapter

➤ Understanding that people are people—not cogs in a machine

➤ Recognizing achievement

➤ Making praise effective

➤ Putting your praise in writing

➤ Honoring team accomplishments

Whether your company works on a team basis or uses the traditional supervisor/ subordinate format, managers should consider their employees as a team. As a supervisor or team leader, your job is to meld your team members into a cohesive group and help them to develop the motivation to reach the team's goals. Successful managers start the process of developing team spirit by taking the time to get to know each of their employees as individuals. Team members are humans—not robots—each with his or her strengths and weaknesses, personal agenda, and style of working. Learning and understanding each person's individualities are the first steps toward building a motivated team, and the topic of this chapter.

Different Strokes for Different Folks

Maybe you think that all you really have to know about your associates is the quality of their work. Wrong! Knowing the people with whom you work requires more than just knowing their job skills. Sure, that's an important part, but it's only a part of their total makeup. Learn what's important to each person—his or her ambitions and goals, family, special concerns—in other words, what makes each of them tick.

Getting to Know Your Associates

The best way to get to know anybody is to talk with them, ask questions, and get their opinions on various matters. Maybe you think that this is too intrusive; you don't want to be nosy. Okay, you don't have to ask personal questions directly. By observing and listening, you can learn a great deal about your colleagues.

When they speak to you, listen to what they say—and to what they don't say. Listen when they speak to others—eavesdropping might not be polite, but you can learn a great deal. Observe how your team members do their work and how they act and react. It doesn't take long to identify their likes and dislikes, their quirks and eccentricities. By observing, you can learn about the things that are important to each of them and the "hot buttons" that turn them on or off.

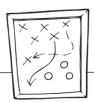

Tactical Tips

Encourage your associates to express their ideas, especially when they differ from yours. Their disagreements not only provide you with new ideas; they give you insight into the ways in which your employees approach problems. This knowledge will help you to work more effectively with them.

By observing and listening, you might realize that Claudia is a creative person. If you want to excite her about her role in an assignment, you can do so by appealing to her creativity. You notice that Mike is slow when he's learning new things but after he learns them, he works quickly and accurately. To allow Mike to do his best, you know that you'll need patience.

It's easy to remember these individual characteristics when you supervise a small number of people. However, if you're involved with larger groups or have high turnover in your department, it's not so easy. You need help. Keeping track of the following items for each of your team members can help you keep an informal reminder of their traits:

➤ Spouse's name/children's names and ages

➤ Hobbies and interests

➤ Schools and colleges

➤ Specific behavioral traits

People Crave Recognition

Human beings crave recognition. People like to know that others know who they are, what they want, and what they believe. Recognition begins when you learn and use people's names. Of course you know the names of the men and women on your team; but you also will coordinate work with other teams, internal and external suppliers, subcontractors, and customers. Everyone has a name. Learn them. Use them. It's your first step in recognizing each person's individuality.

When Seth quit his job with the Building Maintenance Company, he was asked what he liked most and least about the company. Seth responded that, although the salary and benefits were good, he never felt that he was part of the organization. "I always felt that I was looked at as nothing more than a cog in the machine," he said. "During the nine months I worked in the department, I made several suggestions, offered to take on extra projects, and tried to apply creative approaches to some of the work assigned to me. My boss didn't recognize the talents I could have contributed."

One of the basic human needs is that of being recognized as an individual. Even if the manager disagreed with Seth's suggestion, discussing it, explaining why it wasn't accepted and encouraging future creative ideas would have solidified the relationship between the two of them.

Providing Positive Reinforcement

An autocratic boss continually criticizes, condemns, and complains; and never forgets negative performance. However, he or she always takes good performance for granted. When people hear continual criticism, they begin to feel stupid, inferior, and resentful. Although someone might have done something that wasn't satisfactory, your objective is to correct the behavior; not to make the person feel bad. Managers today are more aware of the value of reinforcing the good things their associates do rather than harping on mistakes and inefficiencies.

The famous psychologist B.F. Skinner noted that criticism often reinforces poor behavior (the only time an offender gets attention is when he or she is being criticized). He recommended that we minimize our reaction to poor behavior and maximize our appreciation of good behavior. Rather than bawl out a person for doing something wrong, quietly say, "You're making some progress in the work, but we still have a long way to go. Let me show you some ways to do it more rapidly." When the work does improve, make a big fuss over it.

Tactical Tips

By focusing on positive things, by giving attention and appreciation to the good things people do, you reinforce their desire to "do the right thing." You also help build their self-image and spur positive thoughts, which help develop a positive attitude.

Showing That You Care

Just as you have a life outside the company, so does every member of your group. A job is an important part of our lives, but there are many aspects of life that are of greater importance: health, family, outside interests, and so on. Show sincere interest in each of your employees as a total person.

197

For example, Virginia, the head teller of a savings and loan association in Wichita, Kansas makes a point of welcoming back associates who have been on vacation or out for several days because of illness. She asks them about their vacation or the state of their health and brings them up to date on company news. She makes them feel that she missed them—and it comes across sincerely because she means what she says.

Everyone Needs Praise—But What If It's Not Deserved?

Human beings thrive on praise. Praise helps feed our egos and makes us feel good about ourselves. However, you can't praise people indiscriminately. Praise should be reserved for accomplishments that are worthy of special acknowledgment. How can you sincerely praise someone who hasn't done anything particularly praiseworthy?

Maria faced this situation in her group of word processors. Several marginal operators had the attitude that, as long as they met their quotas, they were doing okay. When they were praised for meeting quotas, it only reinforced their belief that nothing more was expected of them. Criticism of their failure to surpass the quota was greeted with the response "I'm doing my job."

Maria decided to try positive reinforcement. She gave one of the operators a special assignment for which no production quota had been set. When the job was completed, Maria praised the employee's fine work. She followed this practice with all new assignments and eventually had the opportunity to sincerely praise each of the word processors.

Look for Praiseworthy Situations

You might tend to look for things to criticize rather than things to compliment. Because you expect your group to perform well, you concentrate on strengthening areas of weakness. Douglas, a regional supervisor for a California supermarket chain, made regular visits to the eight stores under his jurisdiction. He reported that when he went into a store he looked for problems. He criticized store managers for the way products were displayed, for slow-moving checkout lines, and anything else he noticed. "That's my job," he said, "to make sure that everything is being done correctly."

As you can guess, everyone working in the stores dreaded his visits. When Douglas's boss discussed this problem with him, she agreed that it was important to improve what was wrong. However, she also pointed out that, because the stores exceeded

198

sales-volume forecasts and kept costs down, the managers needed to hear compliments on their successes. She suggested that Douglas seek out good things and express his approval. Douglas was encouraged to continue to make suggestions for improvements, but not to make them the focus of his visits.

Although it wasn't easy, Douglas followed his boss's advice. Within a few months, store managers looked forward to his visits. They began to share new ideas and seek his counsel about store issues. Clerks and other store staffers soon overcame their fear of the "big boss" and welcomed his comments and suggestions.

Personnel Perils

Beware of overpraising. When you praise every little thing, you dilute the power of praise. Save it for significant improvements, exceptional accomplishments, and special efforts.

Five Tips for Effective Praising

As important as praise is in motivating people, it doesn't always work. Some supervisors praise every minor activity, diminishing the value of praise for real accomplishments. Others deliver praise in such a way that it seems phony. To make your praise more meaningful, follow these suggestions.

➤ **Don't overdo it.** Praise is sweet. Candy is sweet, too, but the more you eat, the less sweet each piece becomes—and you might get a stomachache. Too much praise reduces its benefit—or loses its value altogether.

➤ **Be sincere.** You can't fake sincerity. You must truly believe that what you're praising your associate for is actually commendable. If you don't believe it yourself, neither will your associate—you come across as phony.

➤ **Be specific about the reason for your praise.** Rather than saying, "Great job!" it's much better to say, "The report you submitted on the XYZ matter enabled me to understand more clearly the complexities of the issue."

➤ **Ask your associates for advice.** Nothing is more flattering than to be asked for advice about how to handle a situation. However, this approach can backfire if you don't take the advice. If you don't agree with the employee's suggestion, rather than rejecting it outright, ask questions about it that will enable the person who suggested it to see its inadequacies.

➤ **Publicize praise.** Just as a reprimand should always be given in private, praising should be done (whenever possible) in public. Unless the praiseworthy matter is a private issue, it's often appropriate to let the entire group in on the praise. If other employees are aware of the praise you give a colleague, it spurs them to work for similar recognition.

In some cases, praise for significant accomplishments is extremely public, such as when it's given at meetings or company events. The Mary Kay cosmetics company is known for its policy of giving recognition to associates who have accomplished outstanding performance. In addition to receiving awards and plaques, award winners are feted at company conventions and publicized in the company magazine. Attending a Mary Kay convention is similar to attending a victory celebration. Winners are called to the stage and presented with their awards to the cheers and applause of an audience. Award winners report that recognition from senior executives and acclaim from peers is as rewarding as the award itself.

"Look What the Boss Gave Me"

Telling people that you appreciate what they've done is a great idea, but writing it is even more effective. The aura of oral praise fades away; a letter or even a brief note endures. You don't have to spend much money. It doesn't take much time. Let's look at how writing the praise has worked for some managers.

Thank-You Cards

At the A&G Merchandising Company in Wilmington, Delaware, supervisors are given packets of thank-you cards on which "Thank You" is printed in beautiful script on the front flap; the inside of the card is left blank. Whenever someone does something worthy of special recognition, that person's manager writes a note on one of the cards detailing the special accomplishment and congratulating the employee for achieving it. The recipients cherish the cards and show them to friends and family.

Something to Hang on the Wall

No matter what type of award you give to employees—large or small (cash, merchandise, tickets to a show or sports event, or a trip to a resort, for example)—it's worth spending a few more dollars to include a certificate or plaque. Employees love to hang these mementos in their cubicles or offices, over their workbenches, or in their homes. The cash gets spent, the merchandise wears out, the trip becomes a long-past memory; but a certificate or plaque is a permanent reminder of the recognition.

Keep a Success File or Journal

Alberta, the sales manager of a large real-estate office in Florida, makes a practice of sending letters of appreciation to sales staffers who do something special.

Accomplishments include selling a property that has been difficult to move, obtaining sales rights to a profitable building, or taking creative steps to make a sale.

With the first of these letters that she sends to a salesperson, Alberta encloses a file folder labeled "Success File" with this suggestion: "File the enclosed letter in this folder. Add to it any other commendatory letters you receive from me, other managers, clients, or anyone else. As time goes on, you might experience failures or disappointments. There might be times when you don't feel good about yourself. When this happens, reread these letters. They're the proof that you're a success, that you have capability, that you are a special person. You did it before; you can do it again!"

The recipients of Alberta's letters repeatedly tell her how rereading the letters helps them to overcome sales slumps, periods of depression, and general disenchantment when things aren't going well. It "reprograms" their psyche by reinforcing their self-esteem and enables them to face problems with new strength and confidence.

Unfortunately, many accomplishments won't be recognized by a letter. Yet they, too, are successes you might wish to remember. Suggest to your people that they add to their success files a journal in which they can enter these achievements. This adds to the list of successes to reflect on when morale sinks and a lift is needed.

Effective Recognition Programs

Any form of sincere recognition can be effective—some, for short periods of time; others, much longer. Recognition programs that affect the entire organization usually are developed and administered by the human resources department. Managers participate in implementing the programs in their teams or units. But even if there's no company-wide program, with a little imagination and initiative, you can create your own.

Employee of the Month

Choosing an associate every month for special recognition probably is the most popular form of formal recognition program. The method of choosing employees and deciding which rewards and recognition to offer vary from company to company. Following are some of the methods used in running an employee-of-the-month program:

➤ **Selection**   In most companies, each team leader or department head nominates candidates for an award. A committee weighs the contributions of each candidate and chooses the winner. In some organizations, peers make nominations in each department and, increasingly, employees are encouraged to make a nomination by writing a note or filling out a form. The committee makes its choice by comparing the nominees against a list of criteria and against each other.

➤ **Awards**   Awards vary from company to company. The most frequently awarded prizes are cash, a day off with pay, or merchandise.

➤ **Recognition** Almost all companies with employee-of-the-month programs have a plaque prominently displayed on which the winners' names are engraved. A photo of the winner also might be displayed during the month. In addition, individual certificates or plaques are given to monthly winners. In some companies the employee of the month is given a preferred parking space. Awards often are presented at luncheons to which all nominees for that month are invited. The winner often is interviewed for an article in the company newsletter and press releases are sent to local newspapers, radio, and TV stations.

As with anything else, there are drawbacks to the employee-of-the-month program. Here are a few:

➤ **Resentment** Some people might believe they are more suited for the award than the winner and resent not being chosen. Resentment and envy are difficult to overcome—but there will always be unhappy losers.

➤ **Overexposure** After a while any monthly program can become overdone. It's difficult to maintain excitement and enthusiasm month after month.

➤ **Lack of team recognition** When people work in teams, individual efforts are subordinate to team efforts. When recognition belongs to a team, no single member of that team should be singled out for recognition. In order to encourage teamwork, some companies minimize commenting on individual achievements. The assumption is that successes are the result of team action and what any one team member does is augmented by the others. Praise and recognition is reserved for the team.

Team Recognition

When individual commendation is undesirable, companies have instituted team recognition programs. One such company is Xerox. In its successful program, individuals receive awards for special achievement but, to encourage teamwork, recognition also is given to teams. These awards include honors to teams that perform outstanding work and special recognition to teams for "excellence in customer satisfaction."

Another way in which Xerox recognizes teams is by holding an annual Teamwork Day. On the first Teamwork Day, held in 1983 in a company cafeteria in Webster, New York, 30 teams showed off various projects. They received no rewards or cash; just thank yous. A combination of word-of-mouth and a company newsletter article helped ensure the participation of 60 teams the following year and an audience of 500 visitors.

In the third year of Teamwork Day, hundreds of teams wanted to participate, but there was room for only 200 (1,000 people attended the exhibits). In the fourth year the company rented the convention center in Rochester, New York and 5,000 people attended. In its fifth year, the program expanded internationally; teamwork fairs were held in Rochester, Dallas, London, Amsterdam, and elsewhere. Teamwork Day now is a highly anticipated annual event.

Peer Recognition

In the total quality management movement (TQM), the commitment to work toward continuing improvement of quality has made every member of a team more aware of the importance of customer satisfaction. One way that companies can increase this awareness is by considering other employees with whom they interact as *internal customers* or *internal suppliers.*

Encourage your associates to recognize any special achievements of their internal suppliers, and any special assistance an internal customer receives that enables him or her to serve more effectively. Supervisors, managers, and team leaders aren't the only people who see the special efforts their associates make. All team members and co-workers are exposed daily to each other's efforts. Enabling them to recognize the work of peers brings to the forefront any accomplishments that might not have been recognized by managers. It also makes both the nominator and the nominee feel that they are part of an integrated, interrelated, and caring organization.

Meanings and Gleanings

An **internal customer** is a member of your team or another team to whom you provide materials, information, or services. An **internal supplier** is another person in your organization who provides you with materials, information, or services. You might be a "customer" in some aspects of your work and a "supplier" in others.

Minicircuit Labs, which has plants in Brooklyn, New York and Hialeah, Florida, encourages this concept by providing all its members with a "You made my day" form. The form indicates who did what and what it meant to that person. The form then is sent to the supervisor or manager of the department and to the human resources department.

Special Awards for Special Achievements

At the Mary Kay cosmetics company, the highest and most coveted award is the famous pink Cadillac. To win one of these cars, salespeople must meet a series of challenges. It's not easy to win the award, but every year more Mary Kay associates make the grade.

Mary Kay doesn't give the cars away; the cars are lent to them for one year. Anyone who wants to keep a car or upgrade to the next year's model must continue to meet the standards. What an incentive to keep up the good work! As a result, relatively few winners have to give up their cars.

Management Miscellany

ABCD awards are given for performance that's truly above and beyond the call of duty. This type of special recognition pays off in continued efforts to achieve superior performance.

In some organizations, special awards are given, not as part of a formal program, but on a manager's initiative. During the pre-Thanksgiving rush at Stew Leonard's food market in Norwalk, Connecticut several office personnel noticed the long, creeping lines at checkout counters. With no prompting from management, they left their regular work duties to help cashiers bag the groceries, which helped speed up the lines.

Stew, the owner of the market, resolved to do something special for the employees who helped out. After the holiday rush was over, he bought each of the employees a beautifully knitted shirt with the embroidered inscription "Stew Leonard ABCD Award." The inscription stands for "above and beyond the call of duty." By giving special recognition to associates who did more than their jobs require, he not only gave credit where credit was due; he let everyone know that he appreciated the extra effort.

Motivating Off-Site Employees

There is a rapidly growing number of telecommuters, independent subcontractors, and others who do most of their work away from the central facility. Motivating these people and keeping them from feeling like outsiders is a challenge for managers. Here are a few suggestions to keep these individuals motivated:

➤ Schedule meetings either monthly or bimonthly with all employees working on a project. If the people are scattered all over the country, it might be more feasible to hold the regional meetings at a convenient location. This enables them to get to know each other and to kick around ideas face to face. It also builds up a feeling of community among them and a closer relationship to the company. They don't feel left out.

➤ Encourage managers to telephone off-site people on a regular basis. Frequent but brief calls to touch base and occasional conference calls to the entire project team solidify team spirit.

➤ People working off site should be invited periodically to come to the home office to meet with staff. The personal contacts between on-site and off-site employees build up feelings of belonging.

➤ Managers should make periodic visits to the locations where off-site people work.

➤ Send a weekly newsletter to all off-site people, telling them about the latest developments in the company. Make it newsy, and include human-interest stories about employees. In addition to or instead of a newsletter, provide a Web site that is updated daily to keep everybody current on company activities. Add some humor. Make it a site they'd want to read every day. Be sure that all telecommuters are on the company intranet so they are aware of and can comment on all the same information that people working on company premises receive.

The Least You Need to Know

➤ By showing sincere interest in each of your associates, you establish a climate that's conducive to cooperation and team spirit.

➤ Provide positive reinforcement by seeking out and praising accomplishments instead of concentrating on faults that need correction.

➤ To make praise truly sincere, specify the reason for the praise.

➤ Put your appreciation in writing. Brief notes, letters of commendation, and certificates of achievement give long-term value to the act of praising.

➤ Create ongoing programs to recognize the achievements of individuals and teams. Find original ways to keep these programs exciting and rewarding.

➤ Don't ignore your off-site employees. Recognize that they are an integral part of your team.

Chapter 18

Employee of the month gets to drive the Giant Robot.

Building Motivation into the Job

In This Chapter

➤ Making a job more worker friendly

➤ Redesigning job content

➤ Motivators that work

➤ Fear as a motivator

➤ Career pathing as a motivator

➤ Empowering employees

Remember Frederic Herzberg's research on what motivates people (see Chapter 14, "The Compensation Conundrum")? He asserted that it takes real motivators to inspire people to extend themselves on the job. These include recognition, control over one's own work, and gaining satisfaction from the job. In this chapter we'll explore how these motivational factors can be built right into the job itself.

Enjoy Your Work

If you enjoy your work, if the job gives you satisfaction, if you can't wait to go to work every morning and hate to leave each evening, there's no need for any other type of motivation. Are there such jobs? Although many new jobs in growth industries have the ingredients for enjoyment and satisfaction, a large number of jobs are routine, dull, and sometimes tedious. It's difficult—if not impossible—to generate excitement about these jobs.

One way to make dull jobs more "worker friendly" is to redesign them. Rather than looking at a job as a series of tasks that must be performed, study it as a total process. Make the job less routine by enlarging the scope of the job. Focus on what has to be accomplished rather than on the steps leading to its accomplishment. You can do all of this by redesigning the manner in which the job is performed.

Try looking at each of the jobs you supervise from the viewpoint of the person performing it—not just for efficiency in performance, but as a vehicle for using his or her talents and creative powers. The following sections have some ideas for accomplishing this.

Management Miscellany

"No one likes to feel that he or she is being sold something or told to do something. We much prefer to feel we are buying of our own accord or acting on our own ideas. We like to be consulted about our wishes, our wants, our thoughts."

—Dale Carnegie

Involving Everyone in Planning

There are many types of work for which production quotas are established. Word processing operators are given the number of letters they must complete each day; production workers are given hourly quotas; salespeople must meet monthly standards. Management usually sets these quotas. Most workers don't like having quotas imposed on them. Worse yet, if management wants to raise quotas, employees are resentful and resistant.

A solution is to have your staff participate in setting quotas for their own jobs. You might think that they'll set low quotas that are easy to meet, and this might happen. That's why the process is *participatory*. As a manager, you don't step out of the picture completely; you are one of the participants. Your role is to ensure that realistic goals are set. In most cases people do set reasonable quotas; because it's their goal, they accept it and work to achieve it.

Motivators That Work Well

There's a great deal of controversy over what motivates people most effectively. From my many years of working with both managers and employees on motivation problems, I have culled the following as some of the best techniques for motivating people to commit themselves to superior performance:

➤ Encourage participation in setting goals and determining how to reach them.

➤ Keep all employees aware of how their jobs relate to others.

➤ Provide all employees with the tools and training necessary to succeed.

➤ Pay employees at least the going rate for jobs within their fields.

➤ Provide good, safe working conditions.

➤ Give clear directions that are easily understood and accepted.

➤ Know each person's abilities and give assignments based on the ability to handle those assignments.

➤ Allow people to make decisions related to their jobs.

➤ Be accessible. Listen actively and empathically.

➤ Give credit and praise for a job well done.

➤ Give prompt and direct answers to questions.

➤ Treat employees fairly; with respect and consideration.

➤ Help out with work problems.

➤ Encourage employees to acquire additional knowledge and skills.

➤ Show interest and concern for people as individuals.

➤ Learn what motivates each employee and deal with him or her accordingly.

➤ Make each person an integral part of the team.

➤ Keep people challenged and excited by their work.

➤ Consider your team members' ideas and suggestions.

➤ Keep people informed about how they're doing on the job.

➤ Encourage your people to do their best and support their efforts.

You can determine the greatest motivators for the people you supervise by getting feedback on the various approaches you use and revising your methods based on your findings.

Avoiding Negative Motivation

Sometimes threatening to fire people if they don't work is effective—at least temporarily. When jobs are scarce and people know that they won't have a job if they get fired, they do the work. But how much work do they do? Some folks work just enough to keep from getting fired—and not one bit more.

Fear of being fired isn't real motivation; real motivation spurs people to produce more than just what's necessary to keep their jobs. Additionally, fear of being fired becomes less a motivator as the job market expands. If comparable jobs are available in more amenable environments, why work for a tyrant?

Yet, there are people who do respond to negative motivation. Maybe they've been raised by intimidating parents or have worked under tyrannical bosses for so long that it's the only way of life they understand. Good leaders must recognize each person's individualities and adapt the motivators they use to what works best for him or her.

Career Pathing—A Motivator for the Ambitious

Not everybody is interested in promotion. Lots of workers are happy to just do their jobs, get their annual raises, and not worry about taking on added responsibilities. For these people, offering opportunity for advancement is not a motivator. However, if a person is ambitious and looks forward to moving ahead in the company, opportunity for advancement can be a major motivator.

This is not necessarily a negative factor. Such people can be the rock foundation of a company. They are trading advancement and raises for their preferred lifestyle. This is common for some older workers, and is more and more prevalent among young parents who opt to devote more time to their growing families.

Meanings and Gleanings

To promote the careers of employees and meet expanding needs, companies have instituted **career pathing** programs. Employees are assessed to determine their potential and the steps they must take to move up in the company. They are placed on a career path to positions that will be of greatest value to the company—and to themselves.

Some companies have formalized their advancement strategies by identifying promotable people early in their careers and working with them to enhance their capabilities. A good example is Kevin, an employee of Southeast Utilities. When he was hired, Kevin went through a series of evaluations and was assigned to a training program. When the program was completed, he was assigned to a team in the technical support department. Over the first few years he was given progressively more important assignments and did very well in each of them.

At his third annual performance review, he was informed that because of his excellent record, he was chosen to participate in the company's *career pathing* program. This program served a dual purpose: It gave top-level employees the opportunity to advance and ensured that the expanding needs of the company would be met. Each year several men and women are selected to be assessed and trained to move up the corporate ladder.

The first step in this process was to report to an assessment center where Kevin was given a series of tests and interviews. He also participated in interactive exercises with other participants. After the results were analyzed, he met with the career pathing team of the HR department to discuss its findings, his own ambitions, and the opportunities available in the company.

The HR staff told Kevin there were many opportunities in the organization for a person with his talents and suggested several areas he should consider for his career path. They pointed out that to become better equipped for growth within the company, he should acquire more knowledge in the information technology areas and develop managerial skills.

To start the ball rolling, he was advised to sign up for an advanced computer training program. When he completed this successfully, he would be transferred to a position in the IT department where he could hone these skills. In addition, to prepare him for eventual promotion to management, he was counseled to enroll in an MBA program at the local university under the company's tuition reimbursement plan.

Career pathing programs take much time and effort on the parts of both the management and the selected employees. They pay off in building a highly motivated group of potential managers. To make the career pathing program even more effective, assign a mentor to each "career pather"—a senior manager to guide him or her over the bumps and hurdles.

The Power of Empowerment

When you read about or attend meetings on motivation, the one word that almost always pops up is "empowerment." You're told that if you empower people they will be motivated. What exactly does that mean? Empowerment means sharing your power with the people over whom you have power. Team members are given the authority to make decisions that previously were reserved for managers.

This is easier said than done. Some leaders don't want to give up their power—and some people don't want to take the responsibility that goes with power. Let's look at empowerment as a motivating factor.

Who Got the Power?

In most companies, power is in the hands of management. In a typical hierarchy, the power flows downward from the CEO through the layers of management. Each layer has power over the one beneath it. Your boss gives you an assignment; you look it over, determine how it should be done, and assign various components of the job to your subordinates. Your job is to follow it through until it's completed.

Empowerment changes this process. You share with your staff the power to make decisions about an assignment. Rather than telling each person what to do, you work together to plan and execute the entire project.

The concept of empowerment isn't entirely new. For years companies have engaged in a variation called participative management. Empowerment carries participation one step further. Team members not only participate in decision making; they are authorized to make decisions on their own without seeking approval from higher-level managers.

Here's an example of empowerment at work: The installation of a new sprinkler system at the Woodbury Golf Club was the biggest job that All-Star Landscaping had ever received. Bill, the owner/manager, had just attended a management seminar on empowerment and thought that this project was a good chance to put into practice what he had learned in the course.

Tactical Tips

To create enthusiasm and commitment on a job, get the people who will do the job involved in planning it.

A few weeks before the job was to begin, Bill invited his team members to his home for a breakfast meeting to discuss the job. He outlined the project and asked for ideas about how to proceed. One associate suggested that, while completing their routine landscaping work at the club, they could identify the best locations for the sprinkler heads and save the time and cost of a special survey. Another volunteered to examine the current system to determine which parts, if any, could be incorporated into the new system.

At their next meeting, the team planned the entire job and agreed on who would complete each part. When the work began, the team went to work full of enthusiasm because they had been completely involved in the planning. During the installation, as problems arose, the team members were empowered to make independent decisions to correct them. Bill reported that if he had just assigned the work to his team members and required them to come to him to solve every problem, it would have taken longer and cost more. The workers would have looked at it as just another job.

What Empowerment Does

Empowerment has its upside and its downside. Let's look at some positive effects of empowering employees.

Idea Generation

You've heard the expression "Two heads are better than one." Perhaps 10 heads are even better. People who work on a job know a great deal more about what's going on in their working environments than many managers realize. They see things that are done inefficiently, and they have ideas for improvement. By eliciting their input about new projects and assignments, you're likely to pick up ideas that might not have occurred to you.

Synergy

When a group of people work together to generate ideas, a suggestion made by one participant can trigger ideas from another. This process leads to an abundance of ideas from an empowered team, often called synergy. However, synergy isn't limited to generating ideas. Synergy is defined as "two or more units (people, in this case) working together to achieve a greater effect than individuals can do by themselves." This is what happens in an empowered team.

If Bill's landscapers had worked individually to perform the sprinkler installation, it would have taken longer and most likely mistakes would have been made. These mistakes would have to be corrected, taking more time. By working as an empowered team, each person knew what the others were doing and, if help was needed, could pitch in.

When all members of an empowered team are engaged in the same type of work, each person should be trained to do all aspects of that work. However, some teams are multifunctional—they consist of people from different disciplines. Although each member of a team made up of marketing, engineering, and finance specialists cannot be expected to do the jobs of their colleagues in other areas of expertise, their total involvement in the planning process lets them know exactly what each team member is doing. The results are a coordinated effort and goals that are easier to achieve.

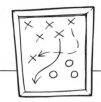

Tactical Tips

By making each participant in the group feel that he or she is a full partner in the development and implementation of a project, you will enhance his or her commitment to its success.

Problems of Empowerment

Empowering workers is not a magic formula. Empowerment can be a great way to motivate people to accomplish superior work—but it doesn't always work. Some managers are reluctant to empower people and some people don't want to be empowered. Let's look at some of these problems.

Refusal to Give Up Power

People who have worked hard to be promoted to managerial positions often believe that empowering their subordinates will diminish their own positions. Some managers feel they are losing status by sharing power with the team; this simply isn't true. The difference is not in rank or position, but in methodology. Rather than being "boss," you teach, inspire, and motivate your team. Being the leader of an empowered team is a position high in status.

Some managers worry about losing control. They ask, "If I'm still responsible for this department, how can I give up my power without losing control?" You don't have to lose control when you share power. You're a member of the team. You're directly in the midst of every activity and know how each team project is progressing. You are aware of this, and so is every member of your team. Control becomes team control. As team leader, you guide your team to meet performance standards.

Fear of Being Empowered

Wendy was perplexed. She thought that her team members would be excited and enthusiastic about their company's move to empowered teams. Instead, she realized that several people were upset. Here are some of the things they said:

"I'm not paid to make decisions—that's your job."

"Just tell me what to do, and I'll do it."

"I work hard enough as it is. I don't want more responsibility."

As you can see, not everyone is thrilled to be empowered. Sometimes you have to sell people on the idea. Your first job as team leader of a newly empowered team is to convert people who think this way into enthusiastic supporters of the new method. Here are some suggestions that might help you do this:

➤ Understand why some people don't want to stretch their brains. Employees often are happy doing routine work in a routine way. Find the true reason they feel this way. Perhaps they don't believe that they have the ability to do more than routine work. Sometimes you have to work with the team to build up self-confidence.

➤ Help people understand their new roles. Take the time in the beginning to explain the true meaning of empowerment. Time spent in good orientation pays off in better team efforts.

➤ Train your team members to generate ideas. Show videos about team participation; teach team members to brainstorm. Have members of another team that has been successful in empowered activities describe how empowerment has worked for their team.

➤ Get the program underway slowly. Choose assignments or projects that easily lend themselves to participatory effort in the beginning. Gradually progress to the point at which team members tackle all projects collaboratively.

The Manager's Role

Some managers fear that their company will have no need for them once empowerment becomes the way of organizational life. If everyone is involved in what managers traditionally do, what role is left for managers? In some companies, the job of the team leader has been redesigned. Variations of *self-directed* teams, which usually have no permanent team leader, replace traditional teams.

Rarely does a company have entirely self-directed teams. Instead, the team chooses a project leader (or two or more leaders) for each project. Because most teams work on multiple projects, a permanent team leader usually serves the important purposes of coordinating all team activities and providing training and support.

Making Empowerment Work

Empowerment isn't a panacea for curing all management problems. Rather, it enhances collaborative efforts to get a job accomplished by giving every member of a team the power to get things done. When management is sincere about empowerment and applies it in a meaningful manner, the chances of success are increased.

In General Motors's Saturn division, any assembly line worker can push the button that stops the line if he or she sees something that needs correction (a power most companies reserve for managers). One GM employee reported on television that he "pushed that button once," after he realized that a part had not been inserted properly on a chassis. The correction took just a few seconds, but the employee said that it made him feel good that he had the power to stop the line and that he was able to help maintain the quality of GM's cars.

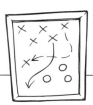

Tactical Tips

Empower people who deal with customer problems to do so without the delays and red tape that result from the need to seek approval from management. At Nordstrom department stores, any sales clerk can make exchanges, give refunds, or provide special service.

Guidelines for Empowerment Programs

Keep in mind that for your empowerment program to succeed, the program must have full support from top management. Empowerment works most effectively when a company's CEO empowers its senior management group, which in turn, passes that empowerment down through the organization. Because many companies assume that the transition to empowerment is more difficult for rank-and-file employees than for team leaders and managers, often they concentrate their training on that group. However, because the program is collaborative, team leaders and team members should be trained together by consultants or others who are knowledgeable in this type of work.

All team members should be given full information about team projects. They should have support to acquire necessary skills and techniques, and freedom to interact with the team leader and any team member to accomplish goals. It also is very important for upper management to encourage team members to use initiative when planning and implementing projects.

Many organizations have excellent training programs for orienting and starting an empowered team program. However, once the program is underway they assume that it will work smoothly. As teams mature, many initial problems are overcome, but new problems do occur. Reinforcement training meetings should be held periodically to discuss and resolve complexities that develop. In addition, counseling should be available to assist people who have difficulty adjusting to the new techniques.

In theory, everyone can be trained to be a leader; in practice, it doesn't always work. Some people aren't emotionally suited for leadership roles; they just aren't motivated to assume these types of duties. These people will not or cannot change their patterns of behavior from authoritarianism to participation. Allowing these types of employees to remain in leadership positions is destructive; they must be removed. Highly motivated, well-trained, committed team leaders are essential to the success of empowered teams.

The Least You Need to Know

➤ One way to make dull jobs more worker friendly is to redesign these jobs and change their focus.

➤ Let your staff participate in setting quotas for their own jobs.

➤ To promote the careers of their employees, companies have instituted career pathing programs. Employees are assessed to determine their potential and what steps they must take to move into positions that will be of greatest value to both the company and to themselves.

➤ Empowerment is sharing with employees the power to make decisions when planning and implementing a job.

➤ When you empower your team, management doesn't have to lose control. Empowered teams work with managers to ensure that performance standards are met.

➤ Some team members might not want to be empowered. Win them over with a well-planned orientation and, if necessary, augment it with individual counseling.

Chapter 19

Keep 'Em Safe and Healthy

In This Chapter

➤ Living with OSHA

➤ Your rights and obligations when inspected

➤ Setting up safe-working programs

➤ "Right to know" laws

➤ Making employees safety conscious

➤ Keeping employees healthy

➤ Dealing with alcohol and drugs on the job

It makes good sense to maintain a workplace that is safe and healthy to work in. Work-related accidents and illnesses are expensive. The added costs of workers' compensation premiums are only a small part of this expense. Lost time, lost productivity, and low morale take an even greater toll on the organization.

The concern about health and safety has been increased since the passage of the Occupational Safety and Health Act (OSHA) in 1970. In this chapter we'll explore the problems companies face in complying with this law and developing programs to keep employees safer and healthier.

OSHA—What It Is and What It Does

The federal Occupational Safety and Health Act governs safety and health in the private sector. It applies to every private employer involved in interstate commerce. All companies, regardless of size, are covered. The law requires that every company establish safety standards for each of the occupations involved; for the plants, offices, and other facilities; and for the equipment and material used.

Representatives of the Occupational Safety and Health Administration (also called OSHA), an agency of the U.S. Department of Labor, are empowered to make inspections of any facility without prior notice. In addition, employees must be notified by posters and other company communications of the address where complaints can be made. Employees also must be advised that they are protected from retaliation if such complaints are lodged.

Some states have similar laws, which might be stricter than the federal law. States with approved plans are called "state-plan states"; state inspectors—not federal inspectors—enforce the laws. Check with your local authorities to determine whether you are in one of those states. In this book we concentrate on federal laws; all states must meet at least these requirements.

Basic OSHA Standards

Many OSHA directives cover specific industries; however, all companies fall under the *general duty clause*. This clause requires that all employers furnish a workplace that is free from safety and health hazards. Any unsafe condition that is not specifically covered is understood to be covered by this general duty clause.

Some specific items covered by OSHA regulations are as follows:

➤ Walking and working surfaces, guarding openings, ladders, scaffolds, power lifts, and housekeeping

➤ Exits: emergency exits, emergency plans, and fire prevention plans

➤ Environmental control: ventilation, noise exposure, radiation, hazard signs, and tags

➤ Hazardous materials: gases, flammables, explosives, hazardous waste, and emergency response

➤ Personal protective equipment: protection of eyes, face, head, feet, and respiratory organs

➤ Fire protection: extinguishers, sprinkler systems, and detection and alarm systems

➤ Materials handling and storage

➤ Guarding and operating machinery

➤ Operating handheld equipment

➤ Training and operation in welding, cutting, and glazing

➤ Electric wiring and electrical equipment

In addition, specific standards are set up for certain industries such as pulp and paper, textiles, bakeries, laundries, sawmills, and logging. In recent years special standards have been issued for employees working on computers to protect eyesight and reduce muscle stress.

It is the responsibility of management to become familiar with the applicable standards and to ensure company compliance. For example, if special protective clothing such as hard hats, safety goggles, or shoes is mandated, management must see that all employees use them at all times. These requirements should be included in company rules and regulations, published in the appropriate manuals, posted at the workplace, and enforced by supervisors.

OSHA requires that companies with 11 or more employees keep records for each work location of occupational injuries and illnesses. Occupational illnesses must be reported regardless of severity. Occupational injuries that result in death, loss of consciousness, one or more lost workdays, restriction of work, transfer to another job, or medical treatment must be reported. Companies in retail, finance, insurance, real estate, and most service industries do not have to keep such records or make such reports.

Your Chances of Being Inspected

With the vast number of companies covered by OSHA, it's obviously impossible to inspect every one. To ensure that the companies most in need of inspection are dealt with, OSHA has set up a priority system in order of potential perils as outlined here:

1. Report of situations in which there is imminent danger.

2. Catastrophes, fatalities, or accidents resulting in hospitalization of five or more employees.

Personnel Perils

Companies have the right to assign a management representative to accompany an OSHA inspector on the inspection. Take advantage of this. Make careful notes on everything noted by the inspector.

Management Miscellany

OSHA rules are complex and are changed from time to time. Companies can obtain copies of the rules from regional OSHA offices (see government listings in the phone book) or OSHA, Department of Labor, 200 Constitution Avenue, Washington, DC 26210; telephone 202-693-1999; Web site www.osha-sic.gov.

3. Valid employee complaints of standards violations, or unsafe or unhealthy working conditions.

4. Industries, occupations, or substances that are considered highly hazardous or injurious to health.

5. Follow-up inspections to determine if previously cited violations have been corrected.

Citations and Punishments

Inspectors who find a violation usually issue an immediate citation telling the company the nature of the violation and the amount of time allowed for the correction. The employer must post a copy of each citation in or near the place of the violation until the violation is corrected. Penalties for violations vary from moderate fines for first offenses to very large fines up to $500,000 for repeated offenses or willful violations.

Preventive Programs

OSHA encourages companies to develop safe working conditions without the need for formal inspections. Companies can request free on-site consultation from federal or state OSHA. These consultants help employers identify hazardous conditions and recommend corrective measures. No citations are issued and consultants' files cannot be used as a reason for formal inspections. There also are private firms that provide consulting services of this type.

OSHA also provides a variety of informational services to employers and conducts training programs in safety and health. More than sixty courses are available at the OSHA Training Institute in Des Plaines, IL. More information can be obtained from the OSHA Web site www.osha.gov.

Right to Know Laws

To protect workers who might not be aware of the dangers they face when using certain chemicals in their work, about 30 states and the federal government have passed laws generally referred to as the "right to know" laws. As these laws varied from state to state, OSHA published its own rules that apply nationally. Known as the Hazard Communication Standard (HCS), these laws apply to all employers that use, produce, import, or distribute hazardous chemicals.

These rules make it the responsibility of the manufacturer or importer to determine whether its products are hazardous under OSHA guidelines; if so, it must provide a data sheet for each hazardous chemical. The manufacturer or importer must clearly label all dangerous materials and employers must train the workers exposed to them on how to identify and use them.

In addition, employers must develop and implement a written hazard communications program for its workplaces that describes how hazardous materials are labeled, what chemicals are present in the workplace, and how the company will train for and keep employees alert to these dangers.

Creating a Safe Work Environment

Even before OSHA and other government safety regulations were issued, companies instituted programs to promote safety in their facilities. It made good sense to prevent accidents. In most companies the responsibility for safety is in the jurisdiction of the human resources department. Safety committees that include representatives from manufacturing, engineering, and other departments often implement these programs. In companies that have contracts with labor unions, representatives from the local union also are included.

Making Employees Safety Conscious

The basic step in most programs is promoting safety awareness throughout the plant. If you've ever walked through a factory, warehouse, or other industrial facility you've undoubtedly seen safety posters and bulletins posted all around. They might be simple signs saying, "Wear your hard hat," elaborately designed posters showing how to operate a piece of equipment safely, or illustrated instructions on using safety equipment.

Most firms supplement these with periodic pamphlets that reinforce this information, articles in company newsletters, and special safety bulletins. In addition, most companies give training classes on a regular basis in which specific safety situations are discussed. In these programs, films or videos are shown, and equipment experts are brought in.

Tactical Tips

A good source for obtaining safety awareness information is your workers' compensation insurance carrier. Most of these organizations have excellent safety programs and offer them at no cost to their clients. Manufacturers of industrial equipment also can send specialists to train your workers to operate the equipment safely.

Setting Up a Workplace Program

There are two basic approaches to reducing accidents: controlling the work environment and motivating employees to think and act with safety in mind. To implement these approaches a company must have a clear safety policy. This policy should start with a statement of the company's commitment to safety and then specify the procedures for accident reporting, investigations, and correction of safety problems. It also should provide for safety training and education, and indicate penalties for violation of safety regulations. Once this policy is in place a safety program can be implemented.

A typical safety program might include the following:

➤ Studying safety records to uncover the causes of accidents and eliminate the hazards that threaten employee safety.

➤ Making regular inspections of facilities to identify and correct hazards.

➤ Appointing a safety committee.

➤ Developing and using safety training, education, and motivational programs.

➤ Developing plans and arranging drills for emergency evacuations (such as fires, chemical spills, or natural disasters).

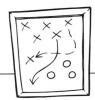

Tactical Tips

The goal of any safety program is to reduce accidents. One way of accomplishing this is to offer incentives to employees who maintain accident-free records over a period of time. Some companies give bonuses to everybody in a department in which no accidents occur over a specified time period. Other systems involve giving points for each day or week in which no accidents occur. At the end of the year, the points can be redeemed for merchandise or cash.

Maintaining a Healthy Work Environment

The "H" in OSHA stands for health. Although safety has long been a concern of industry, health has been given less attention, except for major hazards such as the debilitating lung diseases that plagued coal miners and the perils of exposure to some chemicals. The following discusses some common work-related health hazards and offers some suggestions for keeping workers healthy.

Health Hazards

Companies are obligated to control the environment in which their employees work. This includes identifying any health hazards that exist and taking steps to eliminate them. As most companies do not have staff members who are experts in this, it is wise to hire specially trained consultants to evaluate the environmental conditions in the facility. Often, such specialists can be recommended by the health-insurance provider. Among the health hazards that have been probed by OSHA are …

➤ Air and water pollution

➤ The effects on workers of regular exposure to all types of chemicals

➤ The effects of cigarette smoking in the workplace

➤ Possible radiation effects of video display terminals

➤ Muscular aches and pains caused by repetitive work

➤ Eye strain, posture problems, and excessive noise that are common to many jobs

As technological innovations change the way work is done, attention must be given to how new techniques affect the work environment. Will using new equipment lead to muscle stress or posture problems? Will the new chemicals or paints affect the health of workers? Will pressure to increase production cause emotional or mental health problems. Managers must keep alert to the effect of such changes.

Keeping Employees Healthy

In most companies employees are not exposed to health hazards; however, it's to the advantage of the company to have healthy employees. Not only does this reduce absenteeism; to quote an old adage, everybody's goal should be "a sound mind in a sound body." Many companies now have wellness programs, designed to keep their employees in good health. These programs provide information and facilities for regular exercise, proper nutrition, weight control, drug and alcohol counseling, stop-smoking programs, and health management.

In some larger organizations, employees often have the use of fully equipped gymnasiums; smaller firms might have an exercise room containing exercise equipment. Exercise classes might be available before or after work or during lunch hour. Lectures and seminars on nutrition, quitting smoking, and other health matters also are sometimes offered. Pamphlets and books on health matters usually are available as part of these wellness programs.

Alcohol and Drug Problems

A frequent problem managers face is the employee who is an alcoholic. Alcohol has been a workplace problem from the beginning of time. It interferes with productivity—and a person who has had even one drink can be impaired both physically and mentally. It can lead to accidents, carelessness, difficulties with co-workers, and loss of productivity.

Suppose one of your employees seems to have an alcohol problem. You've never seen this person drink or come to work drunk, but you often smell alcohol on the person's breath. He or she is frequently absent; especially on Mondays. You can't ignore this situation.

Tactical Tips

To prevent any misunderstandings or ambiguities, every company should have a formal policy prohibiting drinking on company premises or during working hours. This policy should be in writing and reviewed periodically with all employees. Restrictions should specifically include beer and wine in addition to "hard" liquor.

Speak to him or her about it. Prepare to hear all sorts of denials: "Me, drink? Only socially" or, "Alcohol breath? It's cough medicine." Rather than talking about a drinking problem, talk about job performance, absence from work, and other job-related matters. Inform the person that if the situation continues, you'll have to take disciplinary action. If this behavior pattern continues, bring up your concern about the drinking and suggest or insist on counseling.

It isn't easy to discuss a sensitive and personal matter such as an alcohol problem. The U.S. Department of Health and Human Services suggests some approaches in its *Supervisor's Guide on Alcohol Abuse* pamphlet. You can obtain the pamphlet from the U.S. Department of Health and Human Services, 200 Independence Ave, SW, Washington, DC 20202 (1-877-696-6775) or obtain more information at the Web site www.os.dhhs.gov.

In most companies, showing up at work drunk or drinking on the job is a punishable offense. However, it's not always easy to prove that a person is drunk; appearing to be drunk isn't enough. Even a police officer cannot arrest a suspect for driving while intoxicated unless he or she substantiates the claim with a breath or blood test.

If one of your employees seems to be drunk, your safest course is to send the person to your medical department for testing. If that's not possible, don't allow the person to work—send him or her home (in a taxi, if necessary). The next day, discuss the situation and state that if it occurs again, you'll take disciplinary action. Also, make sure to suggest counseling. A note of what transpired should be placed in the employee's personnel file as documentation.

Testing for the use of drugs is becoming an increasingly routine practice in many companies. A survey of more than 3,500 companies showed that 48 percent test job applicants and that 43 percent periodically test employees. Although some companies do conduct random drug tests, most of them test employees only when they suspect drug use.

HIV/AIDS in the Workplace

Despite all the articles and TV programs that make clear that AIDS and HIV is spread primarily through semen and blood, many people still have an unreasonable fear of even casual contact with someone who is infected with HIV or AIDS. When it becomes known that an employee of a company has HIV or AIDS, many co-workers refuse to work with that person. If the person with AIDS is in your group or works in conjunction with it, this attitude can disrupt its activities.

Not only is this bad for morale, but if the company doesn't take action to avoid these situations, it may be sued under the Americans with Disabilities Act (ADA). To deal with this, companies have instituted programs to inform employees of the true facts about the virus and the disease. HIV/AIDS-awareness programs include videos, pamphlets, articles in the company newspaper, and doctor-facilitated lectures. (You can obtain literature about HIV/AIDS and information about AIDS awareness programs from your local health department or from the CDC National AIDS Clearing House at 1-800-458-5231.)

The Least You Need to Know

➤ The federal Occupational Safety and Health Act governs safety and health in the private sector. It applies to every private employer involved in interstate commerce. All companies, regardless of size, are covered.

➤ Companies can request free on-site consultation from federal or state OSHA. These consultants help employers identify hazardous conditions and recommend corrective measures.

➤ To protect workers who might not be aware of the dangers they face when using certain chemicals in their work, about 30 states and the federal government have passed laws generally referred to as "right to know" laws.

➤ There are two basic approaches to reducing accidents: controlling the work environment and motivating employees to think and act with safety in mind.

➤ Companies are obligated to control the environment in which their employees work; this includes identifying any health hazards and taking steps to eliminate them.

➤ Employees with alcohol or drug problems should be encouraged to get counseling. If behavior doesn't change, disciplinary action should be taken.

Chapter 20

Employee Problems and Problem Employees

In This Chapter

➤ Absenteeism—causes and cures

➤ Reporting to work—on time

➤ Sensitive, emotional, and negative employees

➤ Stress, burnout, and pressures

The people with whom you work are human beings with all the idiosyncrasies, attitudes, moods, and problems that each of us has. We don't leave our problems at the door when we come to work; we take them with us. One of the great challenges of being a leader lies in recognizing and dealing with the special needs, personalities, and problems of the members of our group. In this chapter we'll look at some of the problems that managers must deal with day by day.

Controlling Absenteeism

Absenteeism has always been a problem. People do get sick and have personal matters that need to be attended to, or maybe just feel like they need a day off. Absenteeism is one of the most chronic and expensive problems companies face. It costs in loss of productivity, breakdown of programs, failure to meet deadlines, and dissatisfaction of customers. It has been estimated that absenteeism costs employers an average of $600 per worker, per year, totaling a loss of anywhere from $10,000 for small employers to $3 million for large corporations.

Crime and Punishment

Some firms punish absentees. If an employee is absent more than a certain number of days over a specified period of time, they are suspended; if absences continue, eventually they are fired. Does this work? At best, it deters some people from staying home for trivial reasons when they are on the verge of being fired; but as soon as the time period is over, they start again. In the long run, punishment doesn't work. When you fire someone, you might lose an otherwise good worker, and there's no guarantee that the replacement will have a better attendance record.

Rewarding Good Attendance

If punishment doesn't work, what about giving rewards for good attendance? This helps somewhat, but still doesn't solve the problem. Invariably, the people who win the attendance rewards are those who would have been there anyway. The chronic offenders are still absent. The main value of reward programs is with marginal types of workers—those who, before the reward system, would get up in the morning, sneeze, and think, "I've got a cold; better stay home." When staying home will cause them to lose the reward, they might think twice before deciding to stay home.

Tactical Tips

In dealing with a chronic absentee, look for factors in his or her personality, background, or attitude that might cause the problem, and try to find a way to help that person overcome the problem.

Rewards reduce absenteeism somewhat, but they are not a panacea. There's no one way to curtail absenteeism because there's no one cause for it. It must be approached differently with each person.

There is another downside to reward programs. Employees who are sick and should stay home come to work so they can qualify for the reward and infect other employees.

Sick Days as an Entitlement

If your company provides a certain number of sick days, you probably have employees who make sure that they take every one of them. Even if they can be carried over to the next year, some people watch the calendar and when the close of the annual period nears, they make a point of "getting sick."

When I questioned several "December" absentees about this, the general attitude was that sick leave was an entitlement. When I pointed out that they might need those days the following year if they had serious illness, the responses ranged from a shrug of the shoulders to "I never get sick" or "Who knows if I'll be working here next year?" To counteract this, some companies are experimenting with a system that lumps vacation, personal leave, and sick days into one big "paid time off" pool. Workers have the option of using the time any way they see fit.

One of my clients converted to a paid–time-off system four years ago and the company executives are pleased with the outcome. The company provides workers with 27 paid days off a year, not counting 8 paid holidays. Except in emergencies, supervisors are given adequate notice so they are not hit with unexpected absences and can plan accordingly. In addition, it reduced the bureaucratic paperwork associated with more traditional systems that require workers to submit doctors' slips to take extended sick leave.

Getting to Work on Time

In every company there are some people who just can't seem to get to work on time. This is particularly disturbing when people work as a team; the tardiness of just one member affects the work of all. One of the first steps in orienting new employees should be to instill in them the importance of being on time. Have other team members who live near the new employees talk to them about the best routes to get to work, traffic patterns, and the optimum time to leave for work to ensure promptness. Reinforce this by talking with latecomers at their very first lateness. Enforce your disciplinary procedures if subsequent lateness occurs.

Excuses, Excuses

When an employee reports to work late, speak to him or her about it immediately. Bring the offender into a private place and discuss the matter. If it's a first or second offense, sell the employee on the importance of being on time. Get a commitment to be on time in the future. If the person has a previous record of tardiness, have the data with you so you can give specific dates and times. Let him or her know how seriously you take the matter and what will happen if this continues.

Flextime: One Solution for Tardiness

Flextime, or flexible hours, has helped reduce tardiness in many organizations. Although there are many variations, a typical flextime program requires all employees to be on duty during the "core" or busy business hours. The starting and quitting times vary.

Flextime is not always appropriate. If the work of a team requires all the members to be together all the time to accomplish the work, all team members must be on the same time schedule. Another problem with flextime is the role of the supervisor.

Meanings and Gleanings

Flextime, or flexible hours is a program in which work hours are staggered so that instead of all employees working the same hours, some employees come in and leave early; the others come in and leave later in the day.

The supervisor is not expected to be at work during all of the hours that the department is open. Managers must feel confident that the early birds and the late stayers can be trusted to work effectively without direct supervision. Controls can be designed to deal with this but unless the employees are committed to their work, flextime will not be successful.

Dealing with Sensitive, Temperamental, and Negative People

Most supervisors and team leaders find one or more members of their groups difficult to work with. These employees can make your life miserable or make it an ever-changing challenge. You can't ignore these folks; you have to deal with them.

Working with Oversensitive People

No one likes to be criticized—but most people can accept constructive criticism. However, some people resent any criticism. When you criticize their work even slightly they pout, get defensive, and accuse you of picking on them.

How do you deal with these people? Be gentle. Be diplomatic. Begin by praising those phases of the work that they have done well. Then make some suggestions about how they can do better in unsatisfactory areas. But be careful, if the only time you praise a sensitive person is as a prelude to criticism, it will backfire. Be lavish with praise when they have accomplished something. This will build up their self-esteem.

Kathy is a good example of a sensitive person. Her fear of being criticized has made her overly cautious in all areas of her work. Rather than risk a slight error, she checks, double-checks, and then rechecks everything she does. This process may minimize her exposure to criticism, but it's so time-consuming that it slows down the entire department. Worse, she stalls in making decisions, claiming that she needs more information. Even after she gets the information, she passes the buck to someone else.

Here are some guidelines to help you deal with sensitive people like Kathy:

➤ Assure them that, because of their excellent knowledge in their field, their work usually is correct the first time and doesn't have to be checked repeatedly.

➤ Point out that occasional errors are normal and that they can be caught and corrected without reflecting on the ability of the person who made the errors.

➤ If you agree that they need more information before making a decision on what to do about a problem, guide them toward resources to help them obtain it. If you feel that they have adequate information, insist that they make prompt decisions.

➤ If members of your group ask you what to do, tell them that they have the resources to make their own decisions on how to deal with a problem and insist that they do it.

In most cases, overly sensitive people have the expertise and do make good decisions. All they might need is your reassurance to help convert their thinking into action.

Watch Those Temper Tantrums

Have you ever had an employee lose his or her temper? It isn't easy to work in an environment in which people holler and scream—particularly if you're the target. Because the poor victims of a tirade might be unable to work at full capacity for several hours afterward, this type of situation cannot be tolerated.

If the person you're criticizing begins to cry or throw a tantrum, walk out. Say that you'll return after he or she calms down. Wait 10 minutes; then try again. Assure the person that this isn't a personal attack but a means of correcting a situation.

Tactical Tips

When dealing with a person likely to have a tantrum, don't meet in your office. Use a conference room instead. It's not a good idea to leave an upset person alone in your office.

Negating Negativity

You probably have negative thinkers in your group. Whenever you're for something, they're against it. They always have a reason that what you want to accomplish just can't be done. These people can tear down your team with pessimism.

The reasons for negativity vary. It might stem from some real or perceived past mistreatment by your company. If that's the case, look into the matter. If the person has justifiable reasons for being negative, try to persuade him or her that the past is past and to look to the future. If misconceptions are involved, try to clear them up.

Often negative people are resistant to change. Even people with a positive attitude are reluctant to change. It's comfortable to keep doing things the way they've always been done. Positive-thinking people can be persuaded to change by presenting logical arguments; negative people resist change just for the sake of resisting. No argument ever helps. They often do everything they can to sabotage a situation so that the new methods won't work and they can say, "I told you so."

When you present new ideas to negative people, encourage them to express their objections openly. Tell them, "You bring up some good points, and I appreciate it. As we move into this new program, let's carefully watch for those problems. We must give this new concept a try. Work with me on it, and together we'll iron out the kinks."

Another problem caused by negative employees is the impact on team morale. Just as one rotten apple can spoil a whole barrel of apples, one negative person can destroy the entire team's morale. Because the negativism spreads from one person to another, it's tough to maintain team spirit under these circumstances.

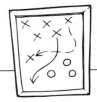

Tactical Tips

Refer people with problems to your Employment Assistance Program (EAP). Chapter 16, "Personalizing the Benefits Package," contains a discussion of how these EAPs can help you and your team when faced with problems that hinder job effectiveness.

Have a heart-to-heart talk with negative people to let them know how their attitude affects your team's morale. Amazingly, many negative-thinking people have no idea that their behavior is disruptive to others. You might suggest that they enroll in a personal improvement program or seek counseling.

Playing "Gotcha"

Have you ever worked with an associate whose greatest joy in life is to catch other people—especially you—making an error? People who play this game are trying to show their superiority. Because usually they have no original ideas or constructive suggestions, they get their kicks from catching other people's errors, particularly their boss's. They try to embarrass you and make you uncomfortable.

Don't give them that satisfaction. Make a joke about it by saying, "What a blooper!" or smile and say "Thanks for calling it to my attention before it caused real problems." If Gotcha-mongers see that you're not riled by their game, they'll stop and try to get their kicks elsewhere.

Stress and Burnout

All jobs have their share of stress. If they didn't, they would quickly become boring. It's when "stress" becomes "distress" that problems occur. This distress might show up as changes in the employee's behavior. People who had always been patient become impatient. Calm people might become tense. Employees who have always been cooperative rebel. All these signs show up when people are under excessive stress.

People under stress might show physical symptoms or complain that they have trouble falling asleep or in sleeping through the night. They're often tired all the time—even if they do get a good rest. They might have stomach pains, a fast heartbeat, or frequent headaches.

Burnout

People are not light bulbs. A light bulb shines brightly and suddenly—poof!—it burns out. People burn out slowly and often imperceptibly. Although some burnouts result in physical breakdowns such as a heart attack or ulcers, most are psychological. People lose enthusiasm, energy, and motivation, which shows up in many ways. They hate their jobs, can't stand co-workers, distrust the team leader, and dread coming to work each morning.

Burnout can be caused by too much stress, but that's not the only cause. Some other reasons are frustration: Promises made weren't kept or the employee was passed over for an expected promotion or salary increase. Some leaders and managers burn out because of the pressures of making decisions that, if made poorly, can cause catastrophic problems. Others just burn out from working excessively long hours or doing unrewarding work.

Often the only means of helping someone recover from burnout is to suggest professional help. However, there are some things you can do to help put a burned-out team member on the road to recovery:

Personnel Perils

If a person is constantly fatigued from work, suggest that he or she see a physician for a thorough medical examination to rule out physical causes and for suggestions to relieve fatigue and stress.

➤ **Be a supportive person.** Demonstrate your sincere interest by encouraging the person to talk about and assess his or her concerns and put them into perspective.

➤ **Consider changing job functions.** Assigning different activities and responsibilities or transferring the person to another team changes the climate in which he or she works and provides new outlets that might stimulate motivation.

➤ **Give the team member an opportunity to acquire new skills.** This helps him or her focus on learning rather than on the matters that led to the burnout and makes the person more valuable to your company. If, despite your efforts, he or she doesn't progress, strongly suggest professional counseling.

Coping with Pressure

When pressure on a job becomes so great that you feel like you're going to break down, follow these suggestions:

➤ **Take a break.** If possible, get out of the building. If you work in a city, take a walk around the block. If you work in an industrial park, walk around the parking lot. If the weather is bad, walk around inside the building. In 10 or 15 minutes, you'll feel the stress dissolve and be able to face your job with renewed energy.

➤ **Exercise.** If you work in a crowded office, it's obviously not expedient to get up in the middle of the room and do jumping jacks or push-ups, but you can choose from several relaxation exercises without being obtrusive. Books and videotapes are available to show you how. If your company has an exercise room, get on the treadmill for five minutes (not enough to work up a sweat but enough to relax your mind).

➤ **Change your pace.** Most people work on more than one project at a time. If the pressures are too great on your current project, stop for a while and work on another one. When you return to your original assignment, it will go much more smoothly.

When There's Too Much Work to Do

When companies downsize, there are fewer people to do the work. Everybody must work longer and harder. Your team is overburdened. They've reached the limit of their time and energy. You decide to speak to your boss about this.

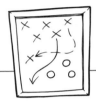

Tactical Tips

When you're asked to take on a special assignment that won't help you meet your team's goals, decline diplomatically. Explain that you realize it's an important project but that you're already involved with several high-priority assignments and, as much as you want to help, you just can't.

Before you approach your manager, thoroughly analyze the jobs your team is doing. Indicate how much time is devoted to each project and determine each project's importance to the accomplishment of the team's goals. Reexamine your boss's priorities. Decide with your team what they can do to work smarter rather than harder.

If you still feel after this analysis that your team has more work than it can handle effectively, meet with your boss to review its results and try to reorder your team's priorities. Your boss might agree to defer certain time-consuming jobs because others are more important; reassign some jobs to other groups; or fight to get additional personnel.

Sometimes the pressure results from you or members of your group volunteering for special projects. Learn to say no. Keep your people aware of your team's priorities. Let them know it's not an indicator of laziness or unwillingness to cooperate if they reject requests to handle special projects outside the team's activities.

Managing Stress

If you're under severe stress, consult a physician who can treat stress with anti-depressants or other medication. However, for the type of stress likely to be faced on the job, you can take other steps to help manage your own stress. For example, keep in tip-top shape, learn to relax, keep learning, develop a support team, accept only commitments that are important to you, and seek new ways of using your creativity. Managing your own stress is the first step in helping the people in your team or department to manage their stress. A stressed-out boss leads to a stressed-out team.

The Least You Need to Know

➤ There's no one way to curtail absenteeism because there's no one cause for it. It must be approached differently with each person.

➤ When an employee reports in late, speak to him or her about it immediately. Get a commitment to be on time in the future.

➤ In dealing with negative people, acknowledge their arguments and persuade them to work with you to overcome their perceived problems so that the project can move along.

➤ Managing your own stress is the first step in helping the people in your team or department to manage their stress.

Chapter 21

Working with a Diverse Workforce

In This Chapter

➤ Understanding sexual harassment

➤ Dealing with racial prejudice

➤ Making accommodations for religious requirements

➤ Working with people from diverse cultures

Before you read this chapter, you might want to review the employment laws for women and minorities in Chapters 2, "You Gotta Know the Laws," and 3, "Still More Laws," respectively. During the first 20 years of these laws, most complaints related to hiring and firing. Although these types of charges are still prevalent, more and more complaints in recent years have involved on-the-job problems such as sexual harassment, and treatment of minorities and women in the workplace. In this chapter we'll explore some of the major issues managers face in applying these laws on the job.

Sexual Harassment

Articles about sexual harassment appear again and again in the newspapers and on television. In one case, the president of a famous cosmetics company was accused of sexually harassing 15 female employees; the company paid the women $1.2 million in an out-of-court settlement. In another, a U.S. senator was forced to resign because he was accused of sexually harassing at least 26 women who worked for him.

Management Miscellany

Although sexual harassment on the job has been illegal since 1965, relatively few cases were filed until Anita Hill brought sexual harassment charges against Clarence Thomas during his confirmation hearings. This made the public aware of this aspect of the law. In the three years preceding these hearings, 18,300 sexual-harassment complaints were filed with the EEOC. In the three years following the hearings, 40,800 cases were filed.

Tactical Tips

Companies can protect themselves from charges of sexual harassment by clearly notifying all employees that such behavior will not be tolerated and by establishing and publicizing a procedure for dealing with complaints. A senior executive should administer this policy; all complaints should be quickly investigated and, if verified, quickly corrected.

It's not only company presidents and senators who are accused of sexual harassment. Organizations of all sizes and types face sexual harassment charges by both female and male employees. Allegations involve managers at all levels and even nonmanagerial employees.

The Supreme Court Ruling

In 1998, the Supreme Court handed down two major decisions related to sexual harassment. In one case, it ruled that a company can be forced to pay damages to workers who are sexually harassed by a supervisor at any level. The general ruling was that companies and public employers are automatically liable for sexual harassment. A company can be liable even if it knew nothing of the harassment. In effect, companies must prove their innocence if a worker claims sexual harassment on the job; when in doubt, the company is liable. As such, the burden of proof is on employers.

However, the ruling did contain some good news for employers. If sued, companies can sometimes successfully defend themselves by proving that they have a strong policy against sexual harassment and that they respond quickly to complaints. They also must show that the victim failed to take advantage of this policy by failing to file a complaint.

In another case, a Chicago woman claimed that her boss made repeated comments to her with sexual innuendos. He urged her to wear shorter skirts, and told her that she was not "loose enough" to suit him. He commented he could make her life very hard or very easy.

After a year the woman quit and sued the company, Burlington Industries. A lower court judge threw out her claim because she had not suffered a "tangible job consequence," such as a demotion, for refusing her supervisor's advances. However, the U.S. Court of Appeals in Chicago overturned the lower court's decision, holding Burlington liable for the supervisor's harassment even though no specific job consequence had been involved.

The Supreme Court agreed. Although the woman had not suffered a tangible job action at the hands of her employer, Burlington was still subject to liability for her manager's action. To defend itself, the company would have had to prove that it "exercised reasonable care" to prevent harassment in the workplace. Having a written policy on sexual harassment—publicized to employees and enforced by management would be considered "reasonable care."

What Exactly Is Sexual Harassment?

What one might assume is sexual harassment isn't always the same as what the courts have defined it to be. The legal definition of sexual harassment covers much more than just demanding sexual favors for favorable treatment on the job (naturally, these types of demands are included).

The courts and the EEOC define sexual harassment as any unwelcome sexual advances or requests for sexual favors or any conduct of a sexual nature when …

➤ Submission is made explicitly or implicitly a term or condition of initial or continued employment.

➤ Submission or rejection is used as a basis of working conditions including promotion, salary adjustment, assignment of work, or termination.

➤ Such conduct has the purpose or effect of substantially interfering with an individual's work environment or creates an intimidating, hostile, or offensive work environment.

What does this mean in plain English? Let's see how this concept works on the job.

Subtlety Is No Excuse

You would think that corporate presidents and senators would have enough common sense to refrain from making explicit sexual demands, and most do. People in positions of authority who sexually harass their subordinates usually use much more subtle tactics. The harasser doesn't make any actual demands; the demands are implied. References are made to other employees who have benefited by being "more friendly." Comments about a person's physical attributes and similar remarks are made. These can be interpreted as harassment.

Personnel Perils

Unless you know someone well, don't hug, don't pat, and certainly don't kiss—greet him or her with the traditional handshake.

"Wait a minute! If I tell a woman that she's attractive, that's harassment?" It depends on what you say and how you say it. A comment such as, "That's an attractive dress" is much different from the comment, "That dress is sexy." The statement, "I like your new hairdo" is also acceptable, but the statement, "Wearing your hair like that excites me" is not acceptable.

Creating an "Intimidating and Hostile Work Environment"

As noted earlier, according to its legal definition, sexual harassment isn't limited to demands for sexual favors. It also includes conduct that creates an "intimidating and hostile work environment." This may include subtle mistreatment of women or actions that have been accepted as "normal" for years but really offended minorities or women.

Ken's team had always been all male; now two women have been added to his group. Some of the men resent this "intrusion" on their masculine camaraderie; as a result, they make life unpleasant for the female team members. The men make snide remarks, give the women incorrect information that causes them to make errors in their work, and exclude them from work-related discussions. No actions are taken that can be interpreted as "sexual" in nature, but it still qualifies as sexual harassment. The men have created a hostile work environment for the women.

Tina works in a warehouse. The street language some of the men continually use offends her. When she complains she is told, "That's the way these guys talk. They talked this way before women worked here, and they're not going to change now. Get used to it." Because people might find that this dirty language creates "an offensive work environment," it can be legal grounds for a complaint.

If a similar situation occurs in your group, talk to the people using the inappropriate language. Point out diplomatically that this behavior is unprofessional and offensive to both women and men and that it isn't appropriate to use it in a business environment. Inform them that such behavior can cause legal problems for the company and for them as individuals. Tell them that if they continue to use street language they will be subject to the same type of disciplinary action as is given for violating other company rules.

Dating and Romance

Cathy was perplexed. Dennis, one of her team members, had gone out a few times with Diane, who worked in another department. It never developed into a romance, but Diane kept bugging Dennis to go out with her again. Diane came into Dennis's office several times a day to talk with him, even though Dennis didn't welcome her visits. Diane's constant attention interfered with his work, and he wasn't interested in seeing her. The next time Diane visited Dennis, Cathy called her aside and told her that social visits were not permissible. Diane never returned, but continued to harass Dennis by telephoning him after work.

Is the company off the hook? Not yet. Even though the harassment has ceased on the job, because both Dennis and Diane are employed by the same company, the company has an obligation to stop Diane from bothering Dennis. Cathy should discuss the situation with Diane's manager and, if necessary, with the human resources department. If Diane continues her harassment, appropriate disciplinary action should be taken.

Intra-Marriage

Dating isn't always unwelcome. Many romances that start on the job develop into marriages. What effect does it have on your group when two associates become romantically involved? This situation can be a delicate one. Some companies, fearing that closely related people working together will lead to complications, actually prohibit parents, children, siblings, and spouses from working in the same department or even in positions in which they must interrelate.

Federal law doesn't expressly prohibit discrimination based on marital status, but it is barred by interpretations of the sex-discrimination clauses by the EEOC. Some states do have specific laws prohibiting discrimination based on marital status. However, companies may still prohibit married couples from working together—but even this is

Personnel Perils

It's not good business to restrict married couples from working in the same company. Why lose productive workers because of an archaic rule? Most married couples work well together and have enough control over their own lives to not bring their personal problems into the workplace.

currently being challenged in the courts. If a company prohibits married couples from working together and two team members marry, which one should leave the team? Some companies base their policy on rank (the lower-ranking spouse leaves) or salary (the lower-paid spouse leaves). However, because it might be more likely for the man to be the higher-ranked or higher-paid employee, this policy discriminates against women. The best way to deal with it is to let the couple make the determination about which one will leave.

Sex Harassment by Others

Suppose a salesperson who comes into your office makes a point of telling off-color jokes to the women who work there. Some of them think he's hilarious, but you notice the look of disgust on the faces of others. Although no complaints have been made, you see that the behavior is creating an offensive work environment. The salesperson doesn't work for your company, but you still have an obligation to do something about it.

The courts have ruled that an employer is responsible for the offensive behavior of all its employees (regardless of whether they're in management). This covers even non-employees when the employer or its agents (that's you, in this case) know about it or should have known about it.

Speak to the person on whom that sales rep calls. Tell him or her to discuss the matter with the sales rep. If the undesirable behavior continues, the company has an obligation to tell the salesperson that it cannot continue doing business with him.

Personnel Perils

Watch those e-mails. Sending or passing along sexually oriented messages, jokes, or addresses of pornographic Web sites has been construed as sexual harassment. Companies can be fined; employees can be fired for using e-mail in this way.

Note that your company is responsible not only when it knows about the offensive behavior but also when it should have known about it. This point is a delicate one. How are you supposed to know about everything that might happen? You can't, of course—but if you're observant, you should know a great deal about what transpires.

Ten Steps to Prevent Sexual Harassment Charges

It's not always easy to understand the implications of the laws and sometimes it's best to consult an attorney for legal interpretations. However, by following these ten guidelines, you can reduce your chances of having sexual harassment charges filed against your company. You also will improve the morale in the company because employees will see that you take this situation seriously.

1. Establish a formal policy prohibiting sexual harassment. Any actions that could be construed as harassment should be clearly indicated. Specify what steps employees should take if they are harassed. Appoint a senior executive to administer the policy.

2. Publicize the policy through bulletins, articles in the company newspaper, regularly scheduled meetings, and training programs.

3. Make it easy for complainants to bring matters to the attention of management. Post notices throughout your offices detailing who to go to and how to do it.

4. Investigate all complaints—no matter how trivial or unjustified they appear to you. Keep written records of all findings (including memos, reports of interviews, and statements from the complainant, the person accused, and witnesses).

5. Never terminate or threaten complainants or potential complainants.

6. Don't make rash decisions. Analyze all the facts. Consult your attorney (remember the matter might wind up in court).

7. Take action. If the complaint is justified, correct the situation. Depending on the case, this might include requiring the harasser to apologize, ordering a cessation of the acts that led to the complaint, adjusting the complainant's salary if the harassment resulted in a loss of income, promoting or changing the working conditions of the persons who have suffered or, in flagrant or repeated offenses, firing the harasser.

8. If the investigation finds the complaint was not justified, explain the decision carefully and diplomatically to the complainant. Keep in mind that if he or she is not satisfied, a charge can still be filed with appropriate government agencies and taken to court.

9. Don't look for easy ways out. Transferring the harasser to another department might solve the immediate problem, but if the harasser repeats the offense in the new assignment, the situation is compounded.

10. If a formal complaint is made to the EEOC or a state equivalent, even if you feel the complaint is groundless, treat it seriously.

Religion in the Workplace

The law requires companies to make reasonable accommodation for an employee's religious practices unless it results in undue hardship on your company. Here we go again. What is "reasonable accommodation" and what is "undue hardship"? These same words were mentioned in discussing the implementation of the ADA (see Chapter 2). You must make an honest effort to accommodate the affected employee as long as it can be done without having a negative effect on your company.

Sometimes accommodation is easy. Suppose your company is open seven days a week and members of your department take turns working on Saturdays and Sundays. Zachary, who is a Seventh Day Adventist, informs you that he can never work on Saturdays but you can schedule him for Sunday work. If you're not open on Sunday and you have other employees who can work Saturdays, you're still required to excuse Zachary from Saturday assignments. The other employees might resent having to work on Saturday, but the unhappiness of other employees doesn't qualify as "undue hardship."

Large companies have a tough time proving that accommodation causes "undue hardship." On the other hand, if your business is small and there aren't enough people qualified in the work to cover the Saturday shift, it might be considered an undue hardship. In that case legally you could have rejected Zachary at the time he applied for the job; if he is already on the payroll, you can terminate his employment.

Harassment Because of Race or National Origin

Although sexual harassment has received most of the attention, there have been numerous cases of employees who have been harassed because of their race or the country from which they came. Unfortunately, there are still a number of people who have strong feelings about members of a race other than their own. Most of the complaints in this area come from employees using the "N" word when talking about or addressing African Americans and blacks. There also have been complaints from members of other groups who have suffered from ethnic slurs.

Personnel Perils

Monitor all e-mail sent on company computers. Hate messages are not jokes. Companies should prohibit such messages and employees who send or forward such messages should be disciplined.

A recent addition to this problem is the plethora of e-mails and other Internet and intranet messages using derogatory terms and telling stereotypical "jokes" about minority groups. *The Wall Street Journal* reported an upsurge in e-mail, graffiti, and even notes depicting nooses—a sign of lynching—sent to African American workers. Companies are required to take strong disciplinary action—including firing—against any employee who engages in such practices.

Working with a Multicultural Workforce

If your employee population consists of men and women who come from different cultures, misunderstandings and conflicts can occur. As a manager, you cannot ignore this situation. Your job is to make your department a smooth-running, collaborative group. It isn't always easy to change a person's deeply ingrained perceptions. Newcomers to America must be taught American ways, and Americans must learn to understand the attitudes and customs of newly arrived immigrants.

Language Problems

"How can I supervise these people when they don't speak English and I don't know their language?" It's not a new phenomenon. A hundred or more years ago when immigrants from Europe flooded this country, their supervisors were faced with exactly the same problem. The usual approach then—and it still works—was to find some employees who did speak the language and use them as interpreters. If the non-English speakers in your company are all from the same country, you can make an effort to learn enough of their language for basic communication. Many companies offer English-as-a-second-language (ESL) programs for their employees.

If you're worried about your non-English-speaking employees' abilities to understand instruction manuals, it's not too difficult to have the manuals translated. It also might be beneficial to use nonverbal tools such as demonstrations, training videos, and graphics to train people to perform manual operations. Unless the need to speak English is job related, you cannot require employees to speak only English in the workplace. Employees who normally speak a different language and are more comfortable conversing in their native tongue cannot be forced to speak English among themselves.

Other Types of Cultural Diversity

Diversity is not limited to integrating persons from other countries into the work force. You also must recognize the other cultures within the American population that must be accommodated. We've noted that to discriminate against the physically and mentally challenged is illegal, and that such employees often bring talents and skills that are valuable to the company. But because accommodations must sometimes be made to assist these individuals or groups, other workers might resent them. This is another challenge of the diverse workforce.

How should organizations cope with these issues? First, decision makers must learn to accept the reality of diversity. This calls for abandonment of traditional stereotypes about workers—who they are, what they look like, and why they work. Rather than arguing over whether or not to support diversity, direct your energy toward designing work systems that anticipate the varying and unique qualities of a diverse work force. One company with workers from several countries, had all of its work instruction manuals redesigned with easy-to-understand diagrams and cartoons so they could be readily followed by workers with little knowledge of English.

Second, focus on developing more objective methods of personnel selection and appraisal. Instead of depending on the traditional interviews in selecting staff, which often perpetuate biases, use methods that test the applicant's ability to actually do the work. Persons applying for jobs calling for manual skills can be asked to actually perform tasks similar to that for which they will be hired. Persons applying for jobs calling for interaction with others may be asked to role play simulated situations. Such techniques can serve two purposes:

Management Miscellany

The American Bankers Association (ABA) has published a guidebook on setting up diversity programs. Copies are free to ABA members and are available to others for $21. Nonmembers can fax requests to 202-663-7543.

1. They increase the chances of hiring talented individuals who otherwise might be rejected under a subjective approach.

2. They protect the organization from legal challenges in instances in which a member of some protected group has been rejected.

The Least You Need to Know

➤ Sexual harassment is not limited to demands for sexual favors. It also includes permitting a work environment that is hostile or offensive to employees because of their gender.

➤ Sexual harassment situations can be prevented by instituting and enforcing a strict policy against that type of behavior.

➤ Companies must accommodate to the needs of employees to observe their religious practices.

➤ Encourage employees from diverse cultural backgrounds to get to know each other as people; not just as members of an ethnic group.

➤ Set up a diversity program in your company to help develop an integrated work force of all employees regardless of race, gender, or ethnic background.

Part 6
Keeping Your Staff on the Cutting Edge

Performance—that's what the boss wants from you and what you want from the people you manage. A method has to be developed by which you can determine in a systematic way how well each member of your group is doing.

Most companies have performance appraisal programs and some are very effective; however, many just provide minimal information. There has to be a better way to really measure how well a person is doing on the job. In this part you'll study several approaches to performance appraisal.

Another concern: Many managers are uncomfortable when they sit down with a staff member to discuss the performance appraisal. In these chapters you'll learn how to do this important but delicate job diplomatically and effectively.

But there's more to keeping staff members on the cutting edge than job performance. There are lots of workers who are technically competent, but other factors detract from their productivity. They might disobey company rules, cause disruption in the workplace, or require discipline in other ways. I'll look into these matters as well in this part.

Evaluating Performance

"How'm I doing?" Everybody wants to know how he or she is doing on the job, and if they are performing up to the expectations of the manager. That's the main reason for performance appraisals—but it's not the only reason. In this chapter we'll look at a variety of systems to measure performance and how to use appraisals to improve performance.

An Overview of Appraisals

Conducting formal performance reviews has long been part of corporate procedures. The annual review—often dreaded by both the supervisor and the employee—was looked upon chiefly as the determination of how much (if any) salary increase a person would receive. Actually, the real reason for such reviews is to look at the performance of the employee and determine how that performance can be improved. Salary adjustment was only part of the program—but it became the one part that dominated the thinking of both parties.

Today, companies are moving away from focusing on salary adjustment—often covering it in a separate procedure—and concentrating on the employee's productivity, goals, and personal growth.

Setting Standards for Individual Appraisals

All employees should know just what's expected of them on the job. Many companies develop and incorporate *performance standards* at the time they create a job description. In other companies standards are established as the job evolves.

In routine jobs the key factors of performance standards involve quantity (how much should be produced per hour or per day) and quality (what level of quality is acceptable). As jobs become more complex, these standards aren't an adequate way to measure performance. Ideas and innovations conceived in creative jobs cannot be quantified, and quality might be difficult to measure. This doesn't mean you can't establish performance standards for these jobs; it requires a different approach, such as the *results-based* evaluation system described later in this chapter.

Performance standards usually are based on the experiences of satisfactory workers who have done that type of work over a period of time. Whether the standards cover quality or quantity of the work, or other aspects of the job, they should meet these criteria:

➤ **They should be specific.** Every person doing a job should know exactly what he or she is expected to do.

➤ **They should be measurable.** The company should have a touchstone against which performance can be measured.

➤ **They must be attainable.** Unless the standards can be met, people will consider them unfair and resist working toward them.

One way to set standards that are understood and accepted is to have employees participate in setting the standards. Encourage them to make a practice of regularly evaluating their own performance against those standards. This way they don't have to wait for formal performance assessments to discover how they're doing. They see for themselves where they stand and if necessary can take corrective action immediately.

Types of Performance Assessments

Most companies conduct formal appraisals of employees on an annual basis. However, annual reviews are not enough. Goals change during the year; performance varies during the year; problems that were never dreamed of when standards were set come up during the year. It would be much better if performance reviews were conducted at least four times a year—but this would be too time consuming and expensive. However, brief, semiformal meetings can be held with employees several times each year—and informal discussions of performance should be ongoing.

The formal and sometimes semiformal review is standardized. A system is used so that all employees are measured in the same manner. In this section we'll look at some of the more commonly used assessment systems.

Check the Box—The Trait System

You've been rated by them. You've probably used them to rate others. The most common evaluation system is the "trait" format, in which a series of traits are listed in the left margin, and each is measured against a scale from unsatisfactory to excellent.

Here is a typical traits-type appraisal form:

	Excellent	Very Good	Average	Needs Improvement	Unsatisfactory
	(5pts)	(4pts)	(3pts)	(2pts)	(1pt)
Quality of work					
Job knowledge					
Dependability					
Ability to take instruction					
Initiative					
Creativity					
Cooperation					

On the surface this system seems to be simple to administer and easy to understand, but it's loaded with problems. Managers tend to fall into the following traps when rating their employees on a trait system:

➤ **Central tendency**   Rather than carefully evaluating each trait, it's much easier to rate a trait as average or close to average (the central rating).

➤ **The halo effect**   Some managers are so impressed by one trait that they rate all traits highly. The opposite of this is the pitchfork effect (see Chapter 4, "Twenty-Five Mistakes Companies Make in Hiring").

251

➤ **Personal biases**   Managers are human, and humans have personal biases for and against other people. These biases can influence any type of rating, but the trait system is particularly vulnerable.

➤ **Latest behavior**   It's easy to remember what employees have done during the past few months, but managers tend to forget what they did in the first part of a rating period.

There are ways to overcome deficiencies in the trait system; some will be described later in this chapter. However, if your company does use the trait method, here are some suggestions to help make it more equitable:

➤ **Clarify standards.**   Every manager should be carefully informed about the meaning of each category and the definition of each trait. Understanding quantity and quality is relatively easy. But what is dependability? How do you measure initiative, creativity, and other intangibles? By using discussions, role-plays, and case studies, you can develop standards that everyone understands and uses.

➤ **Establish criteria for ratings.**   It's easy to identify superior and unsatisfactory employees, but it's tougher to differentiate among people in the middle categories. The great percentage of workers are neither top grade nor failures. To rate effectively those in the middle area, its important to set standards against which differences in performance can be measured.

➤ **Keep a running record of member performance throughout the year.**   You don't have to record average performance, but do note anything special that each member has accomplished or failed to accomplish. For example, some notes on the positive side might say, "Exceeded quota by 20 percent," "Completed project two days before deadline," or "Made a suggestion that cut the time required for a job by a third." Notes on the negative side might say, "Had to redo report because of major errors," or "Was reprimanded for extending lunch hour three days this month."

➤ **Make an effort to be aware of your personal biases and to overcome them.**   For example, Sally believes office employees should dress conservatively. Molly wears bright, colorful outfits. In rating Molly, Sally must recognize that the way Molly dresses has no bearing on her job performance and not let it influence her rating.

Personnel Perils

When you rate your subordinates, don't be overly influenced by their most recent behaviors. Employees know that it is rating time, and they'll be as good as a kid just before Christmas. Keep a running log of their behavior during the entire year.

Record specific examples of team member's exceptional and unsatisfactory performance and behavior to support your performance evaluation.

Results-Based Evaluations

Rather than rating people on the basis of an opinion about their various traits, in the results-based system the supervisors (who do the rating) focus on the attainment of specific results. Results-based ratings can be used in any situation in which results are measurable. This system obviously is easier to use when quantifiable factors are involved (such as sales volume or production units). However, it's also useful in such intangible areas as attaining specific goals in management development, reaching personal goals, and making collaborative efforts.

In a results-based evaluation system, the people who do the evaluating don't have to rely on their judgment of abstract traits. Instead they can focus on what was expected from the person being evaluated and how closely these expectations were met. The expectations are agreed on at the beginning of a period and measured at the end of that period. At that time, new goals are developed, which will be measured at the end of the following period.

Here's how this system works:

➤ For every job, the supervisor and the people doing the job agree on the expected results. These are called key results areas (KRAs) as discussed in Chapter 5, "Starting the Search." Employees must accomplish results in these areas to meet the established goals.

➤ The manager and the employee establish the criteria on which the employee will be measured in each of the KRAs.

➤ During a formal review, the results an employee attained in each of the KRAs are measured against what was expected.

➤ Some organizations use a numerical scale to rate employees on how close they've come to reaching their goals. In others, no grades are given. Instead, a narrative report is compiled to summarize what has been accomplished and to comment on its significance.

Following is a results-oriented appraisal form used in evaluating the performance of a tax accountant. Use it as a model for your own form.

Employee: _____ Date _____

Position held: _____ Dept. _____

Results Expected

Key Results Area #1:

Prepare federal, state, and local tax returns on a timely basis.

Results Achieved

_____

_____

Results Expected

Key Results Area #2:

Advise management of changes and administrative rulings regarding tax laws.

Results Achieved

_____

_____

Results Expected

Key Results Area #3:

Study and report on management policies to determine their tax ramifications.

Results Achieved

_____

_____

Some companies request that staff members submit monthly progress reports compiled in the same format as the annual review. This technique enables both the employee and the supervisor to monitor progress. By studying the monthly reports, the annual review is more easily compiled and discussed.

Although results-oriented evaluations can be more meaningful than trait systems, they're not free of problems. Unless the supervisor and the employee take an objective view of what should be accomplished, they could set unrealistic expectations. They might be set so low that employees attain them with little effort; or set so high that employees have little chance of attaining them. Also, not all goals are equal in importance. Consider the value of the expectation in comparison to the overall goals of the department and the company.

Intangible goals are more difficult to measure. However, even intangible factors have tangible phases that can be identified. For example, rather than indicating that a goal is to "improve employee morale," specify it in terms that are measurable, such as "reduce turnover by X percent" or "decrease the number of grievances by Y percent." Rather than stating a goal as "Develop a new health insurance plan," break it into phases, such as "Complete study of proposed plans by October 31" or "Submit recommendations by December 15."

Collaborative Evaluations

To make the results-based format even more meaningful, use the collaborative model. If performance evaluations are based on the arbitrary opinion of a supervisor, they serve only part of the real value that reviews can provide. Such a model provides a formal evaluation for the purpose of raises or promotions and enables you to tell employees how to improve performance. However, it doesn't involve team members in the process.

A joint review can do this more effectively. The collaborative review is particularly useful for evaluating creative jobs such as research and development or jobs in the arts. These work best in a team setting. Team members join their leaders to determine the standards that are expected, build in the flexibility to accommodate special circumstances, and decide the criteria that will be used to evaluate the work.

The team member and team leader then complete the evaluation form. The KRAs and the "results expected" items are agreed on in advance (usually during the preceding review). The team member and the leader independently indicate the "results achieved."

Self-Evaluations

A variation on the collaborative evaluation is having employees evaluate their own performance before meeting with their supervisors. Both supervisor and employee complete a copy of the appraisal form. At the meeting, similarities and differences in the ratings are discussed, and adjustments in the ratings resulting from the discussions are reflected in the formal evaluation that's filed with the human resources department. In some companies, if the employee still disagrees with the evaluation after the discussion, a rebuttal can be written and filed along with the team leader's report.

At the appraisal interview (described later in this chapter), the supervisor and the employee discuss the comments on the form. During this session, the appraisal begins to move from a report card to a plan of action for growth and teamwork.

Personnel Perils

If the assessee gives himself or herself a significantly higher rating than you do, be particularly sensitive in the discussion so that it doesn't degenerate into a confrontation. Use specific examples rather than statements of opinion to make your points.

Collaborative reviews of performance have the following advantages:

➤ They give people the opportunity to make a formal appraisal of their own work in a systematic manner.

➤ They allow for a thorough discussion between manager and employee about their differences in their perceptions of expectations and results achieved.

➤ They enable a manager to see areas in which he or she might have failed in developing a staff member's potential.

➤ They help the staff member and the supervisor identify problem areas that might easily be overlooked on a day-to-day basis.

➤ They pinpoint areas in which employees need improvement and additional training.

➤ They provide an opportunity to discuss areas in which the employee can become even more valuable.

➤ They provide a base on which realistic goals for the next period can be discussed and mutually agreed on.

➤ They help employees measure performance and progress against their own career goals and determine the appropriate steps to move forward.

Tactical Tips

Supervisors should note their comments on the monthly report form and keep copies in their files. Reviewing the monthly reports when making the annual formal appraisal will result in a much more realistic view of the employee's progress.

In-Between–Reviews Appraisals

As noted earlier, limiting reviews to once a year is not realistic. Members need more frequent feedback to keep on the cutting edge of their jobs. One solution is the mini-review, usually conducted monthly. Employees are asked to evaluate their progress for the past month by responding in writing to a series of questions. Each person should answer these questions to evaluate his or her past month's progress. At the appraisal interview the manager and employee discuss the responses and develop plans to enhance strengths, shore up weaknesses, and set revised goals for the ensuing month.

The 360-Degree Assessment

One type of appraisal that often has been less than satisfactory is the evaluation of supervisors, team leaders, and managers. Just getting their own boss's view of their performance is not enough. An increasingly popular approach to this is *multilevel assessments,* usually referred to as *360-degree assessments.* Managers are evaluated by their bosses, peers, and subordinates; and even outsiders such as vendors and customers.

People do not see themselves as others see them. We perceive our actions as rational, our ideas as solid, our decisions as meaningful. When only your own manager evaluates your performance, it provides insight on how your work is perceived only by that person. However, he or she is not the only person with whom you interact.

Even more complex is the evaluation of senior managers, who frequently are not evaluated at all. When peers and subordinates assess these executives, they might learn things about their management style of which that they were not aware. Many managers are shocked to find that they are perceived by others much differently from what they envision. As a result, many take steps to change their management styles.

> **Meanings and Gleanings**
>
> **Multilevel** or **360-degree assessments** of an individual are made by his or her bosses, peers, subordinates, and even such outsiders as vendors and customers. This gives the company a well-rounded view of how that individual is perceived at several levels.

Despite these advantages of multilevel assessments, there are serious drawbacks. Feedback can hurt. Evaluators aren't always nice or positive. Some people see their role as an assessor as an opportunity to criticize others' behavior on the job.

Another flaw is conflicting opinions. Who decides who is right, or if an appraisal is biased? If the evaluator does not like the person being evaluated, the responses might be skewed negatively; if the assessee is a friend, the evaluation might be skewed positively. Often, people rating senior executives fear it is dangerous to be completely truthful.

To increase the chance of a 360-degree assessment producing change, the following are recommended:

➤ The appraisal must be anonymous and confidential.

➤ To have sufficient knowledge of the person being rated, the appraisers should have worked with the appraisee for at least six months.

➤ Appraisers should give written comments as well as numerical ratings. This enables them to be more specific in their evaluations and produce more meaningful results.

➤ To avoid "survey fatigue," don't use 360-degree assessments on too many employees at one time.

Discussing the Performance Appraisal

An integral part of the performance appraisal is the meeting between the manager and the employee to discuss the appraisal. Managers must carefully prepare for this

meeting. Every effort must be made to ensure that the interview will be a positive experience for the person being appraised and will result in a commitment to continue to improve performance.

Prepare for the Interview

Before sitting down with a staff member to discuss a performance appraisal, study the evaluations. Make a list of all aspects you want to discuss—those that need improvement and those in which the member did good work. Study previous appraisals and note improvements that have been made since the preceding one. Prepare the questions you want to ask about past actions, steps to be taken for improvement, and future goals; then ask how the team member plans to reach those goals.

Reflect on your experiences in dealing with this person. Have there been any special behavioral problems? Any problems that have affected her or his work? Any strong, positive assets you want to nurture? Any special points you want to discuss? By being prepared to deal with these, you'll make the interview a more meaningful exercise.

Face to Face with the Employee

Make your associate feel at ease with a few minutes of small talk. Then point out the reasons for the appraisal meeting. Say something such as, "As you know, each year we review what has been accomplished during the preceding year and discuss what we can do together in the following year." Note the areas of the job in which he or she has met standards, and particularly the areas in which the employee has excelled. By giving specific examples of these achievements, you emphasize that you're aware of the positive qualities, not just the less effective areas.

Encourage the appraisee to comment. Listen attentively; then discuss the aspects of performance or behavior that didn't meet standards. Concentrate on the work—not on the person. Never say, "You were no good." Say instead, "Aspects of your work didn't meet standards." Be specific. Give a few examples where expectations haven't been met. This is more effective than just saying, "Your work isn't up to snuff." Ask what he or she plans to do to meet standards and what help you can provide.

If the employee's problems aren't related to performance but rather to behavior, provide examples: "During the past year, I've spoken to you several times about your tardiness. You're a good worker, and your opportunities in this company would be much greater if you could only get here on time all the time." Try to obtain a commitment and a plan of action to overcome this fault.

Throughout the interview, encourage the team member to make suggestions about every aspect of the review. Of course, he or she might have excuses or alibis. Listen actively! You might learn about some factors that have inhibited optimum performance.

Develop an Action Plan

At the end of the interview, ask the employee to summarize the discussion. Make sure that the person fully understands the positive and negative aspects of his or her performance and behavior. Listen while he or she reiterates the plans and goals for the next review period, and any other pertinent matters. Keep a written record of these points.

Ask him or her to develop an action plan to implement the changes that are to be made. This plan should be specific, listing actions in each pertinent area and timetables when the plan will be started and completed. If new goals are set, list the goals and when and how they will be achieved.

There are times when the employee will be unhappy about the evaluation. He or she may believe that the manager overlooked important accomplishments or overemphasized some shortcomings. In many companies, employees who disagree with an evaluation are given the opportunity to write a rebuttal to be attached to the appraisal. When salary adjustments are based on ratings, some organizations provide a procedure for appealing a review.

In most companies the appraisal form is sent to the human resources department to be placed in the employee's personnel file. Some companies require that a copy be sent to the next level of management—the person to whom the immediate supervisor reports.

Management Miscellany

An appraisal interview isn't the supervisor telling the employee, "This is what you did well, and that is what you did poorly." It's a two-way discussion about performance.

Tactical Tips

If you're an employee who disagrees with your review, send a polite memo to the supervisor a few days after the meeting. Point out some recent achievements that might have been overlooked in your review. Although this might not help in the current appraisal, it will be in your personnel file and will be noted if interim reviews are made before the next formal appraisal.

Even if it's not a formal practice in your company, it's a good idea to give a copy of the appraisal to the employee. It serves as a reminder of what was discussed at the appraisal interview and can be referred to during the year. And, if it includes the goals that the employee and you have agreed on for the year, the employee can reread it from time to time to keep motivated. End the interview on a positive note by saying, "Overall, you've made good progress this year. I'm confident that you'll continue to do good work."

The Least You Need to Know

➤ The chief reason for performance reviews is to look at the performance of the employee and determine how that performance can be improved.

➤ Have employees participate in setting the standards and encourage them to evaluate their own performance against those standards.

➤ Annual reviews are not enough. Problems occur during the year that were never dreamed of when standards were set.

➤ Keep a record of specific examples of exceptional and unsatisfactory perform-ance and behavior of team members to support your performance evaluation.

➤ In a results-based evaluation, the expectations are agreed on at the beginning of a period and measured at the end of that period.

➤ When discussing areas in which expectations haven't been met, give specific examples. Ask what the person plans to do to meet standards and what help you can provide.

➤ At the end of the interview, ask the employee to summarize the discussion. Keep a written record of the points that were agreed upon.

Chapter 23

Doling Out Discipline

In This Chapter

➤ A systematic approach to discipline

➤ Making reprimands effective

➤ Punishment: probation and suspension

➤ Documentation: your first line of defense

When you hear or see the word *discipline*, the first thing that usually pops into your mind is punishment. Look at that word again. Notice that by dropping just two letters in the last syllable (i and n), it turns into disciple, which is a synonym for "student." Both words are derived from the Latin word *disciplina,* meaning "to learn." If you look at discipline not as punishment, but as a means of learning, both you and your employees will benefit. Look at yourself as the coach and your employees as the learners. In this chapter we'll look at the formal approaches to discipline that most organizations use.

The Typical Disciplinary System

When an employee violates company rules, most companies follow a standard procedure to try to get him or her back on track. If this doesn't succeed, they generally punish the offender. This usually is referred to as *progressive discipline.*

Meanings and Gleanings

Progressive discipline is a systematic approach to correcting rule infractions. A typical program has six steps, beginning with an informal warning. If the warning doesn't succeed, the following steps are taken, in order: disciplinary interview, written warning, probation, suspension, and termination (if necessary).

Typically, progressive discipline is a six-step procedure as follows:

1. **An informal warning or reprimand** The supervisor talks to the offender, usually at his or her workstation; discusses the problem, and cautions that the behavior should not be repeated.

2. **A formal disciplinary interview** This usually is held in the supervisor's office or a conference room. The offender is put on notice that future violations will not be tolerated.

3. **A written warning** This step sometimes is included as part of the formal disciplinary interview. Copies are placed in appropriate files.

4. **Probation** The employee is given a specified period of time to shape up and get back on track.

5. **Suspension** The employee is suspended without pay for a specified period of time.

6. **Termination** The end of the line. This will be discussed in detail in Chapter 25, "How to Fire an Employee Legally and Tactfully."

Now let's look at how these steps are implemented.

Effective Reprimands

When you, the manager, note a violation of rules—let's say tardiness—you call it to the employee's attention in a casual way. These chats are friendly but firm, and are not part of the progressive discipline procedure. However, because it may lead to more formal action, it's a good idea to make a note of it in your department records. Although this note is not placed in the employee's personnel file, it can be helpful to prove a pattern of behavior if needed.

The first official step in the progressive discipline system often is called the oral, or verbal, warning. In this step, you take the offender aside and remind him or her that the two of you have previously discussed the problem with lateness. Because this behavior has been repeated, you are officially asserting that tardiness cannot be accepted. Make clear what steps you'll take if the behavior continues.

You might be exasperated about one of your group's failure to keep a promise to be on time. It's normal to be annoyed if your team's work is delayed—but don't lose your cool. Here's how you should *not* do it:

You (angrily): How many times do I have to tell you that we need you here at 8 o'clock? You know that we have a deadline to meet today. Haven't you any sense of responsibility?

Employee (annoyed): I was only ten minutes late. It's not my fault. I ran into a traffic problem.

You: If you had left home early enough, you wouldn't have had a traffic problem. The rest of us were here on time. You just don't have a sense of responsibility.

Employee: I have as much of a sense of responsibility as anyone.

You: If you're late again, I'll write you up.

Did this conversation solve anything? The objective of an informal warning is to alert team members that a problem needs correction. By using an angry tone and antagonistic attitude, you only rile the person without solving the problem.

Let's replay that reprimand in a better way:

You: You know how important it is for you to be here when the workday begins. The entire team depends on all of us being on time.

Employee: I'm sorry. I ran into unusual traffic this morning.

You: We all face traffic in the morning. What can you do to make sure that you'll be on time in the future?

Employee: I've tried alternative routes, but it doesn't help. I guess I'll have to leave earlier every day so that, if I do run into traffic, I'll at least have a head start.

You: That sounds good to me. You're a valuable member of our team, and being on time will help all of us.

Personnel Perils

Never reprimand people when you're angry, when they're angry, or in the presence of other people. Reprimands should be a private matter between two calm people working together to solve a problem.

When you're preparing to reprimand someone, to ensure that you conduct the reprimand in the most effective manner, study the following guidelines:

➤ **Time the reprimand properly.** As soon as possible after the offense has been committed, call the offender aside and discuss the matter in private.

➤ **Never reprimand when you're angry.** Wait until you've calmed down before talking to the employee.

➤ **Emphasize the *what,* not the *who*.** Base the reprimand on the action that was wrong, not on the person.

➤ **Begin by stating the problem, and then ask a question.** Don't begin with an accusation, "You're always late!" Say instead, "You know how important it is for all of us to be on the job promptly. What can you do to get here on time from now on?"

➤ **Listen.** Attentive, open-minded listening is one of the most important factors of true leadership. Ask questions to elicit as much information about the situation as you can. Respond to the offender's comments, but don't let the interview deteriorate into a confrontation.

➤ **Encourage the employee to make suggestions for solving the problem.** When a person participates in solving a problem, there's a much greater chance that it will be accepted and accomplished.

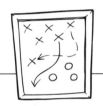

Tactical Tips

If an employee raises his or her voice, lower yours. Most people respond to a raised voice by raising their own. By responding in a soft voice, you disarm the other person. It has a calming effect.

➤ **Provide constructive criticism.** When possible, give him or her specific suggestions about how to correct a situation.

➤ **Never use sarcasm.** Sarcasm never corrects a situation; it only makes the other person feel inadequate and put upon.

➤ **End your reprimand on a positive note.** Comment on some of the good things the person has accomplished so that he or she knows that you're not focusing only on the reason for this reprimand, but on total performance. Reassure the person that you look on him or her as a valuable member of the team.

Asking for a Plan of Action

When you deliver an oral warning, throw the problem back to the employee. Rather than saying, "This is what you should do," ask, "What do you think you can do to correct this situation?" Get people to come up with their own plans of action.

In a simple situation such as tardiness, a plan of action is relatively easy to develop: "I'll leave my house 15 minutes earlier every day." In more complex situations, a plan might take longer to develop. You might suggest that the person think about the problem for a day or so and arrange a second meeting in which to present and discuss it.

Documenting a Reprimand

Even informal reprimands shouldn't be strictly oral. You should keep a record of them. Legal implications mandate that you document any action that could lead to serious disciplinary action. Some team leaders document an informal warning by simply noting it on their calendars or entering it in a department log. Others write a detailed memo for their files. Use the technique your company prefers.

Disciplinary Actions

If an employee repeats an offense after receiving a verbal warning, the next step is the more formal disciplinary interview. In some systems the written warning is given as part of this step; in others it is a separate step given if the employee repeats the offense.

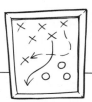

The disciplinary interview differs from a reprimand in that it is more formal. The verbal reprimand usually is a relatively brief session, often conducted in a quiet corner of the room. Conversely, a disciplinary interview is longer and is conducted in an office or conference room.

Tactical Tips

An alert and observant manager can anticipate problems before they develop. Be alert to any deviations from standards before they become problems. By dealing with rule infractions early on, disciplinary procedures can be averted.

A disciplinary interview should always be carefully prepared and result in a mutually agreed-upon plan of action. Whereas a plan of action following a verbal warning usually is oral, the resulting plan in a disciplinary interview should be put in writing. This not only reminds both the supervisor and the employee of what has been agreed on; it serves as documentation.

To ensure that the disciplinary interview is carried out systematically, use the following discipline worksheet.

When administering the disciplinary interview, follow the same guidelines as suggested for the reprimand. However, this is a more formal meeting; comments, questions, and the suggested plan of action should be written. A copy should be given to the employee, a copy kept in the department file, and a copy sent to the human resources department for the employee's personnel file. This is important; if any legal action should ensue from the disciplinary action, this report will serve as documentation to support the position of the department and the company.

Similar distribution should be made of any written warnings—whether issued as part of the disciplinary interview or at a later time. Samples of appropriate documents are shown later in this chapter.

Discipline Worksheet

Part I (Complete before interview begins)

Team member: _____ Date: _____

Offense: _____

_____

_____

Policy and Procedures provision: _____

Date of occurrence: _____

Previous similar offenses: _____

_____

What I want to accomplish: _____

_____

Special considerations: _____

_____

Questions to ask at beginning of interview: _____

_____

_____

PART II (Keep in front of you during interview)

- Keep calm and collected.
- Listen actively.
- Emphasize the *what,* not the *who.*
- Get the whole story.
- Don't interrupt.
- Avoid sarcasm.
- Give *team member* an opportunity to solve the problem.

PART III (Fill out near end of interview)

Suggestions made by team member: _____

_____

_____

Agreed-on solution: _____

_____

_____

PART IV (Action taken: Fill in when interview is finished)

Documentation completed: _____

_____

Discipline Worksheet.

Probation and Suspension

Until now, all attempts to correct performance or behavior have been positive. The supervisor has provided advice and counsel. If nothing has worked, the next step is to put the offender on probation. This step gives him or her one more chance to shape up before some form of punishment is invoked. Most people take probation seriously.

Probationary periods vary from as few as 10 days to the more customary 30 days and sometimes even longer. If an employee makes significant progress, the probation can be lifted. If he or she reverts back to the offending behavior after the probation is lifted, you can reinstate the probation or resort to the next step.

One primary reasons for progressive discipline is poor performance. If this is the problem, probation is the last step before termination. If, despite all the retraining, counseling, and coaching, the employee fails, probation is one last chance to overcome the problem during a definite period. If this doesn't help, suspending the member won't help, either. If he or she can be transferred to a more suitable job, do so; if not, there is no other choice than to terminate that person.

Until this step in the progressive discipline system, there has actually been no punishment. Each step has been a warning with the implication of potential punishment. If probation hasn't solved the problem, the most commonly used form of punishment—short of termination—is suspension without pay.

Although supervisors and team leaders often have some leeway in the length of a suspension, most companies set specific suspension times depending on the seriousness of the offense. Because suspension is a very serious step, union contracts often require consultation with a union representative before suspending an employee. Even when companies aren't unionized, it's best to require approval for suspensions by both the manager to whom the employee's supervisor reports and the human resources department.

Appropriate documentation specifying the reason for the suspension and the exact period of time involved should be made, signed by the appropriate managers, and by

Personnel Perils

It's not a good idea to extend a probationary period. If a person makes some progress by the end of the probationary period but his or her behavior still isn't up to expectations, you can extend the time period—but only once. Continuous probation is bad for morale and rarely solves the problem.

Tactical Tips

The downside of suspending a worker is that the team loses that person's contribution during the suspension period. Make efforts such as training and counseling to keep the person employed so that suspension isn't necessary.

the suspended employee. If an employee returns from a suspension and continues to break the rules, your next step might be a longer suspension or even termination.

"If It Ain't Written Down, It Ain't Never Happened"

In this litigious age, you never know when a current or former employee will sue you. Keeping good records of all disciplinary actions is your best defense in such cases. In addition, written warnings often are taken more seriously than the reprimands or oral warnings. Employees don't want negative reports in their personnel files, and even the possibility that they'll be "written up" serves as a deterrent to poor behavior.

If the written warning concerns poor performance, specify the performance standards and indicate in what way the employee's performance fell short of the standards. Also state what the company did to help the employee meet the standards. This will protect you against potential claims that you made no effort to help that employee.

If the warning concerns infraction of a company rule, specify the nature of the offense and what disciplinary steps were taken before writing the warning (see the following two sample memos). To protect your company from potential legal problems, check any form letters concerning discipline with your legal advisors before sending them to be printed.

Memo for Poor Conduct

From (team leader): _____ Date: _____

To: _____

On (date) _____ , we had a discussion concerning _____
_____
_____

At that time, you agreed to _____
_____

Because you have not complied with this agreement, you are being formally notified that if the above matter is not corrected by (date)_____ , additional disciplinary steps will be taken as specified in Section ____ of the Policies and Procedures manual.

Signed (team leader): _____

Team member's comments: _____
_____
_____

Signed (team member): _____

Memo for Poor Conduct.

Memo for Poor Performance

From (team leader): _____ Date: _____

To (team member): _____

The performance standard for (specify job) _____ is (specify standard in quantity, quality, or other terms)_____

_____

_____

Your performance has not met these standards (give details): _____

_____

_____

To help you, I gave you ____ hours of special coaching. The areas covered include:

_____

_____

Signed (team leader): _____

Team member's comments: _____

Signed (team member): _____

Memo for Poor Performance.

Employee Acknowledgment

Although it's always advantageous from a legal standpoint to have employees sign all disciplinary documents, it becomes imperative when the warning itself is in writing. However, you can't force anyone to sign anything. If an employee refuses to sign a disciplinary document, call in a witness—a person not directly involved in the situation—and repeat your request. If he or she still refuses, have the witness attest to that response on the document.

One tough supervisor reported that he never had trouble getting employees to sign a document. If they refused to sign, he'd turn the paper over and slam it onto the desk and order, "Okay, then just write on the back "I refuse to sign" and sign it. They always did.

The Least You Need to Know

➤ Progressive discipline gives employees several opportunities to correct their behavior before punishment is applied.

➤ When reprimanding somebody, stay cool, be constructive, and focus on the problem, not the person.

➤ Prepare carefully before conducting a disciplinary interview. Get a plan of action from the employee on how the problem will be resolved.

➤ All disciplinary actions should be documented.

Chapter 24

When There's a Union Contract

In This Chapter

➤ Uh-oh ... here comes a union

➤ The recognition process

➤ How unions operate

➤ Negotiating a labor–management contract

➤ Settling grievances

The influence of labor unions on human resources management is far greater than one might think from just looking at the numbers. Fewer than 15 percent of American workers belong to unions; yet unions dominate such major industries as automobile, steel, communications, and transportation. In recent years, unions have increasingly organized commercial companies such as banks and insurance firms. Now a large number of civil service employees at federal, state, and local levels also are union members.

Unions have an influence even on companies in industries in which there is little or no union activity. This is because the wages, salaries, and other benefits they negotiate for their members become benchmarks that set the standards for the rest of the economy. In this chapter we'll look at union-management relations, how unions operate, and the interactions between managers and their employees when a union is in the picture.

The Labor Relations Process

In Chapter 3, "Still More Laws," we reviewed the National Labor Relations Act as amended by the Taft-Hartley Act, which governs the relationship between management and labor unions. Each party has certain rights and obligations that must be adhered to under the law. The National Labor Relations Board sets rules implementing the law regarding union recognition and contract negotiation. Let's see how this works in practice.

Management Miscellany

The highest percentage of union membership in the United States was in 1945 when 45.5 percent of the labor force was organized. This was up from 11.6 percent in 1930. Since 1945 union membership has declined every year; it was down to 13.9 percent in 1999.

Enter the Union

You have a group of disgruntled employees. They feel they're underpaid, overworked, work in unpleasant surroundings, have dogmatic bosses, or have other gripes about the company. They decide they can't get the company to change things by themselves, so they invite a union to come in.

Here's another scenario: A union targets your company and sends an organizer to sell the workers on the need for a union. In either case, the next steps are much the same. The union representative will approach the workers individually or at meetings, discuss their concerns with them, and tell them what steps must be taken to form the union and obtain recognition.

Recognizing the Union

Meanings and Gleanings

An **authorization card** is a statement signed by an employee authorizing the union to act as his or her representative for the purposes of *collective bargaining*, discussed later in this chapter.

The first step toward recognition is to obtain *authorization cards* from each employee. The number of signed authorization cards demonstrates the potential strength of the union. At least 30 percent of the employees must sign such cards before the National Labor Relations Board (NLRB) will conduct a representation election.

Once the authorization cards have been obtained, the union might petition the local office of the NLRB asking that an election by secret ballot be held. The agency sets a date. Before the election takes place, both the union and management conduct intensive campaigns to win workers over to their side.

Most employers fight hard to defeat unionization. However, their efforts are restricted by law. Employers must not threaten employees with loss of their jobs, or loss or reduction of other benefits; or make promises to improve conditions if the union is defeated. However, they can express their views about the disadvantages of being represented by a union. If the union has been involved with strikes against other employers, the company might stress this and warn employees against possible work disruption and loss of income. They might remind them that union dues and assessments can be costly.

Once the union is certified either by consent or by an election, representatives of management and the union bargain collectively to reach an agreement on the labor contract. This may include increases in wages, addition of benefits, and changes in working rules, as well as special rights given to the union and rights retained by management. Once the contract is signed, both parties must live up to its contents.

Personnel Perils

If more than 50 percent of your employees have signed authorization cards, it doesn't pay to go through the expense and aggravation of an election. Unless you feel you have a good chance of changing enough votes, it's better to accept the certification of the union on the basis of the card count.

The *Structure* of the Union

Most unions in the United States are hierarchical. At the bottom is the "local"; then comes the national or international union. All are coordinated by the American Federation of Labor/Congress of Industrial Organizations (AFL/CIO). The AFL/CIO is the central body that coordinates labor activities in the United States and Canada. Its primary function is lobbying congress for labor legislation, coordinating organizing efforts of affiliated unions, and providing public relations on labor-union matters.

Locals

The local is the unit that represents the employees of a particular bargaining unit. The bargaining unit in an *industrial union* might be one department, a division, or the whole company. In a *craft union*, the local usually represents just the employees in that craft. For example, in the same company or department there might be separate bargaining units for the electricians, the machinists, and the draftsmen.

Meanings and Gleanings

Industrial unions represent all workers—skilled, unskilled, and semi-skilled in the same industry, such as all employees of an automobile plant, a textile mill, or a garment factory. **Craft unions** represent skilled craft workers such as machinists, carpenters, plumbers, and similar professionals.

273

National Unions

The locals, whether they are craft or industrial, are the basic units of a national union (also called an international union) such as the United Mine Workers, the Teamsters International, and the National Education Association.

Most national unions have regional offices; however, they are primarily administrative, not policymakers. The national union establishes the rules and policies followed by the locals. It sets guidelines for collective bargaining and provides help in negotiations, legal matters, and grievance procedures to the locals. Most managers rarely see representatives of the national (or international) unions except when an entire industry negotiates industry-wide contracts, or very large companies negotiate blanket coverage for all their facilities.

Who's Who in the Union

There are several layers in the union that managers must recognize. Most of the day-to-day contacts will be with the shop steward or representative of the local. Negotiations and more serious problems might require dealing with representatives of the national (or international) organization. The following sections discuss some of the union roles.

Shop Steward

The shop steward is an employee of the company who has been elected by union members in the department to represent their interests on the spot. This worker does his or her regular job on a full-time basis, but handles matters that arise between workers and managers on a day-to-day basis. Much of this work has to be done after hours; however, when grievances are filed the steward might have to be relieved of regular duties to participate. In these situations, the union makes up for earnings lost by the steward while away from the regular job.

Business Representative

This functionary is a full-time employee of the local union, and may or may not come from the ranks of the company. Among his or her duties are negotiating contracts with the employer, helping union members with job-related problems, counseling the shop steward on interpretations of the contract, and dealing with grievances that can't be resolved by the shop steward. In a small local, the business representative usually is the chief administrative officer of the local.

Officers of the Local

In some locals, the president and other officers are company employees, elected for a specified term. They deal with routine organizational matters such as conducting meetings, collecting dues, dispensing funds, arranging for conventions, and so on. The real leader of the union is the business representative, who handles grievances with the company, settles internal disputes among members, and acts as liaison with the regional, national, or international union.

In other unions, the local president is the real boss of the union. There are numerous cases in which the president of a local dominates the union for years and is paid an unusually high salary. If your employees are unionized, learn who the real boss of the union is. When serious problems arise, it's that person you have to deal with.

Negotiating the Contract

The National Labor Relations Act requires that once a union has been certified, the employer is obligated to bargain in good faith with the union representatives. Collective bargaining is the negotiating between a company and the labor union that has been certified to represent its employees. This collective bargaining involves rates of pay, hours of employment, benefits, working conditions, and other conditions of employment.

To put pressure on management to accede to its demands, unions might threaten and sometimes carry out these tactics:

➤ Strike

➤ Picket

➤ Boycott

Management Miscellany

The number of strikes in the U.S. has declined over the years. According to the Bureau of Labor Statistics, there were only 17 strikes involving 1000 or more workers in 1999 compared to an average of 288 in the 1970s.

The most feared tactic of a union is a strike. Employees walk off the job and refuse to work until their demands are met. This is costly to both the company and the men and women who lose their wages while on strike. Additionally, it causes bitterness, antagonism, and emotional distress, which often last long after the strike is settled.

Some affluent unions can afford to pay strikers at least part of their wages—but usually this is very limited. Most companies continue to operate—on a reduced scale—during a strike. Management personnel roll up their sleeves and take over the strikers' jobs. Non-union members continue to work. In many cases, outside help is brought in through temp services or direct recruiting of *strikebreakers*. Although there have been some long and bitter strikes, most strikes are settled rapidly when parties compromise on the demands. However, even after a short strike there remains rancor between those who struck and those who continued to work.

Management Miscellany

Strikebreakers are persons hired by a company to replace union members who go on strike, or those employees who continue to work during a strike. They are referred to by the union as "scabs." **Pickets** are union members who stand or march in front of a building to discourage entry by nonstriking employees or customers. **Boycotts** are to discourage customers from purchasing products of a company at which the union is striking.

Personnel Perils

A rarely used management tool is the lockout. Instead of waiting for the union to strike to resolve an impasse in the negotiations, the company literally locks union members out of the facility and either closes down completely or hires a new crew. Lockouts are expensive, and once the contract is agreed on they have to re-admit the locked-out people. This results in low morale and a poor public image.

Picketing is one weapon of strikes. Its aim is twofold: Most important is to keep others from crossing the picket line and going to work. You've seen them marching up and down in front of a plant, store, office, or warehouse. They carry signs and shout about unfair treatment.

A *boycott* also can be a powerful tool, particularly when employees of suppliers, repair and service units, and others who are sympathetic to unions refuse to cross the picket line. This prevents delivery of materials and service equipment, and other needed services. In retail and other consumer-oriented businesses, this can significantly reduce business.

The Grievance Procedure

Once the contract is agreed to, most of the contacts between the company and the union will involve grievances. Typical union contracts set up a standard grievance procedure. Every complaint an employee has about the job is not necessarily a grievance. As a matter of fact, most are just gripes. A gripe is an informal complaint about working conditions.

A grievance is a formal complaint concerning a violation of a union-management agreement. For example, the union contract states that supervisors must give employees 24 hours' notice if asked to work overtime. This can be waived under certain specified circumstances. At 3 P.M. Stan's supervisor orders him to work from 5 to 7 P.M. Stan refuses. The supervisor cites him for insubordination and suspends him for three days. Stan files a grievance.

With the assistance of the shop steward, a formal grievance is written and presented to the supervisor. The shop steward presents Stan's case. The supervisor explains the special circumstances that required the overtime. The steward disagrees. He points out that other workers were available to do that work. The supervisor refuses to change his mind.

The next step is to bring the grievance to the next higher level. This might be the department head or plant or office manager, along with the business agent or a local union official. They try to resolve the problem. Most problems such as Stan's over-time can be resolved at this level.

However, if this doesn't succeed, the next step might be handled by the HR manager and the chief union official in the local or the regional office of the union. In more complex matters, the final step before arbitration might be negotiated by a senior corporate executive or attorney, and an equivalent representative of the union. This happens particularly when the grievance involves a major policy matter or sets a precedent that might have extensive impact.

In cases in which no solution is reached at this point, most contracts call for arbitration. The union and management choose a neutral person or group of people to hear the case and make the decision. Typically, a three-person panel might arbitrate. A list of prospective arbitrators is given to each side and an agreement is reached on which three to use. Both parties agree to accept the decision and no appeals may be made.

The Least You Need to Know

➤ At least 30 percent of the employees must sign authorization cards before the National Labor Relations Board (NLRB) will conduct a representation election.

➤ Most of the day-to-day union contacts are with the shop steward or representative of the local. Negotiations and more serious problems might require dealing with representatives of the national (or international) organization.

➤ A strike is the most feared tactic a union takes. Strikes are costly to both the company and the men and women who lose their wages while on strike.

➤ A typical grievance procedure starts with the worker (represented by the shop steward trying to resolve the problem with the supervisor). Next step: union rep with higher-ranking manager; next step: senior union rep with senior executive; if that fails: arbitration.

Part 7

The End of the Line

Jobs are not forever. Sooner or later they come to an end. Some people gracefully retire; others leave voluntarily. However, often the separation from a job is involuntary—and sometimes traumatic. Business slows down and employees are laid off. A worker doesn't meet performance standards and is let go. A troublesome employee is fired after going through progressive discipline—or in some instances on the spot.

Separation and termination present special challenges to managers. Losing employees— whether it's their or your initiative—breaks up teams, upsets morale, requires reshuffling of the work, and if the worker is to be replaced, it brings the headache of hiring and training the replacement.

In this part of the book you'll learn how to cope with both voluntary and involuntary separations. You'll learn how to conduct a separation interview to find out why good people quit. You'll learn about the laws that must be adhered to when you have mass layoffs. You'll learn how to legally and tactfully fire somebody and how to protect your company from potential litigation.

Chapter 25

How to Fire an Employee Legally and Tactfully

In This Chapter

➤ Employment at will—what it really means

➤ Preventing legal complications

➤ Termination when the employee can't cut the mustard

➤ Firing after progressive discipline

➤ Firing disruptive employees

It's never pleasant to fire an employee. Even if you're glad to get rid of him or her, firing is a disagreeable task that most people do reluctantly. Yet sometimes your only course of action is to terminate an employee. As noted in the preceding chapter, a series of disciplinary steps usually leads to this final act. However, circumstances occasionally warrant an unplanned discharge.

Terminating employees is a serious matter that needs careful consideration. In most companies, before a supervisor or team leader can terminate anyone, approval must be obtained from both the manager to whom the supervisor reports and the human resources department. This step is necessary to ensure that company policies and legal requirements are fully observed. This chapter examines the importance of this process.

Employment at Will

"I'm the boss. I can fire anyone I think deserves it." Right or wrong? Most modern managers will answer "wrong." But they are only partly correct. True, there are a few

legal restrictions on firing. However, because of employment at will, most managers can fire any employee for any reason or no reason at all. The only exceptions are those reasons specifically banned by law.

Understanding the Law

Unless there is an employment contract with an employee or the employee is covered by a union contract, the employee is considered an *employee at will*. This concept has governed employment since colonial times. Bosses always had the right to fire employees—and it works both ways. Ever since slavery was abolished, employees have had the right to quit; only recently have these concepts been challenged.

To understand employment at will, you first have to know a little about our legal system. Americans are subject to two kinds of law: statutory law and common law. Statutes are the laws passed by Congress, the states, and local governments. Common law is based on accepted practices as interpreted by court decisions over the years.

The primary difference between the two types of law is that common law can be superseded or modified by legislation and can be changed in individual cases by mutual agreement between the involved parties. A violation of common law is not a criminal offense and is handled in a lawsuit as a civil action. Legislated statutes can be changed only by amendment, repeal, or court interpretation.

Employment at will is a common-law principle. Over the years various statutes have modified it. For example, there are laws that prohibit a company from firing or refusing to hire someone for union activity, race, religion, national origin, gender, disability, and age. The right under common law to hire or fire at will is therefore restricted in these circumstances.

This principle also means that employment at will can be waived by mutual consent. Employees can sign a contract with a company in which they agree not to quit and the firm agrees not to fire the employee for the duration of the contract. Or, the company and a union can agree that no union member will be fired except under the terms of the contract. In both cases, the company has given up its right to employment at will.

Employment Rights When No Contract Exists

During the past several years, a number of court cases have extended employees' rights not covered by specific legislation. Courts in several states have ruled that although a company's policies and procedures manual isn't a formal contract, it can be considered to have the same effect as a contract.

In one case, a New York publishing firm fired a supervisor without going through the progressive discipline process. He sued on grounds that the policy manual called for progressive discipline before terminating an employee. He pointed out that when he had to discharge one of his staff members, he was required to follow the manual. However, when he was fired the company didn't follow the procedure. The company's contention was that the manual was intended only as a guide and not as a rigid procedure. The court ruled in favor of the employee. It ruled that if a policy is published in a manual, employees could expect that it will always be followed.

> **Personnel Perils**
>
> Although an employee can waive a common-law right by contract, he or she cannot waive a legislated right. For example, an employee cannot agree to work for less than the minimum wage.

To avoid this type of problem, attorneys advise their clients to specify clearly in their company policy manuals that they are "at will" employers. This statement also should be included on employment application forms. A typical statement on this is shown in Chapter 7, "Screening Candidates."

Oral Commitments

Quite often when interviewing prospective applicants, the interviewer might make statements or promises that obligate the company. For example, during an interview, Stella was told that her job would be permanent after a six-month probationary period. A year later, the company downsized and Stella was laid off. She sued. She said, "I left my former job to take this one because the manager assured me that it was a permanent job." The manager's response: "I made that comment in good faith. Our company had never had a layoff, but circumstances changed." That's not good enough. The court ruled in Stella's favor and awarded her a large settlement.

Preventive Maintenance

As this is a very sensitive area, managers should be extremely careful when discussing the nature of a job whether it be to an applicant or to a current employee. What you say—often in good faith—may backfire if circumstances change. To avoid these types of complications, follow these guidelines:

> ➤ All managers and team leaders should be trained in termination procedures and adhere to them.

> ➤ Management should never make commitments concerning tenure or other employment conditions orally or in writing.

Tactical Tips

The following clause or one similar to it should be printed on all
applications for employment and
in employee handbooks: "This
company follows an employment
at will policy and employment
may be terminated for any reason consistent with applicable
federal and state laws. This policy
cannot be changed verbally or in
writing unless authorized specifically by the chairman or president of this company."

➤ Make written job offers only after consulting
with legal specialists.

➤ Never use the term "permanent employee." NO
ONE is a permanent employee. If your company
must differentiate between full-time staff and
temporary or part-time staff members, refer to
the full-time people as "regular employees."

➤ On all documents and records relating to employment conditions, state that the company
has a policy of employment at will.

Following these guidelines will keep you out of trouble when it's necessary to fire an employee.

Termination for Cause

There are two basic causes for terminating an employee. One is for inability to perform the job—poor
performance; the other is for poor conduct—violation
of company rules. Although the final steps of the termination process are much the same in both cases,
what leads up to those steps differs.

Inability to Perform the Job

A set of performance standards should be established for every job. These often are
included in the job description. These standards should be clearly explained to all
people performing the job.

A major responsibility of a supervisor or team leader is to work with each person to
ensure that the standards are met. If work is substandard, coaching, added training,
and special attention should be provided. If at any time an employee's work falls
below the set standards, it's incumbent upon the supervisor to do all that is possible
to help correct the problem.

Some employees just don't have the talent necessary to perform the job. In these
cases, after a reasonable effort to help, it's best to remove him or her from the job. If
possible, transfer the employee to a more suitable position. If not, the only recourse
is termination.

Before firing anybody for poor performance, every effort should be made to bring the
performance up to standard. In some companies, employees who were fired for this
reason sued on the grounds that they were not notified that their performance was
below standard and management made no effort to help them. To protect against

such charges, give the employee every chance to improve, document what you do, and use the sample memo form for poor performance from Chapter 23, "Doling Out Discipline."

Termination for Poor Conduct

Employees who have gone through the steps of progressive discipline (see Chapter 23) should never be surprised when they get fired. Presumably, at every step along the way they were told what the next step would be. When an employee is suspended—the next-to-last stage in the disciplinary process—it must be made clear that if he or she doesn't improve in the problem areas, the next step will be termination.

Preparing for Firing

Firing employees is a sensitive situation. You must do it diplomatically and be fully aware of the legal implications. Ask your human resources department for advice about dealing with this situation.

Some managers get more upset about having to fire someone than about losing the person who is being fired. Here are some suggestions to help you prepare:

➤ Review all documents so that you're fully aware of all the reasons and implications involved in the decision to terminate the employee.

➤ Review all that you know about the employee's personality:

  ➤ What problems have you had with the person?

  ➤ How did he or she respond to the preceding disciplinary steps?

  ➤ How did you and the employee get along on the job?

  ➤ How did he or she relate to other team members?

  ➤ What personal problems does the person have that you're aware of?

➤ Review any problems you've had in firing other employees, and map out a plan to avoid those problems.

➤ Check your company's policy manual or discuss with the human resources department any company rules that apply.

Make sure you relax before the meeting. Do whatever helps you clear your mind and calm your emotions. If you've done your job correctly, you've made every effort to help him or her succeed. The progressive discipline system has given the person several chances to change, so you don't have to feel guilty about the firing.

You're Fired!

You've stalled as long as you can. Now you're ready to sit down with the employee and make clear that this is the end of the line. Find a private place to conduct the meeting. Your office is an obvious spot, but it might not be the best one. A conference room is better because, if the fired employees breaks down or becomes belligerent, you can walk out.

Most people who are fired expect it and don't cause problems. They might beg for another chance, but this isn't the time to change your mind. Progressive discipline gives people several "other chances" before they reach this point. Don't let the termination meeting degenerate into a confrontation.

If the employee gives you a hard time, keep cool. Don't lose your temper or get into an argument. It's a good idea to have another person in the room at a termination meeting. A person being fired might say or do inappropriate things. Also, you might become upset and be tempted to say something that's best left unsaid. The presence of a third person keeps both you and the employee from losing your temper and from saying or doing something that can lead to additional complications.

The best "third person" in a termination meeting is a member of the human resources department. If such a person isn't available, call in another manager or team leader. If the employee belongs to a union, the union contract usually stipulates the presence of a union delegate.

Having a third person in the room when you terminate an employee also provides a witness if an employee later sues your company. Suppose a former employee files an age discrimination suit several weeks or months after being fired for poor performance. He or she claims that during the termination meeting, you stated that the company needs younger people to meet production standards.

Although the claim is false, you'll have to spend time, energy, and money to defend your company against it—and it's your word against the other person's. If a third person is present at the termination meeting, former employees will be less likely to file false claims—they know they'll be refuted by a witness.

In most organizations when a termination meeting ends, the employee should be escorted to the human resources department to handle the administrative procedures needed to complete the separation. When there is no human resources department at the facility, the supervisor usually has to take care of this. Make sure to follow the company's procedures carefully. Use the following termination checklist to ensure that you take the necessary steps when terminating an employee.

Management Miscellany

Most companies fire people at the end of the workday on Friday afternoon. Psychologists say it's better to terminate employees in the middle of the week, so they have a chance to begin looking for a new job the next day and won't brood about the firing over the weekend.

Termination Checklist

Name of employee: _____ Date: _____

Part I: If discharged for poor performance, steps taken to improve performance:

Date   Action

_____

_____

_____

Comments: _____

_____

_____

If discharged for poor conduct, list progressive disciplinary steps taken:

Date   Action

_____ Informal warning

_____ Written warning

_____ Disciplinary interview

_____ Suspension

_____ Other (specify) _____

Comments: _____

_____

_____

Part II

Have you reviewed all pertinent documents?   _____

Have you treated this case in the same way as similar cases in the past?   _____

Has this action been reviewed by your immediate superior?   _____

By human resources department?   _____

By legal department?   _____

Does employee have any claim pending against company?   _____

Any workers' compensation claims?   _____

Other (specify): _____

Termination Checklist.

Part III: Termination interview

Conducted by: _____

Date: _____ Place: _____

Witness: _____

Comments: _____

_____

_____

Final actions: _____

_____

ID and keys returned? _____

Company property returned? _____

Final paycheck issued? _____

Additional comments: _____

_____

_____

Termination Checklist (continued).

Spontaneous Termination

Are there times when you're so annoyed with an employee that you wish you could be the old-school boss and just say, "You're fired"? Of course. That's why progressive discipline was instituted—so that supervisors don't let the emotions of the moment dictate their actions. Progressive discipline protects the employee from being fired by ruthless bosses and protects the company from the litigation that could result from such actions. However, under certain circumstances progressive discipline can be waived.

When You Can Do It

There are times when termination without warning is permitted. These occasions are rare and usually limited to a few serious infractions that are clearly delineated in company policies. Serious offenses include drinking on the job, fighting, stealing, and insubordination.

Because these charges aren't always easy to prove, be very careful before you make the decision to fire someone without progressive discipline. You must have solid evidence that can stand up in court. Law books are loaded with cases in which people, because of a rash firing decision, have sued former employers for unlawful discharge, defamation of character, false imprisonment, and whatever else their lawyers can dream up.

Insubordination, which is one of the most frequent causes of spontaneous termination, isn't always easy to prove. If an employee simply fails to carry out an order, it's not enough grounds for termination. Unless a failure to obey instructions can lead to serious consequences, such as engaging in actions that endanger other workers, it's better to use progressive discipline. On the other hand, if a team member becomes unruly in his or her refusal (if he or she hollers and screams or spits in your face, for example), spontaneous discharge might be appropriate.

Documenting a Spontaneous Discharge

When you fire someone after progressive discipline procedures fail, you have an entire series of documents to back you up. In spontaneous termination you have no such documents. Immediately after the termination, write a detailed report describing the circumstances that led up to it. Get written statements from witnesses. If you can, get the employee to sign a statement presenting his or her side of the story. If the discharge is later challenged and the terminated employee presents a different version of what happened, having his or her immediate comments will protect you.

You Can't Fire Me—I Quit!

You've worked hard to bring Mike's performance up to par. Despite your efforts he just can't do the job. You tell him that you have to let him go. You explain that if he quits voluntarily, it will look better when he applies for another job. This option might sound sensible, but what happens if Mike applies for unemployment insurance and is told that he's not eligible because he quit? If you give someone the option of resigning, be sure to inform the person about loss of unemployment insurance and any other negative factors.

Now suppose you try to be shrewd in getting rid of the person: "If I fire him," you figure, "he'll give me problems; so I'll just make his life so miserable, he'll quit." Over the next few weeks you give him as many unpleasant assignments as you can. You time his returns from breaks and even how long he spends in the restroom. You chastise him for every minor violation of company rules and, after a few weeks, he quits.

Meanings and Gleanings

Rather than fire employees, some managers make life miserable for them so that they quit. When an employee quits because of intentional unfair treatment, it is "constructed" by the courts as equivalent to being fired and is referred to as **constructive discharge.**

Don't be shocked when the person sues your company for unlawful discharge! When you tell the court, "I didn't fire him, he quit," the judge will respond "Not so. This is a *constructive discharge*—your treatment forced him to quit." You might be ordered to pay the person back wages, rehire him, or make a satisfactory financial settlement.

The Least You Need to Know

➤ Other than for reasons prohibited by law or waived by contract, an employer can fire any employee for any reason or for no reason (employment at will).

➤ Prepare for a termination meeting by studying all the pertinent documents, reviewing the employee's personal characteristics, and psyching yourself up for the meeting.

➤ Check with your human resources department to ensure that all policies are followed and laws complied with.

➤ Invite a third party to participate in and witness termination meetings.

➤ Use spontaneous termination only for extreme infractions.

➤ Oral commitments to an employee about tenure or conditions of employment are as binding as written agreements.

Chapter 26

"I Quit"

In This Chapter

➤ Seeking the real reason people quit

➤ Making separation interviews more meaningful

➤ Some questions to ask at the separation interview

➤ What to do when an employee gives notice

➤ Counteroffers—yes or no?

Every time an employee leaves a company—whether it's voluntary or involuntary—it costs the company a great deal of money. The investment involved in hiring, training, and supervising that person in addition to the enormous administrative expenses that are incurred are lost forever. The company loses production output until a replacement is hired and trained. Additionally, the interaction among team members is disrupted every time there's a change in the makeup of the group. Team leaders must make every effort to keep turnover down.

Firing people was discussed in the preceding chapter; layoffs and downsizing will be discussed in the following chapter. But separation is not always involuntary. Retaining good people is a major problem. To minimize turnover, we must find out why people we want to keep leave. In this chapter we'll concentrate on voluntary quits.

Losing Good People

Nothing is more frustrating to a supervisor than having a top-producing associate quit. It often takes months or years to bring a person up to optimum productivity—then suddenly he or she leaves. This disrupts the momentum of the team's work. Additionally, it has negative effects on the other team members—unless, of course, the person who quits is universally disliked.

Why Employees Say "I Quit"

You ask the person why he or she quit. Often your answer will be that it's for personal reasons. Duncan decides to go back to college; Vicki's chosen to be a full-time mother; Jane's father's illness requires her to take over his business; Sam's spouse is transferred to another city. Or, maybe it's a career move. Ben has gone as far as he can in your company; Geri is offered more money by another firm; an opportunity arises in a different field—one in which Doug is particularly interested. Hilary's going into her own business.

However, often the reason given is not totally true. Yes, Doug did go to an industry in which he has particular interest—but would he have made that decision if he were satisfied in his current job? Geri is leaving for more money. Sure, she would like more money, but perhaps she wouldn't have even looked for a new job if she had been happy with the supervisor's management style.

Probing for the Real Reasons

Every time someone quits, it's important to determine the true reason. This isn't easy—it might not even be clear to the person who leaves. It might be something deeply embedded in the culture of the company that has subtly made the person discontented.

People might feel they are not making the progress they had hoped for, that their salary is too low, that working conditions are unsatisfactory, or that the job has become boring. Some are reluctant to divulge the real reason for deciding to quit. This is particularly true if the real cause of discontent lies with the supervisor or other employees.

When Should the Separation Interview Be Conducted?

Too often companies do not know why they lose good employees. *Exit interviews* or *separation interviews* are designed to probe for the real reasons people leave a job. The interviewer, usually a member of the HR staff, tries to obtain information about the job or the company that might have caused discontent.

Traditionally, separation interviews are conducted as part of the exit process. The employee is given the final paycheck or told when it will be mailed, advised of the status of benefits, and the paperwork is completed. He or she then might be asked in a formal or informal way a series of questions to determine the reason for leaving.

There are several serious problems in this procedure. First, is this the most appropriate time to obtain this important information? The major objective of the separation interview is not only to learn why the employee has quit. This is important, but even more important is to find out as much as possible about the conditions that propelled the employee to make the decision to quit.

Meanings and Gleanings

A **separation interview** is an interview with employees who voluntarily quit to determine the real reason for their decision to leave (also called an **exit interview**).

However, even well-structured interviews might not bring out the pertinent facts if conducted at the time of separation. Employees who leave might be reluctant to tell the whole story at that time. Often they are still too close to the company culture to evaluate it objectively. Sometimes they are concerned that anything negative that they say might be held against them and reflected in any references the company might be requested to provide. Some people are just reluctant to get into a conversation that could become unpleasant.

Some companies have found that by conducting interviews with former employees six to eight months after they have left the organization they can elicit much more meaningful information than in the traditional exit interview. The employee has had a chance to reflect on his or her experience with that firm; concern about hurting the feelings of a former supervisor or fear of reprisal has been lessened. In addition, comparison with the new job gives them a sounder basis for judgment.

I recently compared the responses from interviews taken at the time of leaving and interviews with the same person six months later. Although the original exit interviews had provided helpful information, the post-separation interviews added significant and valuable insights into aspects of the job environment, corporate culture, and supervisory attitudes that were minimized at the time of separation.

Does this mean that exit interviews should be delayed for six months? Not necessarily. A well-conducted separation interview can give the company much insight into how employees view the organization and even identify critical areas that must be corrected immediately. However, to obtain a substantial and profound analysis of the events leading up to the employee's departure, a follow-up interview six months after leaving can be worthwhile.

Questions to Ask at the Separation Interview

In too many exit interviews, the questions asked are of such a superficial nature that no significant information is obtained. To get meaningful information that will enable the company to identify and correct problems that cause turnover, a well-structured interview must be conducted.

Personnel Perils

The immediate supervisor of the person who is leaving should not conduct the separation interview. It's best that a more objective individual, such as a member of the human resources staff or another manager, conduct it.

Just as in an employment or appraisal interview, it is best to start a separation interview by building rapport. The process should begin with a general question that will not put the employee on the defensive. The question of why he or she is leaving the company should never be the first one asked.

A better start might be: "Tell me about the kind of work you've been doing in your most recent assignment." This will get the conversation going and enable the interviewer to evaluate the kind of work one might expect to do in that job. One reason people leave jobs is because it was not what they thought they'd be doing. A market researcher might be spending all her time on statistical compilations when she expected to be doing in-depth analyses of specific marketing activities.

Questions to Ask About the Job

There are many reasons a person might leave. To ensure that all points of contention are covered, list the questions you plan to ask by category. The following are questions to ask about the job.

What did you like most and least about the job? When listening to the answer, consider whether these are job factors or personal factors. If you find similar answers to this question from several employees, it indicates that the problem lies within the job and not the individual.

How do you feel about your compensation? Many people leave one job for another with higher pay. Others feel they should have made more money even though they were being paid the going rate for the work. Evaluate the answers to this question in light of the equity of the company's pay scale, the methods used to give pay increases, and whether the firm's compensation adjustment system is properly implemented. This also will enable the interviewer to learn about the methods used to give increases in other companies in the employer's industry and in the community in which it's located.

How do you feel about the progress you've made in this company? Many people claim they have left their jobs because of the lack of opportunity for advancement. Often this masks the real reasons for leaving. However, it's important to examine what a person might have expected in terms of growth in the company. Compare the expectation with the real opportunity for advancement in the job she or he held.

This might reveal poor selection or placement practices on the part of your company. Often companies seek people who are overqualified for jobs because they insist all employees should be potential managers. Unfortunately, the opportunity to reach that goal might be much too limited. As a result, employees become impatient or disillusioned and leave. If failure to make progress shows up often in exit interviews, it might be a signal for the company to reevaluate its hiring standards, training programs, and career pathing.

Management Miscellany

The National Association of Colleges and Employers reported that 10 percent of new college grads leave their jobs within a year. Within five years of employment the turnover rate reaches 24.8 percent.

How do you feel about working conditions? Companies often have picked up information from this question about matters that were unimportant in their eyes. However, these things annoyed employees to the point of causing them to leave. Often these are easily correctable.

Questions to Ask About Supervision

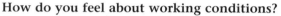

The immediate supervisor is the key person in the relations between a worker and the company. The way that the boss manages is a frequent cause of discontent. The following are some questions about supervision:

What did you like most (least) about your supervisor's style of managing? As many of the problems existing in organizational life involve supervisors, it's important to probe this factor, particularly if there is a large turnover in that department. It will bring out whether the supervisor is dogmatic, stubborn, or authoritarian and whether he or she encourages participation. Probe further to learn how the supervisor deals with complaints. Some leaders tend to be defensive and take any complaint as a personal affront; others take time out to discuss even the most far-fetched grievances. It also helps the interviewer to learn the good points of each supervisor and report them back to him or her. This is positive reinforcement and encourages the supervisor to keep it up and perhaps improve upon it.

Does your team leader or supervisor tend to favor some employees or act unfairly to others? Favoritism on one hand and bias on the other are major causes of discontent. This question also can identify blatant areas of cronyism or, at the other extreme, prejudice and discrimination. If this bias is based on racial, religious, national origin, gender, or age factors, it might alert you to potential legal problems and give the organization a chance to correct them.

What has been your experience in dealing with leaders or managers other than your immediate supervisor or team leader?   This provides an opportunity to get feedback about the organization's leaders from the viewpoint of someone who is not a direct subordinate. This might give insight into other problems not directly related to the employee's supervisor, which also might cause turnover. For example, the major cause of turnover in one firm was due to the arrogant behavior of the team leader's boss, who vetoed team members' innovative ideas after the team leader had already okay'd them.

Additional Questions to Ask

As the reasons for leaving are not limited to specific job or personal problems, a series of more general questions should be asked. The following are additional questions to help uncover special problems:

What might have been done differently here?   A frank answer to this question will bring out some of the real reasons he or she was not happy in the job. It also might offer insight into aspects of the company environment that you'd never considered.

What would have made you stay longer?   When one of my clients asked this of a highly competent technician, he was shocked to learn that the employee had discussed his discontent several times with his supervisor. His supervisor had repeatedly promised the problems would be resolved but nothing was ever done.

Summing It Up

Before closing the interview, ask a few summary questions to ensure that all possible aspects have been brought out. The following are questions to sum up the interview:

If you could discuss with top management exactly how you feel about this company, what would you tell them?   This open-ended question often results in some interesting insights. Let the person talk freely. Avoid leading questions that might influence the response. Encourage him or her to express real feelings, attitudes, suggestions, problems, fears, and hopes about the organization.

If the applicant has accepted a job with another company, ask:

What does the job to which you are going offer you that you were not getting here?   The answer might repeat some of the issues already brought out—but it also might uncover some ways the firm failed to meet the person's hopes, goals, or expectations.

If none of the answers to these questions have brought out the true reasons for the employee's leaving, ask specifically:

Why are you leaving at this particular time?
Some of the problems that come out at the interview have been in existence for a long time. Some of them have seemed unimportant until now. Find out what precipitated the resignation *at this time*. Have things become worse? Is there anything that can be recommended to management that will prevent them from becoming even more serious and causing more turnover?

Because a great deal of turnover occurs during the first months of employment, it's especially important to investigate why this occurs. It might reflect on your hiring practices, your training programs, or your orientation process. It also might indicate that prospective employees are being oversold on the job. Here are some questions to ask people who leave within sixty days after being hired:

Tactical Tips

A good separation interview can take an hour or more, but it can provide insight into how employees who have quit really feel about the organization, how the negatives can be overcome, and the positive aspects of the work environment.

When you first started here what impressed you most about the company? In what way did this change? Why?   Most people starting a new job are very enthusiastic and excited about it. Many look upon it as a challenge and an opportunity. Unfortunately, some are disillusioned almost immediately; others remain positive and optimistic for a while, but it doesn't take long for them to face the realities of the situation. Excitement fades, optimism turns to pessimism; they believe they made a mistake in accepting the job and find a more satisfying position elsewhere. By identifying the factors that caused this, your company can make corrections that could prevent early turnover in the future.

How fully was your job explained to you before you accepted it? During your training for the job, was the nature of the job changed from what had originally been told to you?   Each area of explanation should be complete. The human resources department should have given the applicant enough information to ensure that he or she understood the objectives of the position. The orientation procedure should have given the new employee more details about the job and the company. The training specialist or supervisor should have taught the employee precisely what had to be done. A lot of discontent stems from failure of the organization to clearly explain the nature of the job and ensure that the new employee fully understands it.

Tell me about the job you held before coming to this company. What aspects of that job did you enjoy? How did these things compare to what you were assigned to do with our firm?   From the answer to this question, you can determine possible areas of failure in the hiring procedure. If this had been carefully explored in the selection interview, the company might have saved itself the expense, trouble, and disruption of hiring a person who would not find job satisfaction in the position.

Personnel Perils

Encourage current team members to make a new employee feel welcome but don't leave it entirely to them. Take a personal interest in each new employee and take a proactive role in making him or her feel part of the group.

When did you begin to feel that you had made a mistake in taking this job? What happened at that time to cause that feeling? Often there is one precipitating factor that starts the downward slide in an employee's attitude about the job. It might be the manner in which a supervisor or team leader deals with the new person; it might be a comment by another employee that initiates negative thoughts; it might be a specific assignment. Probe to find this factor.

However, often it isn't one thing, but a general feeling of discontent. Try to determine what caused it. Ask the following:

You commented that you just weren't happy here. Can you tell me what it was about the organization that made you feel discontented? What you are attempting here is to obtain the employee's take on the corporate culture. This might be the key to general discontent and you must probe carefully and cautiously to get to the root causes. Follow up on every comment. For example:

Employee: "I felt I was looked upon as an outsider. Even though my skills were as good or better than my teammates, they never asked my opinion and cut me short when I made suggestions."

Interviewer: "I can understand your frustration. Did all your teammates do this?"

Employee: "Some of the guys and gals were okay. But the team was really dominated by Chuck L. He's one of those know-it-alls and the other members are in awe of him. They don't dare contradict him, as he gets very sarcastic. They agree with his ideas openly or just keep quiet rather than offend him. After I was squelched a few times I complained to the team leader, but he seemed afraid to intervene. All he's interested in is avoiding confrontation and getting the work out."

Often the cause is more ambiguous. It's not any one factor but a general climate. For example, at one company employees left during the first few months because they felt they were always under pressure. At another firm, employees left because it was too bureaucratic. At still another organization, newly hired people felt they were not given enough guidance.

At one high-tech company, the great need was for creative men and women who could take the initiative and work independently on projects. Yet, the culture of the company only gave lip service to this concept. Although told at the interviews that their creativity would be utilized, during the first six months on the job they were kept under very strict control. Innovative ideas were discouraged until "they learned the ropes." Unfortunately, some of the most creative and intelligent individuals became impatient; when their ideas were ignored, they quit.

Because of a series of in-depth exit interviews with short-term employees, the company adjusted its policies to fit the individual needs of new people. This enabled new employees to "learn the ropes" more rapidly and build into their training opportunities to use their creativity.

The results of the termination interview should be shared with the team leader, as a guide for future leadership actions. Simply locking the interview notes in a drawer in the HR department does no one any lasting good.

When Employees Give Notice

Some supervisors and team leaders take an employee's resignation as a personal affront. "How could she do this to me?" Be aware that other employees are carefully monitoring the way you handle this situation. Take care to make the transition smooth.

The following suggestions help reduce the confusion that often results when a person leaves your company:

> ➤ **Don't blow up.**   I once worked for a manager who considered anyone who quit to be disloyal. If someone gave him the courtesy of two weeks' notice, he ordered the person to leave immediately. He then badmouthed the employee to everyone in the company. The result was that employees quit without giving notice, which caused serious production problems.

> ➤ **Agree on a mutually satisfactory departure date.**   You might need time to readjust your work schedules.

> ➤ **Request a status report on the employee's projects.** This will enable you to arrange for others to handle them. Develop a list of vendors, customers, or other people outside your department that the member interacts with so that you can notify them of the change.

> ➤ **Contact your human resources department.**   Ask them to either arrange for an internal transfer or start the hiring process to refill the job.

> ➤ **Let the other team members know.**   Do this as soon as you're notified. Tell them how it will affect their work until someone else is hired.

Your job is to keep the department running smoothly during this period. Plan your schedule so that you have time to do your regular work plus the added activities of refilling the job and training the new employee.

Should You Make a Counteroffer?

In Chapter 9, "Making the Hiring Decision," you were advised on what steps to take to discourage a new hire from accepting a counteroffer from his or her present employer. Now you are in the position of determining whether or not to try to salvage an employee who has given you notice.

Whether or not to make a counteroffer depends on how badly you need that person on your team. If he or she has expertise that is essential to the group, try it. You need that person and sometimes a raise or a change in the job structure might persuade the employee to remain. However, if the reason for leaving is more complex, money or superficial changes won't do the trick.

By acceding to an employee's demands, you also are setting a precedent. Other members of your group will get the message. "Get a job offer from some other company and use it to extort the company to get more money." In most instances, it's best not to submit to blackmail. Let him or her go. Learn from the separation interview the real reason for the resignation and make whatever adjustments are needed to keep others from following suit.

The Least You Need to Know

➤ Every time someone quits, it's important to determine the true reason. It might be something deeply embedded in the culture of the company that subtly has made the person discontented.

➤ The major objective of the separation interview is not so much to learn why the employee has quit, but to learn as much as possible about the conditions that prompted the employee to make the decision to quit.

➤ Carefully prepare the questions you plan to ask at the separation interview to cover not just reasons the employee is leaving but to seek the real underlying causes of discontent.

➤ When an employee notifies you he or she is quitting, don't panic. Set up a plan of action to allow for a smooth transition in your department.

➤ Counteroffers should be made only if the loss of the employee will result in serious detriment to the company.

Chapter 27

Layoffs and Downsizing

In This Chapter

➤ Furloughs and layoffs

➤ Cutting payroll without laying off workers

➤ Downsizing: reducing staff permanently

➤ Notifying employees before layoffs

➤ COBRA: Protecting employees' medical benefits

➤ Helping laid-off workers find new jobs

Even when the economy is good, there are occasions when companies find it advantageous to reduce their payrolls. When there are serious economic downturns, layoffs and downsizing become rampant. Layoffs or furloughs can result from temporary conditions or major upheavals such as poor revenues, mergers or acquisitions, or companies going out of business. In this chapter we'll learn how to deal with employees who are terminated—not because of any fault of theirs, but due to payroll reduction.

Short-Term Layoffs

If you work in an industry in which work is done seasonally (for example, construction, certain clothing manufacturing, landscaping, and the automobile industry), you're accustomed to temporary *layoffs* or *furloughs*. Workers in these fields expect to be laid off at certain times of the year and plan their lives accordingly. They're usually covered by unemployment insurance or, in some union contracts, supplemental paychecks. When the new season begins, most of them are rehired.

Meanings and Gleanings

Furlough is a short-term layoff usually due to seasonal work or temporary problems, after which the employees return to their jobs. **Layoffs,** in which workers are dismissed, occur when companies don't have enough work to keep their workforce busy or when they want to reduce payroll to increase profits. Sometimes layoffs are temporary (until the workers are needed); sometimes they are permanent.

Personnel Perils

As much as you might want to keep laid-off team members available for recall, don't mislead them with false hopes. It is unfair to someone who might turn down another job on the basis of your promise—and it can have legal repercussions. Former employees have sued companies when implied promises to rehire didn't materialize.

Some layoffs are unexpected, even though they're temporary. Business might slow down or a company might cut its payroll for other reasons. In these cases, laid-off workers have a reasonable chance of being re-hired when business picks up—but they have no guarantee. Although some people will wait for a recall, many choose to look for other jobs. This situation poses a problem for the company because many experienced workers won't be available when they're needed.

Alternatives to Layoffs

When employees know that a layoff is for a specified period and that the company has a history of calling back workers after a furlough, they're less likely to seek other jobs. If your company faces an indefinite layoff but it's likely that you will rehire sooner or later, take steps to keep available as many people as you can. Some ways of doing this will be discussed later in this chapter. This way, when the recall comes, your group will be intact and ready to function.

When you're managing a smooth-running, highly productive team, a layoff can be devastating. The loss of some workers means that the surviving members will have to do more work to pick up the slack. Team interaction that had been developed over time is lost and must be rebuilt; morale suffers, and most likely productivity is reduced. The best way to rebuild morale is to find alternatives to a layoff.

Here are some ways companies have avoided layoffs:

➤ Pay cuts

➤ Work sharing

➤ Early retirement

The main reason for most layoffs is to reduce payroll. When companies institute a general pay reduction for all employees (including management), the entire work-force shares the burden. If there is a labor-management agreement, management is obligated to negotiate the pay cut with the union. Many unions will agree to moderate pay cuts if it can save members' jobs.

Where no union exists, a company can arbitrarily cut its payroll. No one wants to take a pay cut, of course, and there are people who are not willing to suffer even a small personal loss to save some other person's job. Unless management can "sell" it to employees by appealing to their nobler motives, a pay cut could cause more problems than it solves.

In a strategy called work sharing, employees work fewer hours each day or fewer days each week; or work full weeks, but fewer weeks each month. With this strategy, hourly pay remains the same but reduced hours decrease the payroll. Work sharing enables companies to keep skilled employees during slow periods and enables teams to stay together. Employees earn less total pay but retain their benefits. Some states have amended their unemployment-insurance laws so that employees can collect some unemployment benefits during work-sharing periods.

Personnel Perils

Careful! Don't even imply that if an older person refuses to retire early—even with an incentive deal—he or she will be laid off or punished in some other way. Even a hint of coercion can lead to legal problems.

One way to minimize the number of employees who are laid off during an indefinite layoff is by encouraging older workers to retire earlier than they had planned. Under the Age Discrimination in Employment Act (see Chapter 2, "You Gotta Know the Laws"), companies cannot compel employees to retire. However, they can offer incentives to make it worth their while. When higher-paid senior employees leave a company, the payroll is reduced significantly.

In most instances, an entire department or team is not laid off. Unless there's a union contract or rigid policy mandating that layoffs be made on a seniority basis, keep your best team members. These are the members who can form the cadre of a new team if some of the laid-off members don't return when they're recalled.

Keep in touch with employees who have been furloughed. Phone them and send them the company newsletter. Let them know that you still consider them part of your team and that you're looking forward to the recall so you can work together again.

Rehiring Furloughed Workers

Seniority in most companies is the basis of both layoffs and recalls. The most senior employees are the last to be let go and the first to be rehired. However, this approach isn't always the most desirable one. If you have no contractual obligation to do so, it might be more advantageous to rehire people according to the skills you need as the work expands. Your immediate need might be for a specialist in one area, but the most senior furloughed member might have a different skill. In this way, you can rebuild your team most effectively.

Downsizing: The Permanent Layoff

The downsizing of major corporations over the past few years has eliminated tens of thousands of jobs, causing disruptions in the lives of laid-off workers and often in entire communities. When a company downsizes, it's not just laying off people; entire jobs are eliminated. A facility might be closed, an entire unit or department eliminated, or an organization restructured by doing away with certain jobs or entire job categories. This section explains how to cope with the fallout from downsizing cuts.

"WARN"—The Law on Downsizing

To ease the burden on employees who are being downsized, Congress passed the Worker Adjustment and Retraining Notification Act (WARN). This law applies to companies that have mass layoffs or plant closings; it exempts companies with fewer than 100 employees. Companies that are covered aren't required to comply with the law when they lay off small numbers of workers. It affects only mass layoffs.

A mass layoff is a layoff or reduction in hours at a single site that affects 500 or more full-time employees or 50 or more if they constitute at least 33 percent of an active, full-time workforce. A reduction in hours means to cut hours worked by 50 percent or more each month for a six-month period or longer.

The law requires that a company must give notice to employees who will be laid off at least 60 days before their final day of work. There are some exceptions to this rule, so check with your legal department to determine how it affects you.

Downsizing and the EEO Laws

Until relatively recently, members of some minority groups and women usually weren't hired or promoted to certain positions because of past company policies or community practices. During the past few years, many companies have made significant strides in bringing minorities and women into the workforce. If seniority is the policy followed during downsizing, minorities and women—who often have relatively low seniority—often are the first to have to leave. This practice can have an adverse effect on a company's affirmative-action endeavors.

The Civil Rights Act of 1964 specifically exempts companies that have established a seniority system for layoffs and rehiring from being charged with discrimination if seniority is the basis for their actions. However, there is an exception: If a member of a protected group can show that he or she personally experienced discrimination that resulted in lower seniority, that person might claim protection.

For example, suppose a woman was rejected for a job as a traveling auditor in 1985 because that company didn't hire women in that category; but she applied again in

1990 and was hired. If she is laid off later because of her lack of seniority, she can sue, claiming that, if not for that discriminatory policy, she would have had higher seniority. Each case is decided on its own merits, of course.

Providing Continuing Benefits

Under the federal law known as COBRA (Consolidated Omnibus Budget Reconciliation Act), employees of companies with 20 or more employees are entitled to maintain their health-insurance coverage for 18 months after they leave a company. Disabled people can maintain it for 29 months. The length of time a person must be allowed to continue coverage depends upon the reason the person left the company. Here is a table covering the specifications:

Reason for Leaving Company	Time
Termination of employee	18 months unless termination was for gross misconduct, in which case no continuation is mandated.
Reduction of hours	18 months.
Disability	29 months for persons disabled at time of termination for any reason.
Divorce	If the spouse of an employee is covered by the company's health benefit plan, he or she is entitled to continue this coverage for 3 years after the divorce.
Death	The surviving spouse and dependents, 3 years.
Retirement	An employee who is retired from a company that goes into Chapter 11 bankruptcy can continue coverage until death. When the employee dies the spouse can continue coverage for 36 months.

The company isn't expected to pay the premiums, however. Former employees, or their widows or divorced spouses, who enroll in COBRA must pay the full premium at the same rate the company had been paying (usually considerably less than if they had to purchase individual insurance) plus a small administrative charge. COBRA also provides for continuing health insurance coverage for survivors of employees who die.

The plan administrator must notify employees or, in case of death, their survivors of their rights under COBRA within 14 days of receiving notice of the separation. The employee or beneficiary has 60 days to decide whether or not to accept the plan. Some people leaving the company might choose not to continue coverage because they have similar coverage from other sources or just don't want to pay the premiums.

Processing Out Laid-Off Employees

In most companies, the human resources department does the separation processing. In smaller companies or at branch facilities that have no HR department, the supervisor or facility manager usually handles the process. These managers should be thoroughly trained in the separation process to ensure that this delicate situation is dealt with in a legal and considerate manner.

Notifying the Employees

If your company is covered by WARN, as discussed earlier in this chapter, you must provide written notice 60 days in advance. If you are not covered by WARN, there's no required time, but it's only fair to give adequate notice to people who will be laid off. For temporary layoffs, two weeks is typical; for permanent layoffs, 30 days.

At the time of the separation, follow these guidelines.

➤ Discuss the continuation of benefits under COBRA, as discussed earlier in this chapter.

➤ Discuss severance pay. No law requires severance pay, but some union contracts mandate it. Many companies voluntarily give severance pay to laid-off workers. The amount varies from company to company and often within a company by job category. Check your company policy.

➤ If appropriate, discuss the callback procedure.

➤ If the final paycheck is not issued when he or she is leaving the company, specify when it will be sent.

➤ If provisions have been made to help laid-off employees seek other jobs, refer the person to whomever is responsible for that function.

➤ Retrieve company property including keys, credit cards, ID cards, tools, company computers, and computer logon IDs. It's usually wise to change computer passwords.

➤ If an employee has incurred expenses for the company that have not yet been reimbursed, such as travel and entertainment, arrange for prompt attention to this matter.

➤ Answer any questions the employees have.

➤ Arrange for employees to clean out their desks, offices, or lockers.

➤ Arrange for forwarding of any mail and messages that are received at the company after the employees leave.

➤ Express your good wishes.

To ensure that all the proper steps are taken, it's a good idea to use a checklist. Once people leave, it becomes more difficult to reach them or gain their cooperation.

Outplacement Services

A relatively recent human resources function is assisting laid-off employees in their search for a new job. Losing a job can be a traumatic experience for some people—particularly long-term employees who might not have had to seek a job for many years. *Outplacement* helps them learn the techniques to find a job more rapidly, and deals with the psychological adjustments that often are devastating to the newly unemployed person.

Meanings and Gleanings

Outplacement is a means of helping laid-off employees find new jobs and reduce the stress caused by the loss of their positions.

The Outplacement Process

There are several approaches to outplacement. The minimum approach is to arrange for facilities where laid-off workers can use the company's computers and photocopy equipment to write and duplicate their resumés, use the telephone, and receive messages. Some companies set aside several vacant offices for laid-off employees to use for a specified period of time after the separation. Other companies prefer not to have laid-off workers use their premises, but provide an off-site facility for this purpose.

More comprehensive outplacement programs do much more than this. Some laid-off workers are invited to orientation sessions where professional counselors introduce themselves and various parts of the outplacement program. They provide help with resumés, letters, appointments, and so on.

In addition, some companies provide professional counselors to help locate sources of jobs, such as directories of companies in their area, publications in which jobs in their fields are advertised, Web sites and other computer-based job sources, and so on. Some programs even include tips on interviewing, providing role-plays of interviews with the counselors and with other participants.

The Pay-Off

Why should a company spend a great deal of money to help people who, at this point in their lives, are unlikely to provide any return to them? Outplacement is not cheap. Typically, an outplacement program consisting of a two-day workshop that all downsized employees attend, plus six hours of one-on-one consulting with each person, would cost $400 to $500 per person.

Some hard-nosed bean counters will raise objections to spending money for outplacement. True, there is no immediate direct return to the company on this investment. However, there is the human element. These men and women have given good service to the company—often for many years. By helping them overcome the loss of their jobs by getting a new position faster and more effectively than they could by themselves, you are in at least a little way rewarding them for past services.

In addition, companies often report that outplacement enables employees to overcome the resentment that often accompanies lay-offs. Many men and women are happy to return to the firm—even several years later—or recommend other talented people to them when jobs open up, because they felt they were treated fairly. Most major companies today include outplacement as part of their separation package, which shows that they consider it a worthwhile investment.

The Least You Need to Know

➤ When business slows down, companies might have to lay off people for short terms or permanently.

➤ Try to find alternatives to layoffs such as work sharing, shorter hours, or general pay cuts.

➤ Keep in touch with temporarily laid-off team members to ensure the likelihood that they'll return when needed.

➤ If your company is covered by the WARN law, it must give 60 days' notice when it closes a facility or lays off a large number of employees.

➤ COBRA mandates that laid-off employees be allowed to continue their medical insurance coverage for a specified period if they pay their own premiums.

➤ Outplacement services are a means of helping laid-off workers find new jobs more rapidly and effectively.

Glossary

ABCD   This is an award given for performance that's truly above and beyond the call of duty. This type of special recognition pays off in continued efforts to achieve superior performance.

active listening   This is not only paying close attention to what the other party says; it is asking questions, making comments, and reacting verbally and nonverbally to what is said.

authorization cards   Statements authorizing the union to act as the signers' representative for the purposes of collective bargaining.

behavioral sciences   The study of how and why people behave the way they do. They include psychology, sociology, anthropology, and some phases of linguistics, economics, and education.

benchmarking   Learning from successful organizations techniques that contributed to their success and emulating them.

bona fide occupational qualification (BFOQ)   This exists when the gender of the employee is essential to performing the job. Some cynics have commented that the only undisputed bona fide occupational qualifications are a wet nurse (for a woman) and a sperm donor (for a man).

boycott, primary   The union asks customers not to purchase items made by the company. Unions may legally picket a store, informing customers about the strike and asking them not to purchase products made by that company. However, it is illegal to tell customers not to patronize the store itself, or to stop suppliers from doing business with the employer. This is called a *secondary boycott* and was outlawed by the Taft-Hartley Act.

cafeteria benefit plans   Employees can choose from a menu of benefits that best suit their needs, up to a specific dollar value.

career pathing   Programs in which employees are assessed to determine their potential and what steps they must take to move up in positions that will be of greatest value to both the company and themselves.

chronological resumés   Presents an applicant's background by listing jobs by the dates of employment.

classified ads   Ads placed in a special section of the paper containing help wanted ads. The format usually is limited to a specific typeface and allows no artwork.

closed shop   A company is required to hire only members of the union with which it has a contract. See *union shop.*

collective bargaining   The negotiations between a company and a labor union, which has been certified to represent its employees.

communication   Takes place when persons or groups exchange information, ideas, and concepts.

constructive discharge   Rather than fire employees, some managers make life miserable for them so that they quit. When an employee quits because of intentional unfair treatment, it is "constructed" by the courts to be equivalent to being fired.

corporate culture (organizational culture)   The shared philosophies, values, beliefs, and attitudes that permeate an organization and upon which their actions are based.

craft unions   Represent skilled craft workers, such as machinists, carpenters, plumbers, and similar jobs. See *industrial unions.*

critical few objectives (CFOs)   The objectives that must be achieved in the first 90 days if the person is to be successful in the new job.

defined-benefits plan   A pension plan in which the amount of retirement pay is specifically stated.

defined-contribution plan   A pension plan that establishes the amount the employer will contribute to the pension fund.

diagnostic interviews   See *structured interviews.*

disability insurance (long-term)   Provides payment to partially cover loss of income for catastrophic illness or accident. Coverage commences at a specified time after the onset of the illness or accident, and is continued until the time specified in the policy.

disability insurance (short-term)   Provides coverage for partially paying employees for loss of income due to non-job-related illness or accident for a specified period of time. Most policies begin coverage after the sick days are used up, and expire after six months.

display ads   Can be placed anywhere in the paper. Display ads can be designed with borders, artwork, photos, and a variety of fonts.

distress, or **bad stress**   The chronic state of anxiety caused by unremitting pressures of job, personal, or societal problems.

diversity   A variety of conditions and activities that create an environment where people can achieve their fullest potential regardless of the many ways they might differ from each other.

downsizing   Not just laying off people; entire jobs are eliminated. A facility might be closed, an entire unit or department eliminated, or an organization restructured by doing away with certain jobs or entire job categories.

employee assistance programs (EAPs)   Company-sponsored counseling service. The counselors aren't company employees; they are outside experts retained to help employees deal with personal, family, and financial problems.

employee relations   See *human resource management.*

employee stock ownership program (ESOP)   A program in which the major portion of the company stock is sold or given to employees so that they actually own the company.

employment at will   A legal concept under which an employee is hired and can be fired at the will of the employer. The employer has the right, unless restricted by law or contract, to refuse to hire an applicant or to terminate an employee for any reason or for no reason.

empowerment   Sharing your power with the people over whom you have power. Team members are given the authority to make decisions that previously were reserved for managers.

executive orders   These are not laws; they are edicts promulgated by the President without being passed by Congress. Executive orders do not apply to the entire population—only to government agencies or organizations that do business with the government. Violation of an executive order can lead to loss of the contract.

executive recruiters   Consultants who specialize in recruiting and screening executives and other top-level personnel. Also called executive search organizations or, informally, headhunters.

exempt employees   Those who are engaged in management, administration, professional work, and others who use "independent judgment" in their work. In addition, outside sales persons are considered exempt. Persons falling into this category can be required to work overtime with no extra compensation.

exit interview   See s*eparation interview.*

flextime or **flexible hours**   Instead of all employees working the same hours, the hours are staggered so that some employees come in and leave early; others come in and leave later in the day.

functional resumés   Present an applicant's background by listing duties, responsibilities, or accomplishments without regard to the job or company in which they were performed.

furlough   A short-term layoff usually due to seasonal work or temporary problems, after which the employees return to their jobs.

going rate   The salary paid for similar work in your industry or community. Another definition: What you have to pay an employee to keep him or her from going to another company.

grievance   A formal complaint concerning a violation of a union-management agreement or, where there is no union, of the company's personnel policies. See *gripe*.

gripe   An informal complaint about working conditions. See *grievance*.

guided interviews   See *structured interviews*.

halo effect   The assumption that because of one outstanding characteristic, all of the applicant's characteristics are outstanding. The opposite—because of one poor characteristic you assume that the person is unsatisfactory in every aspect—called the pitchfork effect.

headhunters   See *executive recruiters*.

health maintenance organizations (HMOs)   Organizations of physicians and other health care professionals that provide health care on a prepaid basis. HMOs generally emphasize preventive care and early intervention.

human resource management   The aspect of management that concerns the coordination of all aspects of employment including hiring, training, compensating, motivating, disciplining, and all day-to-day interactions. Formerly this function was called personnel administration, employee relations, or industrial relations.

industrial relations   See *human resource management.*

industrial unions   Represents all workers—skilled, unskilled, and semi-skilled in the same industry—such as all employees of an automobile plant, a textile mill, or a garment factory. See *craft unions*.

internal customers   Members of your team or another team to whom you provide materials, information, or services. See *internal suppliers*.

internal suppliers   Persons in your organization who provide you with materials, information, or services. You might be a "customer" in some aspects of your work and a "supplier" in others. See *internal customers*.

interview   The word is derived from *inter* meaning "between" and *view* meaning "a look." An interview is not a one-way interrogation. Two parties "look" at a situation and discuss it. A job interview is a look at a job between the interviewer and the candidate.

job analysis Includes a description of the duties and responsibilities of the job *(job description)* and the background required to perform the job *(job specification).*

job bank or **skill bank** A database listing all of the skills, education, experience factors, and other backgrounds of all employees, which can be searched to match job openings against current work force.

job description A description of the duties and responsibilities of a job. Also called *positions results description* or *job results description.*

job enrichment Redesigning a job to provide diversity, challenge, and commitment—in some cases, to alleviate boredom.

job fair An organized recruiting facility at which companies and applicants can meet and discuss job openings.

job-instruction training (JIT) A systematic approach to training people to perform tasks; it involves four steps: preparation (ready), presentation (set), performance (go), and check it out (follow-up).

job results description See *job description.*

key results areas (KRAs) The major aspects of a job that must be accomplished by the employee.

layoffs When companies don't have enough work to keep their workforce busy or when they want to reduce payroll to increase profits, workers are dismissed. These layoffs are sometimes temporary (until the workers are needed) and sometimes permanent.

lifelong learning Providing for continuing education all through one's life to enable people to keep improving their knowledge and skills in their current areas of expertise and broadening their knowledge in other areas.

lookism Overemphasizing appearance in making decisions about a person.

management by objectives (MBO) A philosophy of management through which employees are judged on their success in achieving objectives established through consultation with their superiors.

medical indemnity insurance A policy that pays all or part of medical expenses incurred by a covered employee directly to the health care provider or by reimbursing the patient.

mentor Employee assigned to act as counselor, trainer, or "big brother or sister" to a new member of the organization.

M.O. (method of operation) The method of operation—the patterns of behavior—that a person habitually follows in performing work.

motivators Inspire people to extend themselves on the job. These include recognition, control over one's own work, and obtaining satisfaction from the job. See *satisfiers.*

313

multilevel or **360-degree assessments**   Assessment of an individual is made by his or her bosses, peers, subordinates, and even such outsiders as vendors and customers. This gives the company a well-rounded view of how that individual is perceived at several levels.

needs assessment   Determining just what types of training are worth spending your training dollars on.

on-boarding   A personalized, comprehensive program designed to assist a new employee in adapting to the new company, the new job, and his or her new colleagues.

orientation programs   Help new employees get a better start on the job by making them feel that they are part of the group from the beginning.

OSHA   Refers both to the Occupational Safety and Health Act and to the agency that enforces it, the Occupational Safety and Health Administration.

outplacement   A means of helping laid-off employees find a new job and reducing the stress caused by the loss of their position.

outsourcing   Contracting work that previously has been done in-house to outside sources.

patterned interviews   See *structured interviews.*

performance standards   Define the results that are expected from a person performing a job. For performance standards to be meaningful, all persons doing that job should know and accept these standards. Employee participation in the establishment of performance standards is one way to ensure this understanding.

perquisites   Better known as *perks,* these are the goods or services given to an employee in addition to regular salary and benefits as an incentive to attract and retain personnel.

personnel administration   See *human resource management.*

piecework   A system of compensation in which workers' pay is based exclusively on how much that person produces.

pitchfork effect   See *halo effect.*

policies   Indicate the viewpoint of the organization concerning various aspects of its activities. For example, human resources policies indicate the firm's beliefs on its dealings with its employees.

position results description   See *job description.*

probation   A trial period during which an employee is given the chance to correct poor performance or behavior.

procedures   The techniques specified for carrying out various aspects of the company's policies.

progressive discipline   A systematic approach to correcting rule infractions. A typical program has six steps, beginning with an informal warning. If the warning doesn't succeed, the following steps are taken, in order: disciplinary interview, written warning, probation, suspension, and termination (if necessary).

religious practices   Include not only traditional religious beliefs, but also moral and ethical beliefs, and beliefs individuals hold "with the strength of traditional religious views."

satisfiers   The basic needs such as good working conditions and adequate compensation. These have limited motivational value. They motivate up to the point of satisfaction. See *motivators.*

scientific management   Developing accurate performance standards based on objective data acquired through time studies for every operation, and training employees to work more efficiently by eliminating wasted time.

separation interview   An interview with employees who voluntarily quit to determine the real reason for their decision to leave. Also called *exit interview.*

sexual harassment   Defined as any unwelcome sexual advances or requests for sexual favors, or any conduct of a sexual nature when an employer makes submission to sexual advances a condition of employment. Also can be when submission or rejection is used as a basis of working conditions including promotion, salary adjustment, assignment of work, or termination; or has the effect of interfering with an individual's work or creating a hostile or intimidating work environment.

sick leave   A short-term salary continuation program for employees due to non-job-related illness or injury.

skill bank   See *job bank.*

structured interviews   Conducted using a list of questions that must be asked in exactly the same way in exactly the same order. They also are called *patterned interviews, diagnostic interviews,* and *guided interviews.*

suspension   A stage of progressive discipline in which an employee is removed from the job without pay for a specified period of time.

synergy   The benefit derived when two or more people, by working together get better results than what the individuals can contribute by working separately.

telecommuting   Using technology to perform work at home or at a location remote from the central office by receiving assignments and submitting completed work through the computer.

teleconferencing   A means of bringing together by satellite employees from various units of an organization for the purpose of training or other business meetings. People at diverse locations can see, hear, and interact with each other.

temps (temporary personnel)   People who work for the company but are not employed by the company. They are on the payroll of a temporary staffing or employee leasing service. Usually they are used for short-term assignments such as filling in for absent employees or augmenting permanent staff when needed.

union shop   A company might hire nonunion members, but they must join the union within a specified time after being hired. See *closed shop.*

vesting   Refers to the percentage of an employee's benefit account that he or she is entitled to retain after leaving the company.

wellness programs   Formal programs instituted by companies to keep employees in good health. They usually include exercise facilities, nutrition advice, stop-smoking programs, and healthcare counseling.

Resources

Publications with Articles on Human Resource Management

Managers, team leaders, and others who deal with people problems must keep up with what's going on. The best way to be on the cutting edge of change is to regularly read several of the magazines and newsletters that cover these matters.

Most industries and professions have periodicals devoted to their individual fields, and many have occasional articles on supervision and interpersonal relations. Here is a list of some of the better general publications that either specialize in or have significant coverage of the practice of human resources:

Across the Board
The Conference Board
845 Third Avenue
New York, NY 10022
212-339-0345 phone
212-980-7014 fax
www.conference-board.org

Business Week
1221 Avenue of the Americas
New York, NY 10020
1-800-635-1200 phone
609-426-5434 fax
www.businessweek.com

Forbes
60 Fifth Avenue
New York, NY 10011
1-800-888-9896 phone
212-206-5118 fax
www.forbes.com

Fortune
Time-Life Building
Rockefeller Center
New York, NY 10020
1-800-621-8000 phone
212-522-7682 fax
www.fortune.com

Harvard Business Review
60 Harvard Way
Boston, MA 02163
1-800-274-3214 phone
617-475-9933 fax
www.hbsp.harvard.edu

HR Magazine
Society for Human
Resources Management
1800 Duke Street
Alexandria, VA 22314
703-548-3440 phone
703-836-0367 fax
www.shrm.org

INC
477 Madison Avenue
New York, NY 10022
212-326-2600 phone
212-321-2615 fax
www.inc.com

Management Review
American Management
Association
PO Box 319
Saranac Lake, NY 12983-0319
1-800-262-9699 phone
518-891-3653
www.amanet.org

Manager's Edge
Briefings Publishing Co.
1101 King Street
Alexandria, VA 22314
703-548-3800 phone
703-684-2136 fax
www.briefings.com

*Success in Recruiting
and Retaining*
National Institute of
Business Management
PO Box 9206
McLean, VA 22102-0206
1-800-543-2049 phone
703-905-8040 fax
customer@nibm.net e-mail

Training
50 South 9th Street
Minneapolis, MN 55402
612-333-0471 phone
612-333-6526 fax
www.trainingsupersite.com

Training and Development
American Society for
Training and Development
1640 King Street
Alexandria, VA 22314
703-683-8100 phone
703-683-9203 fax
www.astd.org

Workforce
245 Fischer Avenue
Costa Mesa, CA 92626
714-751-1883 phone
714-751-4106 fax
www.workforce.com

Working Woman
135 West 50 Street
New York, NY 10020
1-800-234-9765 phone
212-445-6186 fax
wwmagazine@aol.com e-mail

Associations Dealing with Human Resource Management

Professional societies are excellent sources of information on the areas in which they specialize. Membership in one or more can give you access to the latest developments in the field—and the experience of other members who deal with issues similar to yours. Memberships also provide opportunities at meetings and conventions to meet your counterparts in other organizations and often, resource material from their libraries or archives.

Here is a list of some associations that may be of value to you:

American Association of Industrial Management (AAIM)
293 Bridge Street
Springfield, MA 01103
413-737-8766 phone
413-737-9724 fax
An association of managers of manufacturing organizations. Provides publications and special reports.

American Management Association (AMA)
1601 Broadway
New York, NY 10019
212-586-8100 phone
212-903-8168 fax
www.amanet.org
Membership is by company. Provides seminars, publications, and library facilities on all aspects of management.

American Psychological Association (APA)
750 First Street
Washington, DC 20002
Industrial Psychology Section
202-336-5500 phone
202-336-5708 fax
www.apa.org
Provides literature and information on issues dealt with by psychologists. For matters related to testing, leadership, management, and employee relations, ask for industrial psychology information.

American Society for Training & Development (ASTD)
1640 King Street
Alexandria, VA 22313
703-683-8100 phone
703-683-8103 fax
www.astd.org

Dedicated to professionalism in training and development of personnel. There are local chapters throughout the United States and there is an annual national convention. Publications include a magazine, special reports, and books.

American Staffing Association (ASA)
Suite 200
277 South Washington Street
Alexandria, VA 22314
703-549-6287 phone
703-549-4808 fax
asa@staffingtoday.net
Source of information on providers of temporary personnel.

Association for Quality and Participation
801B West 8th Street
Cincinnati, OH 45203
1-800-733-3310 phone
513-381-0070 fax
www.aqp.com
Dedicated to participative programs primarily, but not exclusively, related to quality management.

Employee Assistance Society of North America (EASNA)
PO Box 634
New Hope, PA 18938
215-891-9538 phone
215-891-9538 fax
72722.465@compuserve.com e-mail
Source to locate individuals and organizations that provide various types of employee assistance programs.

International Foundation of Employee Benefit Plans (IFEBP)
18700 West Bluemound Road
Bloomfield, WI 53008
414-786-7100 phone
414-786-8670 fax
pr@ifebp.org e-mail
Excellent source of information on employee benefits. Also accredits benefits specialists.

National Association of Personnel Services (NAPS)
3133 Mt. Vernon Avenue
Alexandria, VA 22305
703-684-0180 phone
703-684-0071 fax
www.napsweb.org
Source of information about private employment agencies.

Society for Advancement of Management (SAM)
630 Ocean Drive
Corpus Christi, TX 78412
540-342-5563 phone
512-994-2725 fax
enterprise.tamucc.edu/sam/default.htm
Provides publications and conferences on various aspects of management.

Society for Human Resources Management (SHRM)
1800 Duke Street
Alexandria, VA 22314
703-548-3440 phone
703-836-0367 fax
www.shrm.org
Membership consists of human resources specialists in all types of companies and organizations. Provides publications, special reports, and books. Local chapters throughout the United States conduct monthly meetings and there is an annual national convention.

Women in Management
30 North Michigan Avenue
Chicago, IL 60602
312-263-3636 phone
312-372-8738 fax
Dedicated to special issues of women in management positions.

Helpful Web Sites

To advertise your open jobs or to search for applicants who might qualify for your jobs, use the following Web sites, listed according to their popularity.

➤ www.monster.com
➤ www.careerpath.com
➤ www.careerMosaic.com
➤ www.headHunter.net
➤ www.jobSearch.org
➤ www.hotJobs.com
➤ www.dice.com
➤ www.careerBuilder.com
➤ www.nationJob.com
➤ www.jobs.com

For information about equal employment laws: www.eeoc.gov.

For statistics on jobs, try the U.S. Department of Labor: www.bls.gov.

For information about Americans with Disabilities Act (ADA): www.janweb.icdi.wvu.edu.

For daily reports on the latest developments in the human resources field: www.shrm.org/hrnews.

The following are associations that can provide information about human resources problems:

➤ American Management Association: www.amanet.org

➤ American Psychological Association: www.apa.org

➤ American Society for Training and Development: www.astd.org

➤ American Staffing Association: www.staffingtoday.net

➤ International Foundation of Employee Benefits Plans (e-mail): pr@ifebp.org

➤ National Association of Personnel Services: www.napsweb.org

➤ Society for Human Resources Management: www.shrm.org

Quick References

Twenty-One Ways to Motivate People

1. Encourage participation in setting goals and determining how to reach them.
2. Keep all employees aware of how their jobs relate to others.
3. Provide all employees with the tools and training necessary to succeed.
4. Pay at least the going rate for jobs in your company.
5. Provide good, safe working conditions.
6. Give clear directions that are easily understood and accepted.
7. Know each person's abilities and give assignments based on the ability to handle those assignments.
8. Allow people to make decisions related to their jobs.
9. Be accessible. Listen actively and empathically.
10. Give credit and praise for a job well done.
11. Give prompt and direct answers to questions.
12. Treat employees fairly—with respect and consideration.
13. Help out with work problems.
14. Encourage employees to acquire additional knowledge and skills.
15. Show interest and concern for people as individuals.
16. Learn each employee's M.O.s (modes of operation) and deal with them accordingly.
17. Make each person an integral part of the team.

18. Keep people challenged and excited by their work.

19. Consider your team members' ideas and suggestions.

20. Keep people informed about how they're doing on the job.

21. Encourage team members to do their best and support their efforts.

Six Ways to Make Praise More Meaningful

1. Don't overdo it. Too much praise reduces its value.

2. Be sincere. You can't fake sincerity. You must truly believe that the deed or behavior you're praising actually is commendable.

3. Be specific about the reason for your praise. Rather than saying, "Great job!" specify the accomplishment you are praising.

4. Ask for your team members' advice. Nothing is more flattering than to be asked for advice about how to handle a situation.

5. Publicize praise. If other team members are aware of the praise you give a colleague, it acts as a spur to work for similar recognition.

6. Give them something they can keep. Telling people that you appreciate what they've done is a great idea; writing it is even more effective.

Ten Tips for Improving Mentoring

1. Know the work. Review the basics. Be prepared to answer questions about every aspect of the job.

2. Know your company. Help the trainee overcome the hurdles of unfamiliar company policies and practices.

3. Get to know your protégé. Learn as much as you can about the person you are mentoring.

4. Learn to teach. If you have minimal experience in teaching, pick up pointers on teaching methods from the best trainers you know.

5. Learn to learn. Never stop learning—not only the latest techniques in your own field, but also developments in your industry, in the business, and in the overall field of management.

6. Be patient. Patience is key for success in mentoring.

7. Be tactful. Be kind. Be courteous. Be gentle, but be firm and let the trainee know you expect the best.

8. Don't be afraid to take risks. Give your protégé assignments that will challenge his or her abilities. Failures may occur, but we learn from our failures.

9. Celebrate successes. Let the trainee know you are proud of the accomplishments and progress made.

10. Encourage your protégé to become a mentor.

Twelve Ways to Keep Alert to Your EEO Responsibility

Go along with the spirit as well as the letter of the law.

Offer women and minorities opportunities that were previously denied to them.

Open training programs to minorities, women, and the physically challenged.

Discipline should be administered equitably and be carefully documented.

Be aware of your own biases and work to overcome them.

Use everyone's abilities optimally.

Set realistic performance standards based on what a job really calls for.

Ignore stereotypes; judge people by their individual abilities.

Never use racial epithets or slurs—even in jest.

Encourage all people to deal with their co-workers as human beings.

Sex life and job life must be kept separate.

Support your company's equal employment and affirmative action programs fully.

Follow these suggestions. They add up to GOOD BUSINESS.

Index

ASA (American Staffing
Association), 320
Association for Quality and
Participation, 320
associations as resources,
319-321
ASTD (American Society for
Training & Development), 320
attendance, good attendance
awards, 228. *See also* absenteeism
audiotaping as a training tool,
137
authorization cards (unions),
272
awards
good attendance awards, 228
special achievement awards,
172-173

B

*Be A Better Employment
Interviewer*, 94
behavioral scientists
Abraham Maslow, 6
Douglas McGregor, 7-8
benefit packages
cafeteria plans, 189
EAP (employee assistance
program)
coverages, 189-190
mechanics of, 190
health care plans
clarity of, 188
dental, 182
HMOs (health mainte-
nance organizations),
180-182
life insurance, 182
medical indemnity insur-
ance, 180
optical, 182
shared costs, 182
legalities
leaves without pay, 177
social security, 176-177
unemployment insur-
ance, 177
workers' compensation
insurance, 177
paid holidays, 178
perks, 191-192
personal days, 179
retirement plans, 182
401(k)s, 183
clarity of, 187
contributory, 183

legalities, 184
noncontributory, 183
sick days, 178-179
vacations, 177
biases
communications, 147-148
hiring process mistakes, 47
body language (communica-
tions), 144-145
bona fide occupational qualifications (sexual discrimination
laws), 16
bonuses. *See also* incentive pay
programs, 173
hiring bonuses, 171
profit sharing plans, 173
boycotts, 276
brand-new positions, 52
burnout, 232-234
coping with pressures,
233-234
overworked employees, 234
stress management, 234
business representatives, roles
in unions, 274
Business Week, 317

C

cafeteria plans, 189
candidates. *See* applicants
career pathing (motivation
tactic), 210-211
CareerBuilder Web site, 73
CareerMosaic Web site, 73
CareerPath Web site, 73
case study training programs,
135
certification of truth (application form clause), 81
channels (communications),
148-149
citations, OSHA (Occupational
Safety and Health Act), 220
Civil Rights Act of 1964 (Equal
Employment Opportunity
laws), 13-17
minorities, 14-15
religion, 15
sexual discrimination, 15-17
civil rights laws
ADA (Americans with
Disabilities Act), 20-22
alcohol and drug users,
21
physically and mentally
challenged individuals,
22

ADEA (Age Discrimination
in Employment Act of
1967), 17-18
affirmative action, 18-20
Civil Rights Act of 1964,
13-17
minorities, 14-15
religion, 15
sexual discrimination,
15-17
clarity of communications,
143-144
classified ads as a recruitment
source, 64
clauses (application forms)
certification of truth, 81
employment at will status,
80
permission to investigate,
79-80
clichés, usage guidelines in
written communications, 157
closed shops, 29
closings
interviews, 99
meetings, 150
coaching, training programs,
138
COBRA (Consolidated Omnibus
Budget Reconciliation Act),
305
collaborative evaluations, 255
collective bargaining, 275
colleges
as a recruitment source, 68
updating training programs,
131-132
communication
active listening skills,
145-146
body language, 144-145
choosing your words
knowing your subjects,
142-143
understanding your audi-
ence, 143
feedback, 149
meetings. *See* meetings
path between sender and
receiver, 148-149
speaking clearly, 143-144
state of minds, 146-148
biases, 147-148
emotional, 148
keep an open mind, 147
two-way process, 142
written
e-mails, 157-161
grammar and spelling
concerns, 155

Q–R

T

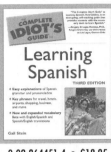

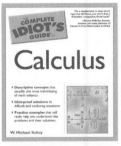